Edited by Irving Drutman

Paris Was Yesterday (*1925–39*) by Janet Flanner
London Was Yesterday (*1934–39*) by Janet Flanner

Good Company

Good Company

A Memoir, Mostly Theatrical

Irving Drutman

Little, Brown and Company/Boston/Toronto

FIRST EDITION
T10/76

Library of Congress Cataloging in Publication Data

Drutman, Irving.
  Good company.

  Includes index.
  1. Drutman, Irving. 2. Performing arts —
United States. I. Title.
PN1583.D7A34   790.2′092′4 [B]   76–18297
ISBN 0–316–19355–0

Designed by D. Christine Benders

Published simultaneously in Canada
by Little, Brown & Company (Canada) Limited

PRINTED IN THE UNITED STATES OF AMERICA

for
Mike

Contents

1

Theater in the Twenties

1

"THEATRICAL REMINISCENCE," wrote Max Beerbohm, precociously ancient at twenty-seven, "is the most awful weapon in the armory of old age."

Half a century later, Max was to make use of that awful weapon himself. Acceding to the inevitable, he willfully let loose over the BBC a barrage of his own early recollections, wallowing in the memory of treasured evenings at the theaters and music halls of the London Nineties.

My own treasured evenings (and matinees) occurred, like Max's, in a city native to me — New York — when I too was in my impressionable teens. Again like Max's — I cling tenaciously to this link since there is no other between us — my youthful theatergoing (in the 1920s) took place during a stimulating, evolutionary period, like that of London at the end of the last century, when the New Drama of Ibsen and Shaw was gaining reluctant acceptance.

Today, when I have become satiated with the theater, I find it difficult to remember the details of a play I saw less than a month ago. But those I experienced in the early years of my theatergoing remain vivid to me. I may have forgotten the plots of many, but I can still recall the titles and the names, not only of the leading performers but of the subsidiary players as well. And most of all I remember the houses in which they were presented. This mnemonic ability (a trick of association, like being able to rattle off old baseball scores) confounds actors of my acquaintance when I correct them about theaters in which they themselves have played. I have even supplied a theater for an entertainment that I insisted had never been produced. When someone mentioned "the Carol Channing musical about Hollywood," I said, with the obnoxious finality of all statistics-collectors, "Nonsense, she never played in a . . . ," then stopped in sudden recollection and added, "It was at the Winter Garden."

Mine is the last of the theater-struck generations (I was born in 1910). Radio — crystal sets — was just beginning and of course television mercifully had not yet been invented, so I remained relatively uncorrupted. Films were the most accessible, and by far the cheapest, form of amusement. There were movie theaters every five or ten blocks or so on the Lower East Side, where I was born and lived until the age of nine, and the same was true of the East Ninety-sixth Street area where I passed my adolescence. During daytime hours on the Lower East Side, prices for children were two for a nickel — this must have been about 1915 or 1916 — and later they were a nickel for each child, when accompanied by an adult. We would stand alongside the box office and accost a grown-up patron with "Mister (or Missus), buy me a ticket?" as we held out our coin. The cynical acquiescence, indeed encouragement of this procedure by the management enabled the theater to keep to the letter but certainly not the intent of the law, which was of course to ensure a responsible guardianship for each child. Once inside we would hastily part company with the obliging stranger and rush to one of the front seats where we could watch the film — always remaining for several showings — at close range. Often, however, especially when one was as small as I was, we would make use of an involuntary guardian and enter free of charge. Men's outer coats

were ankle-length; as a male customer presented his ticket to the
ticket-taker, we would dart under his coat and walk through the
entrance with him, thereafter scurrying down the aisle and quickly
seating ourselves among the other children already there, indistin-
guishable from them and safe from managerial discovery.

My introduction to the "legitimate theater" began with the show
business trade paper *Variety,* a discarded copy of which I picked up
on the sidewalk in front of Ruppert's Brewery at Ninety-second
Street and Third Avenue one afternoon when I was meandering
home from school. In a box on the front page was a bit of raffish
dialogue which, because of its audacity (1923 and I was thirteen), I
can still remember.

1st Chorus Boy: Do you know Nance O'Neill?
2nd Chorus Boy: Maybe. What's his first name?

I wasn't aware that Nance O'Neill was a ranking female star of
the serious drama but of course, as a son of the city pavements,
the irreverent word play didn't escape me. I remember nothing else
from that issue but I must have gone through every page, held
captive by the columns reeking of show biz, each pungent section
headed with disarming formality: VAUDEVILLE, TIMES SQUARE,
BURLESQUE, OPERA AND CONCERT, PICTURES, CABARET, LEGITIMATE.

From then on my reading, which had progressed from *The Sun-
bonnet Babies* and *The Five Little Peppers* through eighty or
ninety of the Horatio Alger series, took a radical turn. I ransacked
the limited drama shelves of my neighborhood library branch on
East Ninety-sixth Street, devouring scores of one-act plays (for
some reason *Where but in America?* — the hired couple can afford
a car but their employers cannot — sticks most in my memory). I
also discovered Burns Mantle's yearbooks of Best Plays with their
invaluable listings of casts, credits and synopses of each of the
season's offerings (they had started in 1919 and under other editors
continue to be published annually).

My father and mother, like the majority of their neighbors who
had emigrated from villages in Russia and central Europe, had no

interest in or even any knowledge of the existence of an English-speaking theater. Once or twice a year they attended a benefit performance, sponsored by my father's *Verein,* of one of the then-numerous Yiddish shows on lower Second Avenue. However, a girl next door was the daughter of White Russian refugees to whom theatergoing, whether as a metropolitan diversion or a cultural habit, was a necessity. I would help her cut out pictures from the drama pages of the New York *Evening Journal* and paste them in a scrapbook, along with programs brought home by her parents. When her family moved from my street, she gave me her scrapbook. In this way I got to know of the historic 1923 visit here of the Stanislavsky-directed Moscow Art Theater, who brought with them a repertory of Chekhov, Gorky, Turgenev. They also brought with them an acting mystique that, later misappropriated by the founders and followers of the Group Theater, lured actors away from traditional techniques into an anarchy that was to bankrupt our theater in twenty-five years.

The next step was my discovery, in the fall of 1923, of the "popular price" Subway Circuit. This consisted of seven or eight houses in the outlying boroughs and in Newark which booked tryouts, road shows, and shows that had just ended their Broadway runs and were picking up a few weeks' extra time before closing permanently. The box office was scaled from a high of $1.00 for straight plays and $1.50 for musicals, down to 25¢ for the second balcony.

I was in my first year of high school and my daily allowance was 50¢ for carfare (5¢ each way) and lunch (from a street vendor: almost invariably, a 5¢ hot dog, a 5¢ pint of milk and a 5¢ Napoleon or chocolate eclair). This left me with a net profit, as I thought of it, of 25¢ a day and 30¢ if, frugally, I walked home. Some of these savings went for after-school candy or a soda at our ice-cream parlor hangout on Third Avenue, but by being careful I could always manage a weekly 25¢ Saturday matinee.

My introduction to the popular-price theater was from the gallery of the cavernous Bronx Opera House as an engrossed spectator of a mystery play called *The Last Warning.* It was the heyday of the genre: of my first half-dozen Subway Circuit entertainments, three others were mystery melodramas — *Whispering Wires, The Bat, The Cat and the Canary* — one was an unfunny musical comedy, *Dew Drop Inn* with James Barton, and one was an elaborate and impressive David Belasco production of *The Merchant of Venice*, with David Warfield's prudent depiction of Shylock, not as villainous as I had imagined the character from readings in school.

I was nearsighted and since my seat was always a great distance from the stage, I passed my early theatergoing years looking down from the heights, without ever seeing the upper half of a set or getting more than a hazy notion of any actor's features. Of course if I had had the vaguest idea of how the actors materialized for their performances, I suppose I could have gone around after the show and waited at the stage door to get a good look at them. But it never occurred to me that these haloed individuals would use an entrance and exit leading to a public street. It took me a while to discover that actors, like schoolteachers, were human beings who had happened to choose esoteric vocations, that in fact either breed could sometimes be seen walking around after working hours just like ordinary people. But by the time I had learned that, I had become too snobbish (and would have been too embarrassed) to stand outside a stage door waiting with the rest of the fans.

I was by then a veteran of a few months of Bronx Opera House matinees. I had also become a between-performance habitué of the Broadway theaters. The school day ended at 2:45. One afternoon, instead of going home, I walked downtown on the West Side. The 48th Street Theater near Seventh Avenue attracted my attention, possibly because a play familiar from school, *Macbeth*, was announced on the marquee. I approached the building and peered into the lobby, afraid to advance any further. To the right was the segregated second balcony entrance (separating the humble from the affluent), which had been left unlocked. I tiptoed up the endless stairs, rebuffed on each landing by unyielding fire exits, until I found a responsive door leading into the gallery.

The house was dark except for the stage, where a dress rehearsal was progressing slowly. James K. Hackett, the portly, fiftyish son of a turn-of-the-century Shakespearean road actor, was preparing a five-act, nineteen-scene version of *Macbeth* under the auspices of the Equity Players. He had already done it in Paris for a single performance, inexplicably receiving the Legion of Honor. "They decorated him because he only played it once," was Lucien Guitry's sardonic explanation.

Almost an hour was spent timing what was supposed to be a quick scene change, a tent dropped from the flies. Hackett, in costume — and anachronistically wearing horn-rimmed spectacles — would step out of character to ask how long the change had taken. He was told two minutes. Too long, let's try it again. The curtain was lowered and they tried it again. Half a minute shorter. Still not enough. Try it again. They tried it again.

I must have gotten bored after a long stretch of so little action and so much repetition, because I got up from my seat in the secluded gallery and began exploring other rows. During one interminable stage discussion, a sudden crash filled the house. In my restless exploration, I had caused a seat to snap down from its springs. At once the attention of the people on the stage was turned in the direction of the second balcony. Who's there? someone called. Who's up there?

But I didn't pause to enlighten them. I raced down the stairs and made my escape into the anonymous Forty-eighth Street afternoon. The episode resulted in the first money I ever earned from writing. I won a prize ($4.00) awarded by the English Department for the best composition by a freshman. My theme was the adventure with Hackett's *Macbeth*. At that, I made more than Hackett did. The production received lackluster notices ("Competent," "he has the god-given gift of mediocrity," "corpulent . . . more of a Falstaff than a Macbeth, who succumbs at Birnham Wood") and closed after thirty-three performances.

Having discovered a new, exotic playground, I returned to it as often as possible. At least once a week I made my exploratory pilgrimage downtown, taking note of the theaters on every street. I soon got over my shyness about entering a lobby. At first timidly, then with bravado, I would attack the box office and ask, "May I have a program, please?" Sometimes I would be refused, but most often the treasurer on duty would reach down under his counter and pass one out to me. Occasionally he would tell me to go inside and help myself from the stack under an aisle seat in the last row. This meant that I could see the auditorium from the expensive orchestra floor. Soon, as I became more knowledgeable about the plan of each house, I would bypass the treasurer and walk boldly inside, get my program, then prowl through the rest of the darkened interior, exploring the lounge and the Gents' and Ladies', quickly (and disdainfully) scanning the first balcony, peering behind the draped boxes, but not daring to breach that sacred altar, the dimly lit stage.

The 39th Street Theater was harboring *Welded,* a new drama by Eugene O'Neill, already marked as our most formidable playwright. I slipped past the box-office man and into the theater to get my program. The unshaded daytime bulb on the stage barely reflected the first act set, a lavish duplex apartment with a full staircase back center. I must see if the staircase was real, if one could actually ascend and descend it. I felt my way down to the pit and hoisted myself over the footlights. I was on a stage at last. Since apparently I had it all to myself, I examined the books on the shelves, the furniture, whatever carefully placed props were lying around; then I headed for the stairs and put my foot on the first tread. Suddenly the stage doorman appeared and asked what I was doing there. I was wearing the customary schoolboy outfit of the day — soiled knickers supporting long black ribbed stockings, a white shirt, and a discarded tie of my father's framed by a rumpled sweater. I carried a scuffed briefcase filled with classroom paraphernalia and I doubt that I looked like a dangerous robber. Nevertheless he pretended not to believe my stammered explanation that I was satisfying my curiosity about the staircase. He told me that breaking into a theater was like breaking into a house, then escorted me to the street and said he'd have me arrested if he ever caught me backstage again.

I stayed away from the district for several weeks after that, but the pull of the forbidden proved too much. A criminal drawn magnetically to the scene of his crime, I soon found myself back to where I had turned my first caper — the 48th Street Theater. By this time a sophisticated footpad, I walked through the second balcony portal as if I belonged in the building. Up the stairs, into the gallery, and I was in luck again. *Macbeth* had closed and what turned out to be a new comedy by Rachel Crothers, *Expressing Willie,* was in rehearsal. On the stage were the star, Chrystal Herne, the leading man, Richard Sterling, and an older gray-haired actress, Louise Closser Hale. The author, also gray-haired and (to my nearsighted eyes and from my usual disadvantageous placement) about the same size and shape as Miss Hale, was directing. Here were professionals secure in their talent; everything was calm and businesslike, as opposed to the fretfulness of the *Macbeth* rehearsal. Of course I couldn't realize that this was early in the game for *Expressing Willie* and also that a small cast was working with a one-set play whereas with *Macbeth* I had eavesdropped on an elaborate and complicated production on the hypersensitive eve of its opening.

I watched the rehearsal for several hours, being careful not to make any noise that would attract attention to my forbidden presence. Finally, the rehearsal reached the end of an act and the cast was dismissed for the day. I left the theater reluctantly, walking slowly down the stairs. Outside, as I passed the stage door, I saw a gray-haired woman coming briskly up the alley. I whipped open my briefcase and brought out a smudged piece of paper and a pencil. As the victim neared me, I thrust out my implements and said, "May I have your autograph please, Miss Crothers?"

She stared at the paper and pencil as though they were lethal weapons. "My autograph?" she said, contracting her lips into a tart vee, "No . . . no . . ." and hastened up the street. Abashed at my temerity, I turned in the opposite direction and, to hide my embarrassment, began to study the photographs on the board in front of the theater. There was Chrystal Herne, there was Richard Sterling, there was Louise Closser Hale. There was a picture of the author. The woman I had approached was not Miss Crothers. The woman I had approached was Miss Hale. Thus began and ended my career as an autograph hound.

2

AT PRESENT WRITING Broadway, the generically termed, nostalgia-infested commercial theater district, has thirty-eight houses; in the full fledge of my program-collecting, rehearsal-surveillance days, there were over seventy. The farthest downtown, on Thirty-fifth Street between Fifth and Sixth Avenues, was the Garrick, away from the mainstream and considered arty because of the then high-minded Theater Guild's tenancy (Benavente, Shaw, Andreyev, Claudel). On Broadway itself, beginning at Thirty-eighth Street, were the musical comedy houses, the Knickerbocker and the Casino (original home of *Floradora* and where the Marx Brothers first transferred from vaudeville to legit respectability with *I'll Say She Is*). One block uptown was Charles Frohman's hallowed red and gold Empire and two and a half blocks further was the George M. Cohan, the only one still standing (it is now called the Globe and shows sex films). Another survivor, but due for demolition, is the National, west of Seventh Avenue on Forty-first Street, now called the Billy Rose after the showman who bought and refurbished it.

On the side streets between Thirty-eighth and Forty-second east of Broadway were the 39th Street Theater; the tiny Princess, home of the famous Kern-Wodehouse-Bolton intimate musicals, where the pampered professional beauties Justine Johnston and Marion Davies appeared and which was to be taken over in the Depression Thirties by the Ladies Garment Workers Union to become the Labor Stage; the marble, patrician Maxine Elliott's, reputedly built as a gift for the canny actress-businesswoman by J. P. Morgan and destined to end its days in a burst of bohemian energy as the flagship of the W.P.A. Theater Project; and the Comedy, which was to end *its* days as the repository of Orson Welles's Mercury Theater, from which the boy wonder mounted his meteor to Hollywood and the world.

These, noble theaters some of them, were on the periphery of the district. The hub of course was Forty-second Street between Broadway and Eighth Avenue, which contained ten houses equally di-

vided on either side of the thoroughfare and even an eleventh
auditorium, seldom used in my day, that had been built on top of
the New Amsterdam as a roof cabaret for Ziegfeld's Midnight
Frolic. What is especially noteworthy now about this cluster of
entertainment emporia is that it is still intact: rundown, squalid,
but continuing to operate as theaters. Second- and third-run movies
on a grind policy have replaced legitimate shows; for me, as doubtless for many others, they remain ghost-haunted, dingy reminders of
the theatrical glamour of my youth.

The most splendid was the *art nouveau* New Amsterdam, which
for many years was identified almost exclusively with Florenz Ziegfeld, Jr.'s, extravaganzas. Here were presented his lavish musical
comedies, *Sally* and *Sunny* and *Rosalie* with Marilyn Miller, *Whoo-
pee* with Eddie Cantor. Here he spent his backers' fortunes Glori-
fying the American Girl in the voluptuous yearly *Follies* series
(when Miss Alison Smith, assistant to drama critic Alexander
Woollcott on the New York *World,* complained that the evening
consisted of one dull beauty parade after another, the self-confessed
roué George Jean Nathan attributed her indifference to the baleful
fact of her gender) .

I never succeeded in getting into the New Amsterdam when it
was dark, since the doors at the end of the long lobby were kept
locked, with a brass chain stretched across the entrance. Nor did I
have any more success breaking into the Apollo, diagonally across
the street, where another of the sybaritic annuals, *George White's
Scandals,* held the stage. Indeed, although I did see the last of
Ziegfeld's *Ziegfeld Follies* at the New Amsterdam — the name was
later sold by his widow to the Shuberts, but the oriental panache of
the master was gone — I never did get to see a *Scandals* until White
tried an unsuccessful comeback with a sodden revue in the late
Thirties.

To the west of the New Amsterdam, the barbaric glitter of the
Ziegfeld shows gave way to simpler and homelier diversions. George
M. Cohan's proletarian musicals, *Little Nellie Kelly, The Rise of
Rosie O'Reilly,* etc., played the Liberty (on the other hand it also
housed such smart Gershwin shows as *Tip Toes* and *Lady Be Good*

with the effervescent Fred and Adele Astaire). The Eltinge, christened in homage to "America's foremost delineator of feminine characterizations," the female impersonator Julian Eltinge, housed the sex farces and melodramas produced by A. H. Woods (*The Masked Woman, Woman of the Jury, Stolen Fruit, Red Light Annie*). The Sam H. Harris and the Frazee — later Wallack's — although named after producers, had no single auspices or set policies; indeed, the *modus operandi* of the latter seems to have been to present an endless succession of flops, the dispirited series being high-pointed by one wildly drunken opening — and as it turned out, closing — performance by a female star. She made one entrance with her evening cape worn inside out and took part of the scenery with her for a rousing exit unintended by the author or director, which ended her illustrious stage career.

The north side of the street was equally eclectic. The *Scandals* and such other musicals as *Manhattan Mary* with Ed Wynn and *Poppy* with Madge Kennedy and W. C. Fields, kept the Apollo fully booked. For *éclat* there were the Selwyn and the Times Square, run by Edgar and Arch Selwyn, with such debonair importations as *Charlot's Revue*, which first displayed Gertrude Lawrence, Beatrice Lillie, and Jack Buchanan in this country, and later Noel Coward's crisp, impeccably stylish *This Year of Grace*.

It was at the Times Square, with its stage door directly on Forty-Second Street instead of at the end of an alley or on the next block, that I caught my first offstage glimpse of a star, Billie Burke. She was appearing there in a musical, *Annie Dear*, produced by her husband, Florenz Ziegfeld, and I was passing by after the midweek matinee had let out when I saw a trio consisting of a man with a reddish mustache — who must have been Ziegfeld's inventive press agent, Bernard Sobel — and two newspaper photographers waiting at the magic portal. "There she is, boys," said Sobel, as pretty, dimpled Miss Burke suddenly appeared. A Dresden china doll in pastel street attire, she posed for a smiling shot and was then whisked off in her limousine.

I believe the sweetest story I ever heard about any star concerns her. From her early days as a Frohman luminary, she toured com-

pulsively with a mountainous assortment of luggage. When a reporter once asked her what was in all those boxes, suitcases, and
trunks, she was puzzled by his ignorance but perfectly willing to
explain. "Why," she gasped, "that's Billie Burke!"

The barnlike Lyric and the Republic, possibly the oldest theaters
on the street, completed the group. The first booked operettas like
The Three Musketeers, with Dennis King as D'Artagnan and Vivienne Segal as the simpering soprano. (Producer Ziegfeld kept her in
those roles for years, without a contract, automatically raising her
salary at the beginning of each season; she only emerged as the
worldly character comedienne of *I Married an Angel* and *Pal Joey*
in the Thirties, at the instigation and inspiration of Lorenz Hart.)
Late in the Twenties, in an unpredictable about-face, it also booked
the chic *Fifty Million Frenchmen,* featuring Cole Porter's first complete professional score.

The Republic, closest to Times Square of the ten, is noteworthy
for having been the home of the notorious *Abie's Irish Rose* — notorious because of its tenacity in triumphing over bad-to-terrible
notices to become Broadway's longest running play of the time.
Some local historians believe it was kept alive by Robert Benchley's
weekly jibes in the old humor magazine *Life.* When it was revived
in 1954 it only lasted for twenty performances. The Republic also
housed the original dramatic version of DuBose Heyward's *Porgy,*
from which George Gershwin derived his famous opera. When the
Minsky organization took over the theater during the depression
and turned it into a burlesque house, it became the first New York
home of the strip act and that act's most celebrated practitioner,
Gypsy Rose Lee.

For some reason, perhaps because it was such a wide, crowded
thoroughfare, I never felt easy about invading the Forty-second
Street theaters. My favorites were embedded in the H formed by
Forty-fourth and Forty-fifth streets and the intersecting Shubert
Alley, between Seventh and Eighth Avenues, with the Martin Beck
forming a sort of cedilla on Forty-fifth west of Eighth. These are
newer structures than those abutting Times Square; the upstairs
sections of most of the auditoriums are on one shelf, eliminating

both dizziness and the humiliation of a separate entrance for customers in the cheapest seats (in the older houses the disparity in rank was further emphasized by the stark newsprint flyer given out as a program instead of the sumptuous slick-paper booklet provided with the more expensive tickets).

This complex remains, after fifty years and with only three displacements for "civilian" structures, the prime group of the entire theatrical district. The capacious 44th Street and the small Nora Bayes in the same building were torn down to make way for the New York *Times* annex and garage. The Klaw, west of the Imperial on Forty-fifth Street, is also now a garage (as, incidentally, are the sites of the Garrick, the Princess, the Comedy, the Vanderbilt, the 48th Street, the Belmont). All the others are intact, although Winthrop Ames's neoclassic Little alternates theatrical performances with lectures and recitals, and the Bijou with films and TV shows.

These theaters retained an individual identity until well into the Thirties. Owned and booked by the ubiquitous Shubert organization (as were and still are two-thirds of the commercial houses), the Plymouth was nevertheless associated with Arthur Hopkins, the Booth as well as the Little accommodated Winthrop Ames's shows, Sam H. Harris was the entrepreneur at the Music Box (with Irving Berlin, he also owned two-thirds of it), and Brock Pemberton produced at the Klaw.

The Shuberts of course put the most promising of the big musicals into the Shubert and the Imperial, while the sixteen-hundred-seat Majestic, which had the largest capacity of any legitimate theater, remained a problem house. There were occasionally some fortuitous and wildly inappropriate bookings in the last; one I remember in particular was an adaptation of Alfred Neumann's *The Patriot,* a drama about Czar Paul I of Russia, which would have suited a medium-sized theater but reeled around dizzily in the vast dimensions of the Majestic.

For the extravaganzas they themselves produced — the *Passing Shows,* Al Jolson's *Big Boy, Innocent Eyes* with Mistinguett, always, the program made clear, "under the personal supervision of Mr. J. J. Shubert" — they seem to have preferred the Winter Garden at

Broadway and Fifty-first. Conversely, and perversely, the theater they had named in honor of mammy-singer Jolson, which adjoined an aromatic horse stable and riding academy on Seventh Avenue and Fifty-ninth Street, was used for such cultural events as the Moscow Art Theater, Maeterlinck's *The Blue Bird*, Sothern and Marlowe's travel-stained Shakespeare productions.

One other street that could serve as a theatrical shopping center, although not by any means considered as desirable as Forty-second Street or the Shubert Alley enclave, was Forty-eighth street between Sixth and Seventh avenues. This block held the Playhouse, where William A. Brady presented adaptations from the Paris boulevards starring his wife, Grace George, and Elmer Rice's neo-realist drama *Street Scene* and where Brady's son in partnership with the farming-implements heir Dwight Deere Wiman produced the first big hit by playwright Robert E. Sherwood, *The Road to Rome*. Up the street was my rehearsal-haven, the 48th, down the street was the Belmont (*Tarnish* with a little-known Ann Harding, and the *Americana* revue), across the street was the Cort, where Laurette Taylor had played her greatest success, *Peg O' My Heart*, and the Vanderbilt, home of intimate musicals (*Merry Merry*, Rodgers and Hart's *The Girl Friend, Peggy-Ann, A Connecticut Yankee*).

From there until the farthest outpost, Daly's 63d Street (where vaudeville singer Mae West made her initial bid for police attention in the first of her dramatic vehicles, *Sex*), the district thinned out with nineteen theaters scattered over the fifteen-block area (*only* nineteen!). They ranged from the smallest, the Punch and Judy on Forty-ninth Street, now showing sex pictures as the World, to the stupendous Century, taking up the entire blockfront between Sixty-second and Sixty-third on Central Park West. The mammoth fortress (it also held the Century Roof for intimate shows) was a Distinguished Citizens' folly, built in 1913 as the New Theater. Intended to be a cultural oasis on the edge of the Broadway desert, it encompassed an area much too vast for its potential audience; customers in the numbers necessary to make it pay were more inclined to thirst for Entertainment than for Art, especially when, as at the New, the twain seldom managed to meet.

Long before I was loping past its forbidding classic exterior, on my way downtown where the action was, it had been taken over and renamed by the Shuberts, who used it as a forlorn catchall for anything they didn't care to book in a better-situated house — for instance, Harry Lauder, the Scottish music hall comedian in his one-man show, or the dying Eleanora Duse in her ghostly last visit to America. Two attempts at revivifying the house were made during the mid-Twenties by the showman Morris Gest, when he engaged Norman Bel Geddes to gut the auditorium and turn it into a cathedral *manqué* for Max Reinhardt's Barnumesque production of *The Miracle,* and later when he imported tons of Continental stars to appear in a Reinhardt repertory, opening with a stately (and, as I remember, somnolent) *Midsummer Night's Dream.*

The establishment in the 1960s of Lincoln Center for the Performing Arts wasn't really an unusual real estate event for the neighborhood, which has a long history as a repository or dumping ground for esthetic stage enterprises. Why the terrain was considered particularly propitious for a Culture concentration is a mystery easy to fathom. The swoop away from Times Square predicted in the early part of the century had failed to materialize, leaving the district after World War I with some wan, difficult-to-fill theaters. They were the first refuge of bookers who, caught with a problem show, must have theorized that suckers in search of the finer things wouldn't mind wandering from the Broadway reservation to indulge their proclivities.

Thus, the Colonial, on Broadway and Sixty-third, once the number two house of the B. F. Keith vaudeville circuit and later host to Negro musicals — *Runnin' Wild, The Chocolate Dandies, Lucky Sambo* — was handed over to Walter Hampden for a Shakespearean repertory. The actor-manager and his co-star Ethel Barrymore, both well into their forties, hardly distinguished themselves as middle-aged, portly Romeo and Juliet, but were politely commended for their later performances in *Hamlet* and *The Merchant of Venice.* Recently, after being shuttered for decades, the theater was garishly redecorated and renamed the Harkness.

On Columbus Circle the Cosmopolitan — into the walls of which

William Randolph Hearst built extensive living quarters for Marion Davies — fluctuated between first-run showings of films starring the owner's favorite and such more cerebral events as Reinhardt's staging of *Dantons Tod*. In the Forties, before it was torn down, it housed Eva LeGallienne's American Repertory Company in moribund productions of Ibsen, Barrie and Shaw. The nearby, aforementioned Jolson's 59th Street, with its polyglot attractions, completed the list of temples in which Mammon was sometimes willing to offer up sacrifices to Thespis.

3

TOWARD THE END of my freshman year, I answered an advertisement for after-school work and got a job with Consoli's Opera and Theater Ticket Agency on Broadway and Forty-first Street, across from the old Metropolitan Opera. My hours were from 3:30 to 9:00 P.M.; my duties, to pick up tickets at the various box offices, to deliver them to the agency's customers, and also to relieve, during his dinner hour, the counterman at the adjacent orange drink stand, which was also owned by Consoli. I was completely guileless and the mores of the counterman world were unknown to me. Conscientiously I would drop into the open cash (wooden cigar) box all the dimes handed me by thirsty passers-by, never dreaming that I could add to my $6.00 weekly salary by pocketing a portion of the proceeds as my rightful if illegal due. Indeed, I was even apprehensive about taking an occasional gulp of the adulterated orange drink, lest I be caught and accused of pilfering. I remember my surprise, when delivering a pair of opera tickets to the office of a Wall Street broker, to have him ask, "Do you have fifty cents?" He looked at me quizzically when I answered "No"; he was asking his partner, who tossed the coin to me as a tip. It was my first job and I simply hadn't got my business legs yet.

Consoli's was a small, independent brokerage, specializing mainly in opera tickets. Apparently a cozy relationship existed with the Metropolitan, but for locations in the legitimate theater the agency had to depend either on box-office treasurers or other brokers. This was the heyday of the "buy"; a producer with a promising show (usually one of the elaborate musicals or a play with a potent star name) could get most of his backing from the big ticket speculators by allocating in advance a certain number of his choice seats for the initial six or eight weeks of the run. A new *Follies, Scandals, Vanities,* any of the aphrodisiac entries, provided practically gilt-edged insurance that the first dozen rows could be sold readily at a high premium, no matter how indifferent the notices. The vivid Ina Claire in a Frederick Lonsdale or Hungarian-adapted frivolity was another guaranteed item for what was then known as the carriage trade.

Occasionally the boys would be caught off guard. The Theater Guild persuaded the newly married Alfred Lunt and Lynn Fontanne to appear for them in *The Guardsman,* a Molnár play which had failed in New York some ten years earlier. Although well known, neither performer had achieved star status; the Guild had a reputation as a highbrow organization forced to subsist on its subscription list. There was no reason for the brokers to suspect that the glowing, still-honeymooning couple would turn yesteryear's flop into a sparkling romp, one of the big hits of the season and the foundation-stone of the Lunts' subsequent legend.

When I started at Consoli's, shortly after the play's opening, tickets for *The Guardsman* were in great demand, with the brokers unable to obtain any until the Guild's rapidly expanding subscription list had been satisfied. On my first day, an elderly man with a beautiful young woman, both in evening dress, came in at theater time and asked for *The Guardsman.* The clerk explained the oppressive circumstances. How about the new Ina Claire comedy (Guy Bolton out of Ernest Vajda), *Grounds for Divorce?* "That sounds amusing," said the young woman. The man — her father? her husband? her sugar daddy? — looked at her sharply. "Didn't you see that in Paris?" Deflated, she mumbled yes, and the resplendent pair walked out. Evening clothes, Paris, the Lunts, Ina Claire

. . . I felt precipitated overnight into the sparkle and glitter of the international fast set.

Consoli's doubtless didn't participate in any advance agency buys since, when a request came in for a show, the clerk would begin by calling the theater's box office for seats; if none were available, he would try one of the bigger brokers. For each ticket, he would tack on an amount above the regular price, usually one dollar for locations obtained from the box office. If the show was a big hit and he was forced to depend upon another agency, the premium would increase correspondingly and it was not unusual for the purchaser to end up paying treble the amount printed on the ticket.

Since the theater brokers, like the brokers on Wall Street, were hardly infallible, they would sometimes be left with scores of tickets for a show they had bought in advance and that had failed to live up to expectations. These were dumped into Joe Leblang's cut-rate agency, an institution that enabled most of my generation of New York theatergoers to see many more plays than otherwise we could have afforded.

Leblang's was strategically located in the basement of an office building on Broadway and Forty-second Street. Peculiarly, it was known to the majority of its customers as Gray's, after the drugstore directly above it on the street level, although there may have been only a geographical connection between the two. The mainstays of Leblang's business were the shows whose initial impact on the critics and/or the public had been negative. These were nursed along for a few weeks, the cut-rate sale frequently helping the producer and the theater operator to clear expenses while waiting optimistically for the piece to catch on.

Some shows managed to do just that. *Abie's Irish Rose,* after its unpropitious opening, was able, through Leblang's, to limp along during its first forlorn months, eventually snaring the audience it must have been written for, to run more than twenty-five hundred performances and turn into the bonanza as well as the laughingstock of its decade. The title, incidentally, is a masterpiece of its kind, elucidating with dispatch both the matter and the manner of the composition it encloses. Mae West's *Sex* was another generous consumer of Leblang customers, as was *The Squall,* a drama about a

Ready for business in the early days of Joe Leblang's cut-rate ticket agency

half-caste wench with her seductive, much-parodied "Nubi like white man" come-on: two initially disdained entries that became long-run bargain-counter triumphs.

Nor did Gray's cater only to the esthetically vile. Many a well-regarded entertainment that failed to attract enough customers at full price could thus keep cozy while waiting for its own box office to thaw. Authors from Bernard Shaw to Zoe Akins, stars from Mrs. Fiske to Ethel Barrymore, producers from the Theater Guild to Gilbert Miller — they were none too august to seek its aid. Shakespeare, Ibsen, most productions of the classics, were almost unfailingly available.

The paranoia of being pointed out as a flop if tickets were offered at cut-rates was then unknown. On a bad weather night or during a slow theater week, even the hit shows would unabashedly send over a last-minute bundle of unsold locations for discount resale. The first play I ever saw from the uncomfortable luxury of a downstairs box seat (at $1.65, reduced from the $3.30 regular Saturday afternoon price) was John Galsworthy's *Escape,* in a high-class presentation by Winthrop Ames. With Leslie Howard at the height of his matinee idol popularity, the play had been doing very well at the small Booth Theater and but for the eleventh hour disposal of a few unsold tickets, I would have missed one of my most fondly remembered theater experiences.

I first learned of Leblang's when I was sent to pick up some tickets for Consoli's clerk, but I didn't become a steady customer until several years later. However, I did wander in constantly while I was on an errand, to look at the big board with its list of entries and half-prices (*The Tantrum*, $1.65, $1.10, 55¢; *Havoc*, $1.65, $1.10, 75¢; *The Chocolate Dandies*, $2.20, $1.10) ; to watch in fascination along about curtain time as some attractions were scratched once their tickets had all been sold; to see that — wonder of wonders — on a stormy night, even a hit like *The Firebrand* was offering a few orchestra seats. My head, which I should have been stuffing with geometry and elementary physics, was instead being stuffed with the ephemera of Broadway. As a result, although the simplest problems in mathematics or chemistry continue to confound me, I could easily win a bet naming the theater that sheltered *What Price Glory?* (it was the Plymouth) .

From the Leblang board I grew familiar with the titles of shows that would find their way shortly to the Bronx Opera House, of which I remained a devoted follower and where I could see my choice at the established gallery price of only 25¢. Beginning with *The Last Warning*, my first season had consisted of fifteen entertainments, including those I've already mentioned: a melodrama, *Red Light Annie,* starring an actress named Mary Ryan who happened coincidentally to be the wife of the influential director; *The Fool,* a morality play by Channing Pollock, which had been a hit of the 1922 season

Daniel: In God's name, who are you?
Poor Man: I am a Jew!
As he speaks, slowly the tree and everything beneath it is il-
luminated by the star of Bethlehem . . . the full choir sings:
"Hark, the Herald Angels Sing," as in black darkness
The curtain falls

(even in my early teens, I could be persnickety about *this* one) ; a musical, *Sally, Irene and Mary,* that sagaciously had cannibalized the titles of the three most popular musicals of the previous few seasons; *Zander the Great,* a comedy about the Wild West in which I first saw one of our best actresses, Alice Brady (she is a hired girl from the East traveling with a five-year-old orphan and they stumble into a clutch of cowboy bootleggers) ; *Merton of the Movies,* George S. Kaufman and Marc Connelly's satire on Hollywood; Mary Nash in *The Lady* (abandoned by her husband, she becomes a cabaret entertainer to support her boy, who in the third act murders one of her customers, etc.) ; Richard Bennett in *The Dancers* (he owns a cabaret and is torn between his society sweetheart and one of his low-born employees, both dancers) ; *Irene* (see above) ; and the ubiquitous operetta *Blossom Time.*

To complete my novitiate I rounded out the fall months of 1924 with the following:

Seventh Heaven, a tearjerker in which Helen Menken was a Paris street urchin whose war lover returns for a last act happy ending — but blind. I like to think of it now in connection with one of S. N. Behrman's memorable anecdotes. The movie version with Janet Gaynor and Charles Farrell was a great success in the early talkie days. Shortly thereafter Behrman inexplicably — since his reputation had been made as a writer of drawing room comedy — was hired for a screen treatment of *Liliom* with the proviso that he excise the death scene and the play's bittersweet ending. Behrman refused, asserting that Molnár's modern classic was too renowned for such a drastic amputation to go unnoticed. "Besides," he argued, "*Seventh Heaven* was a big moneymaker and the hero was blind." The producer (Sol Wurzel) was adamant. "Blind men," he said, "can go to bed." Behrman was punished for his obstinacy by being switched to a remake of *Rebecca of Sunnybrook Farm*.

Laugh, Clown, Laugh, David Belasco's reworking of *Ridi, Pagliaccio,* and one of the last plays in which Lionel Barrymore appeared before retiring into films. His death scene (they enjoyed their stage mortality in those days) I remember as embarrassing me by its histrionic excesses. I also remember the extraordinary, almost wraithlike slimness of his wife and leading lady, Irene Fenwick.

Sweet Little Devil, with an early Gershwin score when Gershwin was still writing for the *Scandals* and was relatively unknown to the general public. I remember about it only the song "Virginia, Virginia, You've Got the Devil in Ya" and Constance Binney with the forefinger of each hand raised over her forehead cutely to simulate a devil's horns.

Rain, the greatest dramatic success of the early Twenties, which both made and unmade Jeanne Eagels's career. She was overpraised for it and the four years she played Sadie Thompson hindered her from enlarging her acting experience, so that when she undertook another role that required more finesse — the gossamer Simone in *Her Cardboard Lover* — she was completely lost (she died in 1930 at the age of thirty-six, reportedly of an overdose of drugs).

Little Jessie James, an intimate musical with a chorus of only eight or nine girls instead of the customary sixteen to twenty-four, each of whom, given a character, stepped out of line to perform her specialty. I can still hear the title song,

> "You've got to hand it to that charming bandit
> Little Jessie James!"

Betty Lee, a big, dull musical with Joe E. Brown as the leading clown. I didn't think he was funny then and had no reason in subsequent years to change my opinion. In 1931 when I made my first trip to Hollywood (hitchhiking all the way from New York) he was appearing on the stage as the dumb ballplayer in Ring Lardner's *Elmer the Great*. I got a taste of Los Angeles theatergoing when, after the first act curtain, I started out to the lobby for an intermission cigarette and was stopped by an usher who said, "Don't you want to see Mr. Brown's specialty?" Sure enough, the star came out in front of the curtain and delivered his vaudeville routine. The curtain then rose for the second act and he blandly resumed his role of Elmer. The audience seemed to take the break in continuity as a matter-of-fact occurrence. They were content to have received a not unexpected bonus. The Big Depression had just started and customers were being bribed with free dishes for each supermarket purchase. Who then could expect the Drama to remain immune to the march of progress?

4

IN 1925, HAVING served my apprenticeship at twenty or so Bronx Opera House performances, I became a full-fledged metropolitan theatergoer. I saw my first play during its initial downtown engagement, I began to read the daily newspapers avidly for reviews of new productions, and I experienced a Broadway opening night.

Mike de Lisio, my friend from grammar school days who lived across from us on Ninety-sixth Street, had been induced by his family to take violin lessons, which he loathed. His teacher, perhaps in an effort to enlarge his cultural awareness, gave him two tickets for the Neighborhood Playhouse, in the heart of the Lower East Side tenement district. Here the wealthy Lewisohn sisters, Alice and Irene, were sponsoring a distinguished company of actors and dancers in an extensive cosmopolitan repertory, giving first New York stagings of plays, pantomimes and ballets by Shaw, Dunsany, Andreyev, the Quintero brothers, Joyce, Lenormand, Sholem Asch, Stravinsky (*Petrouchka*'s local debut). The company, which included at various periods such mimes and mummers as Whitford Kane, Albert Carroll, Aline MacMahon, Dorothy Sands, Paula Trueman, worked together the year round and had, by the time I first experienced them, achieved an enviable reputation for ensemble playing.

The piece we saw was *The Little Clay Cart,* an adaptation from the ancient Hindu. It was one of the Players' most esteemed presentations and an exotic evening for me, exquisitely remote from anything I had yet experienced in the theater. I still remember the romantic setting by Aline Bernstein: with simply a cyclorama for background, the lavish effects on the tiny stage were achieved by the ingenious use of set pieces, props, and elaborately fashioned costumes (Mrs. Bernstein told me, some thirty years later, that she and the staff had sewn them all by hand).

The Neighborhood Players, the Provincetown Players and the Washington Square Players, nucleus of the Theater Guild, were the three exceptional institutions which set the esthetic standards for the theater of the Twenties. Each had been started in 1915 by idealistic amateurs in revolt against the staleness of established drama molds — the women's problem plays, the melodramas, the slick comedies — that still — under whatever guise of contemporaneity — provide the bulk of theater in New York, London, and Paris.

The Provincetown concentrated on new dramatists, producing Susan Glaspell and all the early plays of Eugene O'Neill. They also utilized the artistry of Robert Edmond Jones, whose simplified settings are credited with having stripped the stage of the clutter of Belasco "realism." I never got down to Greenwich Village (unknown territory to me until years later) to see the Provincetown Players; the only production of theirs I ever saw was an uptown revival of O'Neill's *The Emperor Jones.*

The Neighborhood Players, in their East Side home on Grand Street, were slightly more familiar to me; after *The Little Clay Cart,* I was in the audience for their closing event at the Playhouse in 1927, the delicious *Grand Street Follies.* When the Lewisohn sisters withdrew their support of the organization they had founded, the company, reorganized as the Actor Managers, moved into the Broadway area and I saw almost every one of their productions for the two seasons they were in existence.

What sophisticated playgoers found most delightful about *The Grand Street Follies* were the witty parodies, the impudent caricatures of the preceding uptown season. The mainstays of the revues were its three tremendously talented impersonators, Albert Carroll,

Dorothy Sands, and Paula Trueman. Carroll above all was a genius at mimicry, giving his characterizations a diabolic flick that set each meticulously costumed portrait hilariously and memorably askew. In this last of the downtown shows, he made his first appearance in a sketch of his own authorship, *A Fjord Joke,* in which he did an astonishing takeoff of Mrs. Fiske being lectured to on Ibsen by her goggling admirer Alexander Woollcott. One of Mrs. Fiske's recognizable stage props was a kerchief or scarf which she skillfully used to underscore a word or a point; in Carroll's mimicry she kept manipulating this while half-listening to Woollcott's enraptured outpourings, bringing it to her nose in a delicate gesture of admonishment when the flattery became too fulsome. Several times during his passionate monologue (he was beseeching her to let him play Oswald to her Mrs. Alving) she would absentmindedly leave the stage, returning unnoticed by him in time for the end of one peroration and the beginning of the next.

When I interviewed Carroll for the *Herald-Tribune* in 1945, I reminded him of this number. He told me that Woollcott, the critic for the New York *World* at the time, had come backstage after the opening to inform him that he had dined with Mrs. Fiske before going to the theater that evening and had arrived just as the curtain went up on the sketch. "I couldn't believe it," Carroll reported him as saying. "Her voice was still ringing in my ears and there I was hearing it again from the stage."

One of Carroll's most ingenious set pieces, done after the *Follies* had moved uptown, was a double impersonation of Mrs. Fiske and Ethel Barrymore in a highly unlikely co-starring venture as Mistress Ford and Mistress Page in *The Merry Wives of Windsor.* Performing in a bisected costume, he astonishingly gave the illusion of being both actresses simultaneously onstage. His right profile, with appropriate habiliment, would be a replica of Miss Barrymore's, his left uncannily Mrs. Fiske's; rapidly turning sides, he was able to carry on a duologue in the purloined, widely dissimilar voices of each.

Dorothy Sands, I see by my tattered playbill, caricatured the effluent Jane Cowl in Robert E. Sherwood's first hit, *The Road to Rome,* and also roughed up Laura Hope Crews as the overpossessive

mother in a Freudian parody of Sidney Howard's *The Silver Cord*.
Her most memorable cartoon, for me, was in a later *Follies:* on the
Fifth Avenue steps of the classic New York Public Library building,
Mae West as a genial, sluttish Juliet, enticing the morose Romeo —
obstinately speaking in his native tongue — of Alexander Moissi,
the great German star whom Reinhardt had recently brought to
this country (an equally malevolent dissection by Albert Carroll).

Paula Trueman, the third of the miraculous trio, did Mary Eaton
in *Three Little Maids from Broadway Town,* a number poking fun
at stereotyped musical comedy ingenues, and a combination Fran-
cine Larrimore and Jeanne Eagels in an all-star-cast revival of a
Restoration classic called *The School for Rivals*. Her brilliance was
much more in evidence later on in the uptown editions, in one of
which she miraculously caught Ruth Gordon as *Serena Blandish*
("the incredibly accurate imitation," wrote the New York *World*'s
Alison Smith, "was only matched by the bewildering delight of
Ruth Gordon in the audience"). Albert Carroll was her foil in this
sketch, playing Constance Collier to her explicit teeth.

I have gone on at such length about *The Grand Street Follies* not
only because they gave me so much pleasure but also because they
are representative of the coziness, the clubbiness that existed in the
New York theater in the Twenties. Each edition was anticipated
eagerly by habitual playgoers; audiences attending them had seen
all or most of the Broadway season's plays, and were familiar with
the mannerisms of the stars so cunningly burlesqued. The stars
themselves were indulgent with their impersonators and conspired
with them to ensure the perfection of the parodies. Carroll, for
instance, was backstage for weeks at every performance of *The
Furies* while he was preparing his caricature of Laurette Taylor.
When he had finally departed, Miss Taylor shook out her white
chiffon gown before making her first entrance that evening, "just to
make sure Albert Carroll isn't in it."

Bereft of the financial and directorial support of the Lewisohn
sisters, the company tried to put on their own productions uptown.
Under a new name, the Actor Managers, they moved the last of the
home-based *Follies* to the Booth Theater and also presented 1928

and 1929 editions at the Booth and the Little; they attempted *Maya*, a drama about a Marseilles prostitute, which was closed by the district attorney; an adaptation by Robert E. Sherwood of Ring Lardner's trenchant short story, *The Love Nest,* with June Walker as guest star; and a revival of Lord Dunsany's ironic fantasy, *If.* The straight plays were failures and the revues, though mildly successful, couldn't manage to remain self-supporting. After a brilliant twelve-year flowering, the Neighborhood Players, once uprooted, were unable to survive transplantation. An American theater tragedy.

5

THE FIRST Broadway opening I ever attended was really only about three-fifths of a Broadway opening since my participation didn't begin until forty-five minutes or so after the curtain had gone up. One evening toward the end of January 1925, a schoolmate and I took the subway to Times Square with the intention of walking about aimlessly, inhaling the Byzantine splendors of the district. We strolled along Forty-second Street to Eighth Avenue, watching enviously as the entertainment-bound crowds pushed their way through the dazzle. Then back down the northern side of the street, up Broadway to Forty-fourth, west to the middle of the block, across Shubert Alley, continuing north on Forty-fifth, with a stop at each theater to absorb the displays and gape at the latecomers rushing to get into the darkened houses.

At the Martin Beck, across Eighth Avenue on Forty-fifth Street, a musical called *China Rose* was giving its first public performance. Just as my friend and I, shabby-knickered adolescents, approached the theater, two young (probably college) men, gleamingly outfitted in evening suits and the fashionable coonskin coats of the day, came hurtling through the lobby door, having had as much of the show as they could abide. Seeing us, one of them laughingly said, "Do you want to go in?" and handed over two ticket stubs. With trepidation we showed them to the doorman, who waved us inside. The usher glanced at the stubs and led us to our seats, well down front and in the center. On the stage a comedian dressed as a V.I.C. — Very Important Chinaman — was singing in front of a row of girls:

> Oh I know . . . why they make . . . them so beau . . .
>   ti . . . ful
> But why . . . do they make . . . them so . . .
>   go-o-o-d? . . .

The show was terrible (the leading characters were named Bang Bang, O Mi, Fli Wun, Cha Ming, Ro See; the situation: Cha Ming is in love with Ro See, "the only unkissed maiden in the province"). Of the reviews the next day, Percy Hammond's dismissal in the *Herald-Tribune* was perhaps the most urbane.

"Such operettas as *China Rose*," he wrote, "should be treated with veneration. This one in particular deserves the respect coming to those afflicted with second childhood. It is just a sweet old thing, of the kind referred to by this ribald generation as a 'daddy.' Rich, courageous, spendthrift and ornamental in a withered way, it is a florid octogenarian, a sentimental grandsire who has left the blessings of retirement for the cruel discomforts of modern Times Square life."

The occasion was memorable, however, since it was the opening gun in my career as a fairly consistent teenage first-nighter. No one had thrown us out of the theater, no one apparently had thought it the least bit odd that two poorly dressed boys should be rubbing threadbare elbows with the finery of the city's finest, at the most glittering event in the life of any Broadway enterprise. That first invasion had been by accident; subsequent incursions, frequently illegal, were entirely by design. Having checked the newspapers to see what play was opening, I would set out after supper, with my friend Mike de Lisio as an apprehensive accomplice. We would time our arrival at the theater for a few minutes before the first curtain was due to fall. When the crowd poured out of the auditorium for their smokes, we would mingle with them, trying to be as inconspicuous as possible. We soon found that the best way to remain anonymous was to slip into the theater when the warning bell for the curtain sounded and dart downstairs to the lounge, picking up a program meanwhile from the stacks behind the last row of seats. The possession of this tangible evidence, we felt, would disarm suspicion if an usher should have any doubt about our right to be there.

Just as the lights were dimming, we would go upstairs and take places at the rear of the house. Usually, unreserved admissions had been sold and we could become part of a fairly solid block of standees. If the management had decided to forgo this extra first night revenue to have as little disturbance as possible on such a crucial occasion, the chances of detection would be much greater. But there were always nervous persons connected with the enterprise — authors, producers, producers' assistants, scenery and lighting men, costume designers or their helpers — lurking in the rear, and the ushers would be wary of singling out any of us to ask for proof of our lawful occupancy.

Attendance at these first nights enabled us to see and observe, however briefly, many of the most celebrated personalities connected with the arts.

I remember seeing Morris Gest several times, once in curbside conversation with Percy Hammond, wearing (it was his trademark) a flowing black ribbon bow tie and wide-brimmed black fedora. The famous showman had brought to this country the Moscow Art Theater, Max Reinhardt's *The Miracle,* Eleanora Duse on her last tour, and such exotic specialties as Balieff's Russian revue, *Chauve-Souris.* The backing for his ventures usually came from banker Otto H. Kahn, the Maecenas of the Twenties, an openhanded benefactor who lavished money on such diverse institutions as the *avant-garde* New Playwrights' Theater and the conformist Metropolitan Opera. (He was reportedly the first Jew permitted to buy his way onto its impregnably Gentile Board. He was also profligate with stock market tips and in the '29 crash many who had taken his advice lost their money like everyone else.)

I also saw Morris Gest's brother-in-law, David Belasco, producing dean of stagey "realism," wearing his collar reversed ministerial-style, conforming to his self-perpetrated public image. And the old turn-of-the-century producer, Daniel Frohman, withered and shaky, still managing the Lyceum Theater he had controlled since the late Eighties.

Harold Ross, who had rallied the Algonquin group to form a new weekly publishing venture, *The New Yorker* (I had bought the first issue, lured by the advertisement "a sophisticated magazine," an unbeatable category for a fourteen-year-old), was to be seen occasionally in the lobby, tongue habitually protruding from parted lips in an unconscious gesture of ferocity. The columnist F.P.A. was a regular, recapitulating the occasion at week's end in his "Diary of Our Own Samuel Pepys." Another regular was the solemn-faced, bespectacled George S. Kaufman, by then a well-known playwright but reluctant to give up his job as theater reporter for the New York *Times*. I recognized some of their faces from having seen caricatures of them by Herb Roth, Covarrubias, Al Hirschfeld, and Wynn in the Sunday drama pages and in *Vanity Fair;* others I knew through eavesdropping when adjacent first-nighters pointed them out.

At these quieter, workaday openings, I could feel a kinship with the literary-journalist-theatrical figures who were more glamorous to me than any other. Although I was too timid to speak to any of my idols, the fact of their proximity made them part of my world.

Big, splashy, star-encrusted openings engendered no such familial feelings. I thought of the quieter first nights as being almost private affairs, which, as a prospective club member and as part of my apprenticeship, I was obligated to attend. The showier events lured me with their glitter, but they were unnerving. At these my nose was pressed unheeded to a window displaying goods that could never be within my reach.

Every celebrity in town would converge at a really Important Premiere — a production for which the anticipation ran high, like a new comedy by George S. Kaufman and his current collaborator, a new Lonsdale with Ina Claire, a new anything starring the Lunts, or Laurette Taylor, or Ethel Barrymore, or one of a handful of

HERB ROTH

HERB ROTH

THREE STARS OF THE MORNING
WORLD. *Franklin P. Adams (F.P.A.)*,
top left, *Alexander Woollcott*, top right,
Heywood Broun, right

HERB ROTH

great favorites, a new "Charles Frohman presents" (the insignia of Gilbert Miller playing with Paramount Pictures money), a new Arthur Hopkins presents, a new Winthrop Ames presents, a new (for a few seasons) Jed Harris presents. . . . Most of all they would turn out in droves for a big revue like the *Ziegfeld Follies,* or a smart musical by the Gershwins, especially one featuring Fred and Adele Astaire, or a winsome musical with Marilyn Miller and Jack Donahue, or an uproarious Marx Brothers extravaganza, or a musical with songs by Irving Berlin, or Jerome Kern, or Cole Porter.

Porter's *Fifty Million Frenchmen,* containing his first complete Broadway score, drew the most breathtaking agglomeration of chic I have ever seen at the theater. Porter was an especial favorite of the richest international set, he had entertained on a spectacularly lavish scale in Europe, his songs were clever and amusing. This was *their* Cole finally coming into his professional own and no one who could possibly be there was going to miss his opening.

Mike de Lisio and I had no difficulty in mixing with the crowd as it glided out for the first act intermission. But it was not easy to maneuver through the long, narrow lobby of the Lyric to get into the auditorium. And, gate-crashing veterans though we by that time were, it was intimidating to be conscious of the disparity between the two of us, in our nondescript, workaday suits, and all the others in their most splendid finery. Many of the men were in white tie and tails and it seemed that even the most unprepossessing at least wore dinner jackets.

We had both left school by then, and Mike was working as an office boy for *The New Yorker.* To his dismay, he looked up to find the magazine's decorous first reader and movie critic, John Chapin Mosher, staring in vague disbelief, no doubt wondering how he had gotten there. But the fact that we knew someone in the audience, however tenuous the relationship, emboldened us to continue to push our way inside and even contributed to our enjoyment of the show (a comic line the audience seemed to relish inordinately was Helen Broderick's retort to her staid traveling companion, after being shown some feelthy pictures by a rue de Rivoli vendor: "You and your goddam châteaus!"). Also adding some spice to the occasion was the appearance in the cast of the pert, Dutch-bobbed dancer Betty Compton, whose intimate friendship with Mayor Walker was an open, illicit secret.

I don't remember seeing many film stars at first nights but I wouldn't have noticed anyway, since I was then snobbish about the movies. Stage stars were often on view, but not too many could attend, even if they wished to, since they would be working the same hours at their own theaters. They did, however, assemble *en masse* for special events, like the midnight performance (its second) of the smart English revue *Wake Up and Dream*, when the Selwyn lobby was awash with the uniform brown furs of Beatrice Lillie and Hope Williams and the dirty-white ermine of Libby Holman, the ladies set off by the glistening likes of Clifton Webb, Fred Allen, et al.

At the Sunday evening one-woman shows of Ruth Draper and particularly Cecilia ("Cissie") Loftus — as she liked to be billed — the seats and the intermission pavements were crammed with practically every prestigious member of Actors' Equity. Cissie Loftus was the most extraordinary impersonator I have ever seen. A holdover from the London music halls of the Nineties (the young Max Beerbohm had been enamored of her as a teenage prodigy; Toulouse-Lautrec's lithographic depiction of her, swaggering insouciantly in a top hat, is ruefully evocative), she was also renowned as a legitimate actress. But as a mimic she was unsurpassed.

The Loftus *Impressions and Impersonations* encompassed three generations of performers. Her versatility was astonishing. She would recapture such departed stars as Sarah Bernhardt (in a scene from *La Tosca* or from *Izeyl*), Ada Rehan (as the most famous Viola of her day), Réjane (a scene, I think, from *Madame Sans-Gêne*); Victorian and Edwardian favorites of the English halls, like Vesta Tilley, Marie Lloyd and Vesta Victoria; the *belle époque* diseuse Yvette Guilbert; down to such then current stars as Jeanne Eagels in *Rain*, Fanny Brice in her Mrs. Cohen at the Beach monologue, and Florence Reed as *The Shanghai Gesture*'s Mother Goddam.

In the lobby crush at the first Loftus program that we attended (having this time paid for second balcony seats so we could see the entire bill) Mike pulled at what he thought was my coat sleeve, to say in great excitement, "There's Alfred Lunt!" I had moved aside and it was of course Lunt's sleeve he found himself tugging. Most exciting for us, however, was the proximity of our heroes, the critics, and of what was loosely known as the Algonquin Round Table group.

We would see the awesome, waspish Woollcott (wearing, at the dressier openings, an evening cape) ; the charming, soft-spoken Heywood Broun, every disheveled cubic inch of him (and he was a tall, bulky man) living up to his sartorial reputation for resembling a bag of rumpled laundry; the *Evening Post*'s John Anderson, handsome and remote; the dapper George Jean Nathan, handsome and imperturbable (he was always impeccably turned out, so notably that when he was called as a witness in a book obscenity trial — I think Cabell's *Jurgen* was under indictment — the prosecuting attorney in order to discredit his testimony attempted to ridicule him as an unconventionally tailored dandy whose breast pocket was on the right rather than on the left side of his coat) ; the sandy-haired, bristle-mustached Brooks Atkinson, usually hugging a pipe; the emergent young Walter Winchell, prematurely gray, wiry, nervous, just learning the celebrity ropes; the stammering John Mason Brown, who replaced Anderson on the *Post* when the latter joined Hearst's *American;* the jovial, tweedy Gilbert Gabriel of the *Sun; bon viveur* Robert Benchley, usually in evening dress, whose uproarious, infectious laugh was easily identifiable inside the auditorium as well as on the street; and the baroque Percy Hammond, whose full, red, puffed cheeks gave him the petulant look of an unburped baby.

Hammond was one of thirteen first-string critics on daily newspapers of varying degrees of influence. He had been brought to New York from the Chicago *Tribune,* where he had earned an awesome reputation with his graceful, ironic prose style and his facility in wielding a lethal epigram. "The human knee is a joint and not an entertainment," he had admonished the producer of a revue featuring near nudity, and, of a tired vaudeville sketch, "They've played it so often that they can play it in their sleep, which they did yesterday."

Hammond stalked his prey skillfully. He would approach his subject with deceptive gentleness before, as Lewis Nichols said, "twisting the most highly polished dagger in New York into the back of the evening." After the kill, a typical epitaph would be: "A large and patient audience did not molest [the play] with much applause."

He was especially canny in his judgments of actors. When Helen Hayes was just beginning to attract attention as a young comedienne, he deftly assessed both the limitations of her talent and the extent to which she would make it work for her. Her role of Babs, Mary Roberts Rinehart's "sub-deb," he observed, was "written to the brim, and Heaven would have had to help it if Miss Hayes had not. Honest, tricky, brilliant, taking many risks and making few errors, Miss Hayes is one of those artists, apparently, who can dare extravagance, and by her charm and her deft obviousness blur the line between acting and an exhibition. She will be a big thing in the theater before long, I predict."

Ruth Gordon, "a new kind of ingenue," he wrote in 1925, early in this actress's career, "split the difference between Life and the Theater almost as expertly as Miss Laurette Taylor does. I shall read in other journals today that she was the 'hit' of the performance [she did indeed receive extravagant reviews], yet I shall still suspect that she was merely the shrewd and wise showwoman."

"The sweetest and the most polite of the Othellos," he found Walter Hampden. "Even as he chokes [Desdemona] to death you feel that he does so with an underlying courteousness. He sees pink, rather than red. You may recall Beerbohm Tree's Othello, a wild beast feeding upon his jealousy, spitting at the mention of Cassio's name, and chewing Desdemona's rose to pieces. Or Grasso, the Sicilian, who was an amorous Othello and pawed the white arms of his Desdemona. . . . Or Robert Mantell's characterization, which made of the Moor a worthy and a resonant Elk. Mr. Hampden is as none of these. . . . His Othello is of a moderate temperature, self-composed and placidly excitable."

When Mrs. Fiske, toward the end of her lustrous career, appeared in an obvious comedy called *Ladies of the Jury,* he labeled his review "The First Comedienne in a Brash Burlesque" and after amusing himself with details of the plot, ended with, "It is all most laughable and just another of Mrs. Fiske's little personal, jovial frolics. One wonders, however, what she herself would really have thought of it if she had been sitting in front, as we were last evening at the Erlanger. She would have laughed, possibly, just as wryly as we did."

Usually a genial if mischievous observer, he could become downright vicious when his sense of decorum had been aroused. Mae West in *The Constant Sinner,* her "saga of a sexologist," found him at his beastliest: "Since Miss West is established in the Theater as one of its admired institutions, I may have the right to ask 'Why?' The inquiry is inspired by wonder rather than insolence, a desire to be corrected in a false impression. As I see this petted favorite, she has few of the endearing attributes of a successful star. Heaven forbid that I should say that any actress is not beautiful, and I refrain from objecting to Miss West's over-conspicuous charms. She is a plump, almost Circassian blonde whose ample figure overflows her girdles in graceful cascades and whose laborious ambulations suggest that she has sore feet. As the constant sinner in her play, she talks through her nostrils, and in other ways reduces a stage harlot's doubtful fascinations to the minimum. You wonder why she appeals to men. She is so different from anything you have ever seen outside a zoo, you decide that her impersonation is deliberately outlandish. When her various heroes in the drama ply her with jewels, you suspect that they should be feeding her peanuts. What can be done with Miss West and her peculiar manifestations? She is a menace to art, if not to morals, and she is entitled to an investigation."

As a result of the above review, Miss West was reported by the gossip columnist Walter Winchell to have bought a whip with which she planned to chastise Hammond if she should ever encounter him.

Hammond's notices in the *Herald-Tribune* were anticipated with no more eagerness (by the theatergoing public) or dread (by the profession) than were Heywood Broun's in the morning *World* or

Alexander Woollcott's in the evening *Sun*. These three, because the most journalistically readable and amusingly quotable, were I believe more influential than the ten remaining daily critics combined in determining audience potential for a Broadway attraction. Broun conducted his general topics column, "It Seems to Me," on the *World*'s renowned opposite-the-editorial page (Laurence Stallings reviewed books, Deems Taylor and later Samuel Chotzinoff reviewed music events, Franklin Pierce Adams over his famous initials F.P.A. ran "The Conning Tower," a dazzling compilation to which many of the most celebrated writers, especially poets, contributed gratis, and three times weekly Frank Sullivan could be counted upon for a very funny piece of surrealist humor). When Broun decided to give up the theater reviews to devote himself solely to "It Seems to Me," the *World* hired Woollcott to take his place. This gave the paper practically a culture-monopoly of the city — and therefore the rest of the country.

Woollcott was rapidly becoming a legendary figure in New York's theatrical and literary circles, although he was some years away from the national deification of his later "Town Crier" radio career as a love-hateable old grumps, whose benediction or curse on a book could radically alter its sales chart. His chatty play reviews, with their lavishly expressed endorsements and peevishly expressed dissents, made enjoyable reading; his relish for the theater was contagious, so that each evening became a combustible event.

"The Seidlitz Powder of Times Square," George Jean Nathan had dubbed him in a corrosive article in *The Smart Set* magazine (Nathan's original title, which he was dissuaded from using, had been "Enter, Madame," after a then-current play dealing with a prickly prima donna). Any entertainment admired by Woollcott "warmed the cockles of this foolish heart"; a person with an unusual name was referred to as "the playwright who rejoices in the name of Em Jo Basshe"; to express enthusiasm he would almost invariably "toss my hat into the air" — "Where I must admit it seems to be spending the week," he added at the end of the 1927 Christmas period which saw the openings of George Kelly's *Behold the Bridegroom,* Philip Barry's *Paris Bound,* George S. Kaufman and Edna Ferber's *The Royal Family,* and the musical version of the latter's novel, *Show Boat,* with a score by Jerome Kern. In celebration of such euphoric occasions there was, naturally, jubilant "dancing in the aisles."

A typical cozy review (headed "Peche Molnar") described 1927's *The Play's the Thing:* "Sooner or later every playwright — be he George Cohan or Clayton Hamilton, Ralph Murphy or Ferenc Molnar — has to turn out that comedy wherein the play writes itself as it goes along. 'Well, well,' the piece seems to say as the curtain rises, 'we are supposed to have a play here tonight, and here it is 8:45, and what are we going to do about it?'

"Then the comedy takes shape before your eyes with the same engaging lack of secrecy that attends the birth of a Childs' wheat cake.

"Molnar has amused himself by writing one in this vein which he calls *Spiel im Schloss.* It was produced suavely and with spirit last evening at Henry Miller's Theatre, where you will find it hiding sportively behind the title, 'The Play's the Thing.' It is an idle, elegant charade, with that tendency to get winded which is the curse of all conceitful comedies that try to last all evening, but with enough of mockery and gay, good invention in it to make it a most agreeable evening in the theatre.

"Inside this form Molnar has tucked away a fable about a dreamy young man who loves a fair lady and who is ready to leap from the castle rock when, through the thin partition of her bedroom wall, he overhears a passionate and compromising dialogue. It is the notion of a fond and older friend that, by deception, toil, and other rogueries, this lad might be lulled into believing it was no real encounter he had overheard but a mere rehearsal of a play.

"The role of this elder sage is played by the unfailing Holbrook Blinn, for whom, somehow, the most diverse plays seem to have been expressly written. If you would have a Wall Street magnate or a Bowery tough or a Riviera cynic or a Mexican bandit, you must send for Holbrook Blinn. His days in the theatre are more untroubled than most because in the capricious poverty of the American stage there happens to be only one of him.

"But this play of Molnar's is rather the opportunity for Reginald

Owen, an English comedian who has been leaping distractedly from *Little Eyolf* to *The Importance of Being Earnest,* only to find his best chance as the bombastic and tearful actor in *The Play's the Thing.* He has the role of roles in the piece at the Henry Miller, and was, I thought last night, enormously comic and delightful.

"Then there is a fine performance by young Edward Crandall, who shared the honors of *Young Woodley* last season with Master Hunter. This time he has a role which would have been just a dry stick in the underpinning of the comedy had it fallen to the ordinary run of juveniles. I am afraid I shall have to predict that Mr. Crandall is going to be an important actor in the American theatre one of these days. [A vain prediction, as it turned out.]

"And it was good to see Roy Nairn again, grinning his way cheerfully through one of those garrulous servant roles our playwrights resort to whenever smitten with an uneasy feeling that their opus is not going to last all evening.

" 'Why are you so late?' they ask him crossly.

"He explains that he fell downstairs.

" 'And did that take you long?'

"And so on and so on until, I declare, it's eleven o'clock and you don't know where the evening has gone to."

Woollcott spread his prose lavishly, so that in addition to his daily reviewing, at least one and frequently two articles by him could be found usually in weekly or monthly magazines. He cribbed from himself shamelessly and it was not unusual to see the simultaneous appearance of several pieces on the same topic: Mrs. Fiske, the Marx Brothers, novelist Alice Duer Miller, commercial artist Neysa McMein, and the Lizzie Borden murder case were especial favorites for repetition. He was sometimes too precipitate in spreading his copy. When the Theater Guild announced its production of O'Neill's marathon *Strange Interlude,* he wrote a derogatory criticism of it, based upon the published version of the play, for the monthly *Vanity Fair.* The issue appeared on the newsstands a day or two before the opening; since his views were therefore known, the irritated *World* management felt obliged to send a substitute to the performance.

When I began reading newspaper reviews, the New York *Times*

J. Brooks Atkinson, *the man from the* Times

THE NEW YORK *Times*

Percy Hammond, *the man from the* Herald-Tribune

MAURICE GOLDBERG, *Stage*

critic was John Corbin, who had been commenting on plays for various newspapers at least since Clyde Fitch's day early in the century. Corbin's opinions were sober but so, unfortunately, was his prose style. His replacement at the end of that season (1925) was Stark Young, erudite, with an aloof, intellectual rather than an emotional, exhortatory approach to his subject, and definitely too abstruse for general consumption ("Can you write for the common reader?" asked the *Times* management at the end of his first tortuous year. "No," answered Young, terminating his employment. He moved on to the *New Republic,* for whose subscribers his distinguished articles were much better suited).

J. Brooks Atkinson, the new incumbent — he didn't immediately drop the initial from his by-line — had been the book editor before being thrust into the notoriety of a drama critic's post ("Criticism of books employs all the decor of the learned professions. Criticism of the drama is chatter," he was to write a few years later). The *Times* reviews, which had turned torpid since the frisky days of Woollcott, Corbin's predecessor, now began to perk up again. Atkinson's scholarship was sound and he had no inhibitions about expressing enthusiasm for a play or a performance when he thought them deserving. He also had a way with an epigram, as when he categorized the political satire *Of Thee I Sing* as being "funnier than the government and not nearly so dangerous."

Of course, like most writers hampered by the menacing time clock of daily journalism, his adjectival resources soon became strained, so that as the seasons passed more and more actresses were giving "luminously beautiful" performances or performances "of rare loveliness"; innumerable designers were devising "luminously immaculate sets" or "sets of purposeful loveliness"; many a star was "acting in the lucid style of which he (or she) is capable"; many an experienced, middle-aged player was making "a coherent character out of what was nebulous in the script."

He could also occasionally communicate his own moral rigidity. When the musical *Pal Joey* opened, he was appalled by the fact that the leading character was an unscrupulous gigolo: "Although *Pal Joey* is expertly done, can you draw sweet water from a foul well?" Twelve years later, the show was revived, receiving a rave review from Atkinson (had his or the world's sense of morality changed meanwhile?) : "Mr. O'Hara's night-club tout has begun Broadway's new year auspiciously." *Variety*, with a long memory, reprinted excerpts from both reviews under the caption "TIME (S) HEALS ALL WOUNDS."

Frequently he could be ambivalent in the same review, expressing approval in the first half and then taking it all back at the end. This Janus-like critical stance was given amused recognition in a comedy by Robert E. Sherwood, *This Is New York*. Two characters are having a discussion about Atkinson's review of a new play. "Did he like the show?" asks one. The other answers, looking puzzled, "I couldn't make out."

Atkinson, before he retired in 1960, influenced the theatergoing of two generations of playgoers. I think his was the second longest tenure of a drama critic's job in this country (William Winter was the New York *Tribune* man from 1865 to 1909). In the 1930s, after the demise of the morning *World* and the gradual abdication of many of the colorful figures among the critics, he became the most powerful play reviewer in New York. A negative opinion from him (as much because of his reputation for soundness as because of the exalted position of the *Times*) usually killed any production's chances of survival.

Until the late Twenties, however, his voice was not nearly so potent as that of Woollcott, who bore the additional cachet of being the local Johnsonian wit of the Algonquin Round Table. To Woollcott's opinion on a play would be added the frequently similar opinions of the widely read *World* columnists and co-Algonquinites F. P. A. Broun and Frank Sullivan. Critics on the other papers were not so comfortably buttressed.

Most were usually in agreement, however, since the standards were based on a comfortable, parochially orientated drama with a "well-made" structure (experimental forms were condoned rather than welcomed; the "literary" play of ideas was sent back regrettably to the bookshelves because it lacked theatrical urgency). The "realist" plays of Clyde Fitch, Eugene Walter, Charles Klein, Edward Sheldon, with their highflown rhetoric and their punch-line curtains ("Four years ago you took away my name and gave me a number; now I've given up that number and I've got your name!"* "I'm going to Rector's to make a hit, and to hell with the rest!"†) had long been discarded and a new, naturalistic drama had come in, with keyed-down "recognizable" dialogue and acting to match. The daily reviewer's function was to report on how nearly "lifelike" the characters and situations were, how contemporary the theme, and how well constructed for middle-class audience consumption. And, above all, how entertaining. Even as late as 1932, with Chekhov a known quantity in New York, Percy Hammond could write of Jed Harris's laudable production of *Uncle Vanya:* "It is a fine performance of characters in a provincial Chekhov *cul de sac* and a credit to Mr. Harris and his aspirations. But in the remote event that he sends me tickets for a future exhibition of *Uncle Vanya,* you may have them, since I shall be seeking recreation elsewhere."

If the New York newspaper reviewers were generally backward in their knowledge of new trends and classical traditions, however, esthetic standards were higher in the serious weekly and monthly magazines. The criticisms of Edmund Wilson and of Stark Young in the *New Republic,* of Young in *Theater Arts Monthly,* of Joseph Wood Krutch in *The Nation,* even of the flippant George Jean Nathan in *The American Mercury,* were broader in scope, treating the theater as a universal cultural expression rather than as a local sport.

More restricted in approach, but fun to read, were the genial dissertations of Robert Benchley in the humor weekly *Life,* and later as the fashionable first-nighter for *The New Yorker.* At intervals Dorothy Parker would substitute for Benchley, almost invariably ending her pieces with frantic pleas to be relieved of her burden ("Dear Mr. Benchley: Please come home. A joke is a joke"). It was on these occasions that some of her most famous quips were produced, such as her discovery that Katharine Hepburn

---

* *Within the Law*: He had sent her to jail and in revenge she had married his son.
† *The Easiest Way*: Her lover wouldn't give her a second chance so she was going to a notorious café to sell herself to the highest bidder.

ran the gamut of emotions from A to B, and that a sticky play called *The House Beautiful* was "the play lousy."

The Broadway theater in the Twenties was dominated by two sets of despots — the powerful critics, and the even more powerful Lee and J. J. Shubert organization, which owned most of the houses and was interested in keeping them filled. Usually they worked more or less in harmony, but a particularly severe chastisement by one of the former would sometimes lead to an attempted retaliation by the latter. At one time or another most of the forthright critics were barred from Shubert-controlled theaters, but they were always reinstated when their publishers refused to knuckle down to demands that they be fired. When Heywood Broun was denied admission to an opening, even after his paper had paid for the tickets, Broun and his employers sued and won. The brash young Walter Winchell, busily acquiring a reputation with his gossip column on the *Evening Graphic,* was too impatient for such legal shenanigans. Having incurred the displeasure of the petulant brothers, he found himself an outcast from one of the biggest openings of the 1928 season, the Marx Brothers' *Animal Crackers.* Winchell cannily solved the problem by having the sympathetic Harpo Marx sneak him into the 44th Street Theater by way of the stage door, and reviewed the performance from backstage.

6

THE BROADWAY THEATER was at its peak by the mid-Twenties. It did not begin to lose its hold on a wide public until well into the next decade, when talking films, which were to wean away much of its audience, stopped lisping and became a serious threat.

In the season beginning with the fall of 1925 and ending in June of 1926 (then, as now, almost nothing was presented during July and August) 255 productions opened, of which I managed to see only 13. This of course along with my quota of at least one weekly visit to a local movie house (10¢) and one vaudeville show almost every week (25¢) at the Keith-Albee Riverside on Broadway and Ninety-sixth Street or Loew's Orpheum on Third Avenue and Eighty-sixth.

In February of '25 I had been transferred to the West Forty-sixth Street annex of the High School of Commerce (the Romanesque structure that now houses the School for the Performing Arts) around the corner from the Keith-Albee flagship, the Palace. By cutting my last class, I could attend the Monday matinee, the Palace's equivalent of a Broadway first night, when all the out-of-work vaudevillians went to catch the competition.

It was here on one memorable Old Timers' bill that I saw some legendary stars of the Lillian Russell–Diamond Jim Brady era: the classic Dutch comics Weber and Fields, Frankie Bailey of "the million-dollar legs," the enormous Fay ("Little Buttercup") Templeton. On another bill I got my first glimpse of the remarkable Laurette Taylor in an unremarkable one-act version of her recent failure, the pantomime *Pierrot the Prodigal*. It was not unusual for theater stars to pick up some extra money between plays by taking a turn in vaudeville, a custom to which I also owe my first experience of the patrician Ethel Barrymore, in James M. Barrie's *The Twelve Pound Look*.

Talents from the big musicals returned periodically to the medium that had originally nurtured them. Eddie Cantor wailing "If you knew Susie, like I know Susie!"; (Bobby) Clark and (Paul) McCullough in a sidesplitting sketch in which they chased each other over the beds in adjoining hotel rooms; Fanny Brice eternally reprising "My Man" after sidesplitting versions of such genre specialties as "Oi oi I'm an Indian now," and "Becky is beck in the Bellet"; Elsie Janis (who could assume the identity of each of her famous subjects simply by rearranging her hair) adding to her standard burlesqued "impressions" — the three Barrymores, Will Rogers, etc. — a new travesty: Fanny Brice, who was about to appear for the first time in a straight play, under Belasco's management, singing in parody to the Gershwins' song, "Oh do do do, What you done done done before, Davy!"

During the 1926–27 season, 263 theatrical productions were put on, according to the tabulations of *Variety*. Of these I saw 26 (that I can recall and check; I must have experienced unrecorded tryouts on the Subway Circuit that never made it into town). The next season, the century's busiest and in point of sheer theatrical exuberance the most stimulating of the decade, there were 264 productions, of which I attended 57 (again not counting those I saw that failed on the road). In 1928–29, I saw 47 out of 225 produced. The following season the count was 233, of which I witnessed 45; in the 1930–31 season, depletion set in, with 187 openings, but I managed to attend 51.

By 1926, as my obsession with the theater kept growing, so did my financial resources. When my indulgent father refused to give me 50¢ for a Saturday matinee at Werba's Brooklyn because I was supposed to be helping in his upholstery shop, I threatened to quit school and did. That Monday I got my first full-time job, as errand boy for the Belwyn Music Company at $12.00 a week. Belwyn's had no connection with the legitimate theater but was not entirely divorced from the entertainment industry. It was a clearinghouse whose function was to assemble musical accompaniments for silent films. Movie houses all over the country would send in detailed requests for piano or orchestral sheet music to cover general situations (Mozart's Turkish March for lively action, a Chopin waltz for tender scenes, Gershwin's "Lady Be Good" for sophisticated flirtations) or entire scores (of original or public domain material) for individual films, which Belwyn published.

The firm had offices in the Columbia Burlesque Theater Building opposite the Palace on Forty-seventh Street and Broadway. My job was to pick up from individual publishers copyright music that had been requested, which would then be sorted in the office by the head of my department and shipped out. The job was hardly taxing, and it had the advantage of permitting me to roam the city unhampered by a too-restrictive time schedule. My route usually took me from Forty-seventh Street, in and out of the heart of the theatrical district — Harms's confined offices in a narrow building on West Forty-fifth, with its show business ambience, home base of Kern, Youmans, the Gershwins, Rodgers and Hart; the pungent, Tin

Pan Alley-ish quarters of Remick, publishers of phenomenal hits by Walter Donaldson ("How Ya Gonna Keep 'Em Down on the Farm?" "My Mammy," "My Buddy," "Yes Sir, That's My Baby") — across Fifth Avenue to the stately premises of Schirmer's, on East Forty-third, and all the way down to Astor Place and the musty atmosphere of Carl Fischer's.

I would make the daily trips more interesting by dipping into a theater here and there (the old habit) to pick up a program or, if a rehearsal were in progress, to remain for a while to watch it. Belwyn's wasn't too exacting about how long I stayed out just so I came back at a reasonable hour in the afternoon to help with the mailing. After two months, I left when I couldn't get a $2.00 raise, and landed in the office boy department at Macfadden Publications, 1926 Broadway — the building still stands, staring placidly at its ostentatious new culture neighbors directly across the street in Lincoln Center.

Bernarr Macfadden was then publishing, besides such mainstays as *Physical Culture, True Story, True Detective, True Romances,* a monthly *Dance Magazine,* edited by Vera Caspary. (I once delivered an envelope to the Riverside Drive house of the ballet choreographer Fokine; the butler said — it seemed gratuitous — "Madame's dancing upstairs naked again.") Macfadden had also entered the newspaper field with the vivid *Evening Graphic,* whose city room and printing plant were located in a squalid building near the Brooklyn Bridge.

The paper's main circulation attractions were the garishly inventive news stories and the Monday gossip column (or colyum, as he spelled it) compiled by the wide-eyed Walter Winchell. Its celebrated pink front page advertised whatever domestic or extramarital sensation had been uncovered by a diligent staff, illustrated in photo-montage that indeed lived up to the paper's name. Each day's flagrant "on-the-scene" picture would be re-created by models on whose torsos were superimposed the chosen headliners' faces, spouting balloon-encased dialogue — Pop Art forty years before collectors and museums were ready for it.

By contrast, Winchell's premature disclosures of forthcoming "blessed events" and romantic "splituations" seemed almost ingenuous. Starting "Your Broadway and Mine" as a receptacle for Times Square chitchat, he soon enlarged his area of reconnaissance to include the "intelligentsia" — an awesomely indiscriminate grouping that embraced popular fiction writers as well as the humanist elite — and "socialites," an equally carefree blending of the sacred Four Hundred with the merely solvent and gregarious.

Winchell's pungent vocabulary, an amalgam of theatrical slang and underworld cryptonymy, his flair for constructing a picaresque portmanteau language, attracted the attention of the "literati" and he was encomiastically greeted in thoughtful journals like *The Bookman* and *The American Mercury* as the Boswell of Broadway and the latter-day successor to the Elizabethan John Aubrey.

My last chore of the day at Macfadden's was to bring down to the *Graphic* varied interoffice memoranda from the uptown executive offices. I would arrive at the Park Row building at 5:30 or so, about the same time Winchell got there, distribute my envelopes, then preempt an unused desk near his. While he opened his mail, I would telephone a friend and talk aimlessly — and loudly — about what shows I was going to see, what books I was reading, anything that I vainly thought would impress him. The city room was relatively quiet then and my chatter could have driven him to distraction. But because he either was too absorbed in his correspondence or had the ability to shut out impersonal noise, he never acknowledged me as an irritant. The only complaint he ever made was once when my conversation was in counterpoint to his on another phone and he shouted to a passing reporter, "For God's sake, get that kid to keep quiet, this is an important long distance call!"

To Winchell I owe my first outbreak in print, eight lines of verse I sent him, of which he changed the last word so that it rhymed more exactly with its mate (I think I had paired "them" with "men"). I stopped at his desk the afternoon it appeared, introduced myself as the author, and thanked him for correcting and publishing it. He didn't appear to recognize me as the occasional loudmouth of the adjacent telephone.

Much of the gossip of the period's theatrical and literary personalities I garnered from Winchell's column as he breathlessly recorded it. I believe that then, at the start of his ascendancy, he did most of his legwork himself, feeding his curiosity and ours by stalking the nightclubs to get "scoops" at first hand; later when he transferred to the *Daily Mirror* and had become a byword (and a self-appointed Omnipotent), he depended increasingly upon professional informants and his column lost the precocious insatiability which had been its chief charm.

7

BESIDES THE TENUOUS CONNECTION with Winchell, the other — much more substantial — theatrical alliance I formed at Macfadden Publications was with Frances Smith, secretary to the advertising manager of *Dance Magazine*. Frances inducted me into the arcana of the embryonic modern dance movement by giving me tickets to the Sunday night recitals of the experimenting Martha Graham and the Doris Humphrey–Charles Weidman groups.

Martha, as she was spoken of by initiates whether they knew her personally or not, commanded her audiences with messianic ferocity. She was even more ruthlessly demanding of her pupils. Stories would come back of hysterical scenes in the studio, of telephones ripped from their wall sockets in frustration when she realized that there were limits to the pliability of the girls' bodies and to their endurance. The demons of her esthetic possessed her, insulating her against years of ridicule before she was able to tear down public resistance. Much pietistic nonsense has been written about her (doubtless including an article by me in the mid-Thirties called "High Priestess of the Dance") but the overwhelming sincerity of her conviction makes it impossible to treat her conscientiously with levity. At one time, when she had still to gain general public approbation, *The New Yorker* assigned Meyer Berger, an unbeliever who had made his reputation as a crime reporter, to do a

Profile of her, on the assumption that he would have some clear-headed fun with the subject. After a probing period during which he could uncover no trace of phoniness, he abandoned the assignment, a scoffer helplessly converted.

Martha Graham's expressionist abstracts were too highly personal to be absorbed readily by a popular medium (although, ludicrous to contemplate, she had committed the standard adagio and apache routines in a vaudeville act with Charles Weidman and was also an alumna of a *Greenwich Village Follies*), but the Humphrey-Weidman group with its more easily assimilated impressionist metaphors, notably in *The Waves,* was able to make a breakthrough on Broadway. They were engaged first for an *Americana* edition, then for an even glossier revue, *As Thousands Cheer,* by Moss Hart and Irving Berlin, staged by Hassard Short, starring Marilyn Miller, Clifton Webb, Helen Broderick, Ethel Waters — they couldn't have been in more glittering, more accepted company. This in turn led the way in a few years to the hiring of Agnes deMille, a much later arrival on the Sunday night modern dance landscape, to do the "integrated" choreography for *Oklahoma!,* the beginning of the morose New American musical (and the end of the festive Old).

In the early days when Graham, Humphrey-Weidman, Hanya Holm, Helen Tamiris were exploring, expanding, finally graduating from the harsh technique invented by the German von Laban (and at a time when the music and art worlds were bubbling with experimentation), conservative Broadway held to its traditional rite of high kicks, ignorant of and ignoring the *avant-garde* movements. Dance elements in a typical musical comedy consisted of the chorus line, usually made up of from twelve to sixteen girls and eight boys, whose function was to come on periodically with a kicking-in-unison routine, and a "premiere danseuse" (Harriet Hoctor, Nina Olivette), who erupted into an *en pointe* solo for each of the two acts, the first with a Sugar Plum Fairy motif, the second a number with lots of *brio,* both emphasizing acrobatics. Alternatives to the latter would be a tap dancer, male (Harland Dixon, Carl Randall) or female (Ruby Keeler), for whom black satin trousers and a white satin blouse with *bouffant* sleeves was the costume *de rigueur,* or a Spanish dancer (Vanessi), or a Spanish dancing team (Rosita and Ramon), or an airy ballroom couple (Moss and Fontana), or an eccentric comedy pair (towering Clifton Webb and tiny Mary Hay, puckish Fred and Adele Astaire).

"Choreography" was not a word that appeared in the program credits; the perfunctory listing was "Dances by . . ." or in further explication, "Dances and ensembles by . . ." or in cases of extreme flossiness, "Dances conceived and staged by Sammy Lee, Bobby Connelly, Busby Berkeley, Jack Haskell, Seymour Felix, J. C. Huffman" (this last a Shubert standby). The "ponies" of the chorus were usually in their late teens, pretty by mandate, pert *à la mode;* these were the chief hiring requisites. They were not often asked to perform particularly elaborate or intricate movements — the basic exercises taught in dance academies like Ned Wayburn's would be deemed equipment enough — and the quality of their voices was undoubtedly ignored, considering that what came out was of two *timbres,* squeak or bray. The occasionally witty lyrics for ensemble songs were wasted, since in performance the result was derailed cacophony.

The chorus boys were mostly wilting daffodils whose effeminacy was a byword in and out of the profession and whose dancing ability was apparently even less extensive than that of the girls. They were likely to be more along in years than their female counterparts for, despite such shining alumni as Wallace Beery, Cary Grant and, later, James Cagney, their occupation apparently kept them in a rut with little inclination to advance, like the girls, into marriage.

The Messrs. Shubert, who produced or had a proprietary interest in many of the musicals, entrusted the hiring of the ensemble to a staff casting director, a gentleman known familiarly as "Ma" (but woe the misinformed applicant who asked in innocence for "Mrs."). "Ma" was sentimental about his chorus people, re-engaging them from show to show, year after year. In time, some of the boys became rather portly and the girls began to look as if they had just hurried over from a PTA meeting. They would then be shifted to one of the innumerable road companies of *Blossom Time* or *The*

Student Prince, along with those dusty crystal chandeliers from the warehouse. The Shuberts didn't waste a thing.

But if these choruses frequently looked shopworn, those of other producers were spanking. Since musicals were devised not for the edification but for the entertainment of the Tired Business Man, all efforts were bent in that direction. The girls and their stage consorts would start the proceedings with a clatter of welcoming song, explaining (if the words could be understood, which they couldn't) that they were here in Miami, Paree, Venice to find a husband (wife), or that they were on the Van Buren estate in Southampton, Newport, Bar Harbor waiting for Jimmy, Frank, Peter to arrive with his new fiancée. Standard rhythmic gyrations would follow at frequent intervals, bosoms and bottoms enticingly in motion; the soubrette and the juvenile would make their entrances and start the plot rolling; the baritone/tenor or the soprano leading lady, depending on which was the bigger "name," would next appear; the obligatory comic with his trademarked yock or leer, his oversized shoes or painted eyeglasses, would go through his first funny scene, probably a disguised routine out of his burlesque or vaudeville days; the specialty dancer would deliver the first specialty (unless the star was noted as a dancer, in which case no competition would be tolerated); along about ten o'clock the two chief principals would have a misunderstanding on which to bring down the first act curtain. The second act would more or less follow the same procedure, with the plot working itself into a happy finale.

It is difficult to comprehend the fascination of the musical comedies of the Twenties from an unadorned inventory of their assets. Almost without exception the librettos were dreadful. The characters are Mary Vandervere (rich), or Mary O'Brien (poor), Mrs. Gotrocks, "Bubbles" Larue, Archie deWitt, Delphine deLavalliere, "Pinky" Parks (comedian); the chorus, when not grouped under the general head "Ladies of the Ensemble," are given either cozy first names — Lulu, Flo, Peaches, Jerri — or names a college varsity wit would be ashamed of having invented — Miss Doer Die, Miss Walker Home, Miss Rollser Owne, Miss Showser Style.

Whatever the variants, the basic line was adhered to. Here, from the latest Samuel French catalogue (where it is still being offered to amateurs!) is the plot of the very successful *Gingham Girl*, first produced in 1922: "The story tells of John Cousins and his sweetheart, Mary Thompson, who live at Crossville Corners, and of their trials and tribulations. Mary has a recipe for cookies which she is anxious to put on the market. She meets the son of the owner of the National Biscuit Company. The visiting boy becomes interested in her and offers to aid her in putting her cookies before the public, in competition with his father. Johnnie leaves for New York, after making Mary a gift of one hundred dollars, which she refuses to take, except on the condition that the money should be regarded as a purchase price of a half-interest in her business. Johnnie decides to go forth and make an honest living in order that she may be proud of him. In the meantime, Mary has met with wonderful success. Johnnie, unaware of the fact that Mary owns a big factory in New York, comes to the office seeking a position. She sees him, and tells him that he is half-owner of the business, which in the end straightens matters out nicely."

The Gingham Girl was one of the shows I saw during my early theatergoing at the Bronx Opera House, and it was highly enjoyable. Eddie Buzzell, who played John, was a light comedian, somewhat on the order of Eddie Dowling and Jack Haley, who could put across a song acceptably and whose appearance was engaging enough to make him plausible as the love interest. Opposite him was Helen Ford, demure, slightly plumpish, with an expressive musical comedy voice, who was a favorite leading lady of the decade (she starred in many of the early Rodgers-Hart shows). I remember the setting for John's departure from the small town, on what looked like a real train pulling out of the station, and the pleasant anticipation of what might befall him in New York. I didn't yet know that the book was stereotypical; later on, as a more sophisticated spectator, I would sit impatiently through tiresome "story" maneuvers, which were interrupting the comics and the musical numbers.

Yet such plots, entirely predictable, with little attempt at characterization, were hardly sillier than many opera libretti and served, on another level of expressiveness, somewhat the same purpose: to provide a reasonable background for the score and to exploit the interpretive talent of the performers. Each show was built around these latter elements, and was even spoken of by a hard-core public as "the new Kern show," "the new Gershwin show," "the new Bert Lahr show," rather than by its official title. Leading perpetrators of musical comedy books were Guy Bolton, who in the late 'Teens had collaborated with P. G. Wodehouse and Jerome Kern on the notable Princess Theater productions (*Oh, Boy!, Very Good, Eddie, Oh, Lady, Lady!!*), then worked with the Gershwin brothers on *Lady, Be Good!, Tip Toes, Oh, Kay,* and Herbert Fields, son of comedian Lew Fields, who formed an equally fortuitous partnership with Richard Rodgers and Lorenz Hart to turn out the youthfully ebullient *The Girl Friend, Peggy-Ann, A Connecticut Yankee.*

Gradually, with an increasing loss of audience innocence, the tone of these books perforce became more cynical and the dialogue more blasé. Beneath the tough veneer, however, breathed the same old heart of mush: Act One, misunderstanding, Act Two, reunion. When these shows are revived today, it is the attempts at smartness that are trying; the structure that preserves the conventions has become endearing and understandable on its own terms, like Great-aunt Bessie's corset stays.

One of the musicals I remember with fervor is *Peggy-Ann,* based on *Tillie's Nightmare,* a farce which had served as a successful Marie Dressler vehicle earlier in the century. *Peggy-Ann* was both a satire on the prevailing musical comedy form and an attempt to inflict on it some originality. The plot, banal by ironic intent, repeated the theme of the small town ingenue who goes to the big city and triumphs over its wicked elements. The first ten or fifteen minutes after the curtain rose were entirely expository. When the music did begin, we heard not the usual opening chorus but a song by the heroine; the chorus didn't come on until the third number — "Howdy to Broadway" — a daring innovation at the time.

We start out in Glens Falls in the theatrical boardinghouse run by Peggy-Ann's mother. Peggy-Ann (Helen Ford) dozes off and dreams her New York adventures, impressions of the Big Town derived mainly from the tabloid press. Her first stop is Fifth Avenue and Forty-second Street, a parodic interlude with a cop explaining the city's traffic mores. She then encounters the vaudevillian Mrs. Frost, a boarder from the opening scene (played by the wonderful Lulu McConnell, a rasp-voiced matronly comedienne with a rapid-fire, nonstop delivery). "Well, if it ain't Peggy-Ann, may I never live to have my face lifted," says Mrs. F. She explains that Fifth Avenue is where she lives: "Fifth Avenue and 186th Street."

We then switch to Chez Pendleton, a fashionable boutique, wherein the salesladies (Mrs. F. is now one of them) deliberately ignore the customers, a scene containing a line I quoted for years. The customer (Edith Meiser) returns an undergarment, explaining, "I'd like to see something larger." The irritated Mrs. F. snatches the garment from her with a snarl: "That's the largest we have in that size." It still convulses me.

Peggy-Ann's dream takes her on a millionaire's yacht, which founders en route to Havana. Adrift in the open sea, she has a conversation with a futuristic fish. Rescued, she lands in the clubhouse of the Havana racetrack, which features a Texas Guinan-like hostess (Lulu McConnell in a hilariously accurate takeoff, singing a song that begins, "A night club hostess is one of those dames/Whose natural father was Jesse James"). The lights then dim, the dream is over, and we return Peggy-Ann to her humdrum Glens Falls existence to marry her local paramour.

The pert Rodgers-Hart score, one of their best, contains such delights as Peggy-Ann explaining that she is aware of the pitfalls of New York: a little birdie told her to

> Look sharp before you leap
> The narrow path is steep.

Unfortunately, the dialogue that cued into the song is:

> "Peggy-Ann: Oh, mother told me all about how fast New York men are.
> "Mrs. Frost: Fast! Why, they're so fast they can turn off the light and jump into bed before the room gets dark."

All through, the felicitous Hart lyrics counteract the heavy-handed jokes pasted together by Fields.

> If you were my sister, I'd put poison in your coffee.
> If I were your sister, I'd drink it.

was a venerable wheeze even then, and regretfully it is still seeing service. But Hart's bittersweet switch on the obligatory song of optimism ("Where's That Rainbow") remains fresh despite innumerable hearings:

> Where's that sunshine they fling about?
> I know morning will come, but pardon my laughter . . .

Peggy-Ann became a great favorite with what Winchell called the "intelligentsia," meaning members and offshoots of the Algonquin Round Table group, who would drop in at the Vanderbilt Theater periodically for a refresher. A group of these fans attended the final night in 1928, sitting in the first row and gagging up the performance by putting on grotesque, oversized hair adornments and reciting the lines along with the cast. It couldn't have been a more jovial Varsity Night on the old campus.

Theater music in the Twenties was incandescent. The lush Viennese operetta style still survived intact in Rudolph Friml (*Rose Marie, The Vagabond King, The Three Musketeers*) and in Sigmund Romberg's adaptations from the masters (*Blossom Time, The Student Prince*). Jerome Kern could give *schmalz* a modern accent, his great melodic gift enabling him to devise tunes either hauntingly slow or danceably brisk for *Sally, Sunny, Show Boat, Sweet Adeline, The Cat and the Fiddle.*

Vincent Youmans's ingenious harmonies put an individual stamp on the songs for *Two Little Girls in Blue, No, No, Nanette, Hit the Deck, Great Day.* He was parsimonious with his song hits, doling out only a qualifying two for each show. His output remains the smallest (twelve theater scores) of any of his peers, but almost all the outstanding numbers have proved their durability.

In 1958 in the south of France I ran into *Non, Non, Nanette* (the title apparently gave the translator little difficulty), performed with élan by a touring operette troupe. *Smiles,* one of Youmans's last, was the only show of his I ever saw in its original Broadway production. Ziegfeld presented it at his theater in 1930, with Marilyn Miller and Fred and Adele Astaire starring. A flop, it must have been ill-fated from the beginning. During the out-of-town tryout in Boston, Ring Lardner was sent for to help revise the book. Told that the Astaires steal the show, "It's petty larceny," he mournfully replied.

The distinctive flavor of the period's show music was set early in the decade by the dazzling George Gershwin, who periodically burst the bounds of the popular theater, exploding onto concert and opera house stages (to get a Hollywood assignment after composing *Porgy and Bess,* he had to send a wire which his West Coast representative could show to film producers, promising that this esthetic deviation hadn't impaired his hit-writing ability). The Gershwin shows featured in the pit the duo-pianists Phil Ohman and Victor Arden, highlighting the brilliance of the music. Ira's fastidious lyrics were a perfect setting for his brother's tunes, wittily yet unintrusively complementing the restless melodies.

Contrasting agreeably with the urbanity of the Gershwins was the perky impudence of Richard Rodgers and Lorenz Hart, immediate favorites with their first complete score (*The Garrick Gaieties*), in which they engagingly took possession of "Manhattan/the Bronx and Staten/Island, too." Late in the decade, the worldly Cole Porter emerged from an interpolated-song status to the composition of entire scores as exhilarating as the decadent high life they celebrated.

Since only two or three of the potential song hits of each show were destined for phonograph recording — the industry hadn't yet devised original cast albums and we might never again hear the complete score — we used to pay keen attention to each number, trying to cram the most delectable into our heads, to be sung over and over, and slightly inaccurately, until we had memorized them. Fifty years later, many of them, despite innumerable changes of interpretation, remain fresh to our ears as we originally heard

them — "Somebody Loves Me," "Lady, Be Good," "Do, Do, Do,"
" 'S Wonderful," "Mountain Greenery," "My Heart Stood Still,"
"Thou Swell," "Ten Cents A Dance," "Who?," "Ol' Man River,"
"Bill," "I Want to Be Happy," "I Know That You Know," "Let's
Do It," "You Do Something to Me," "What Is This Thing Called
Love?," dozens of others — indestructible, irreplaceable. Unfortunately, because the debilitating librettos make revivals of the shows
impractical, the remainder of the cohesive scores, the cheery openings, the plot numbers, the "smart" songs to accompany dancing,
the comic songs, the finalettos and finales, are lost to us, probably
forever.

In justice to these librettos, it must be understood that they were
seldom written at the original instigation of the authors. Most
often they were composed by request, to suit individual circumstances (such as a prime theater being available for a desirable date
the following season) or to accommodate specific performers. Ziegfeld had Marilyn Miller and Jack Donahue under contract and,
since he found them to be a winning combination, would assign one
of his regulars like William Anthony McGuire to lay out a story
tailored to their talents — a dancing ingenue and a dancing light
comedian. Gertrude Lawrence, having made a big hit here in the
Charlot Revues, would be signed by Aarons and Freedley for her
local musical comedy debut in *Oh, Kay,* with a score by the Gershwins. The popular Victor Moore would take care of the funny
scenes. The plot to be devised must therefore revolve around a
stylish English leading lady and a dowdy, middle-aged American
comic who specialized in quavering, sad-sack types (in this instance,
Miss Lawrence became the sister of a Duke who uses her brother's
yacht to bring liquor illegally into the United States, and Moore
was "Shorty" McGee, a timid Prohibition bootlegger). When the
show was revived a few years ago the score retained its sparkle but
the book fell flat without its original effervescent principals. *Show
Boat* is the only Twenties musical of any distinction that I can think
of which originated with a complete story rather than having one
built to order, and it has shown its indestructibility in countless
revivals.

Sometimes this meticulous tailoring could be altered slightly to suit other personalities for a road production, but never without a sacrifice of gloss. For a *sui generis* performer like Al Jolson, Eddie Cantor, or Ed Wynn, no casting alternate was possible; the vehicle either existed for and with its star or disappeared forever. Nor could these virtuosi inspire memorable scores. Larger than most theatrical life, they seemed to sap the creative energy of everyone surrounding them. *Oh, Please!*, Beatrice Lillie's first adventure with an American book show, has forgettable music by Youmans in a period when he was composing at the top of his form (although it did contain *I Know That You Know*, not written for or sung by the star). Rodgers and Hart's *Simple Simon*, an Ed Wynn vehicle, is among their least winning contributions. Irving Berlin, invincible as a song hit champion, was felled by the Marx Brothers' *The Cocoanuts*, unable to get even one number in the entire show off the ground. The songs of Fanny Brice, including her "signature," the lachrymose "My Man," are unexceptional; the comic songs not funny without her comic spirit to make them hilarious. George Gershwin's "Swanee," the most distinguished song in Al Jolson's extensive repertoire, was not written especially for him but for a movie theater presentation, and was later interpolated into *Sinbad*.

Such performers, burlesque and vaudeville alumni, were happier in a more casual atmosphere where, unfettered by a burdensome book, their genius could take wing. The revue, with its classic mixture of luscious girls and louche comedians, was at the height of its popularity in the Twenties. There were the hardy annuals, Ziegfeld's *Follies*, George White's *Scandals*, Earl Carroll's *Vanities*, Jones and Green's *Greenwich Village Follies*, Irving Berlin's *Music Box Revues*, the Shuberts' *Passing Shows, Artists and Models*, and *A Night In* ——— series (Paris, Venice, Spain, etc.). Then there were the independent and occasional ventures, *Keep Kool, Gay Paree, Nic Nax, Texas Guinan's Padlocks, Ed Wynn's Grab Bag, Rufus Lemaire's Affairs, Great Temptations, Innocent Eyes, Spice of 1922, Nifties of 1923, Vogues of 1924, Puzzles of 1925, Bunk of 1926* (that one was raided and closed by the police and never did get a chance to proliferate).

No matter how many well-known singers or comedians were featured, the actual box-office attractions were the beautiful, long-

stemmed showgirls, haughty caryatids supporting improbable head-
dresses, who did no dancing at all (indeed, even having them walk
across stage seemed an imposition). Their most arduous task was to
impersonate tassels in the Living Curtain tableaus, to pose, arms
outstretched, as carnal candelabra, or to hang draped or suspended
from enormous chandeliers, the few beads covering nipples and
vulva sufficiently identifying them as pink-and-crystal garlands,
pendants, plaquettes.

These showgirls, since they attracted not only customers but
backers, were the spoiled darlings of the producers, coddled as were
no other cast members. Ziegfeld, who could haggle over a straight
man's salary and deny an advance to a needy comedian, would
order $75 shoes for his *houris* and permit them truant vacations in
Florida with no reprimand. He couldn't see why his great clowns —
W. C. Fields, Fanny Brice, Ed Wynn, Ray Dooley, Frank Tinney
— were funny, considering their acts merely necessary interludes to
give the beauties time to dress for the next spectacle number. This
myopia induced frustrations which could lead to some unbridled
backstage behavior. Tinney, waiting resentfully in the wings as the
row of coddled nymphs stuck their heads through cutouts for some
Living Curtain tableau, would sometimes run behind the drop with
a paddle, letting off steam by whacking each undefended *derrière*.
It must have been the only time an audience ever saw any expression
on those faultless, vacuous faces. Ironically, and no doubt inevitably, Tinney's shining career ended with a scandal involving Imo-
gene Wilson, one of the most famous of the Follies fabulosae.

My favorite of the stories about the alleged obtuseness of Ziegfeld's beauties concerns a legendary dazzler who invited a group of
her dressing room mates to her penthouse apartment for a cozy
lunch. They arrived to find that their hostess would not, after all,
be able to preside; discourteously, she had just committed suicide
by hurling herself off the roof. One of the guests later recounted to
a friend the luncheon party's shattering denouement. "Oh, it was
terrible," she said. "None of the girls could eat a thing!"

The Ziegfeld girls were seldom exhibited *au naturel*, since the
Great Glorifier believed a suggestively veiled torso to be more
provocative than one rudely unadorned. Disposed bountifully

about the stage in a tactful Ben Ali Haggin tableau, with a magnificent Joseph Urban background, they were indeed the most voluptuous imaginable bevy of Favorite Flowers, Precious Jewels, King's Mistresses, Sultan's Slaves.

Nymphs in the buff (with the minutest triangular covering to appease the prudish) could be seen much more readily in the bawdier *Scandals, Vanities, Artists and Models, Greenwich Village Follies.* The latter were staged by John Murray Anderson, who had a passion for story-ballets like *The Legend of a Rose,* and who disdained any members of the company whose function it was merely to speak lines (when, years later, he was hired to direct a book show, *The Firebrand of Florence,* Ira Gershwin, one of the authors, dolefully predicted, "I know just how it will be: the chorus rehearsing on the stage and the principals rehearsing in the toilet").

The alignment in the big revues would be ritualistic, with singers, dancers, comics following one another in a routine predicated on the amount of time necessary to set the main stage for the big spectacle numbers. The comedy, except for that in the more decorous Ziegfeld shows, was frequently rough, based mostly upon classic situations out of burlesque. Willie and Eugene Howard were *Scandals* favorites (Willie's fascination with the overripe breasts of a heaving soprano could bring down the house with laughter). The *Greenwich Village Follies* seemed to specialize in robust female impersonators, Jimmy Watts having a field day with the mannerisms of distaff opera stars, Bert Savoy in his outsize, profane delineation of a Broadway tart (he was equally uninhibited offstage: when the block-long Saks–Fifth Avenue was being erected, he rode past it in an open touring car shouting, "I don't care, he can build it for me but I'll *never* live in it!"; he met his death when he was struck by lightning in Long Beach, just after sneering, "Listen to Miss God carrying on!" which, perhaps in Divine Reproach, turned out to be the last words he was ever able to utter).

During the latter part of the Twenties, the lavish spectacles began to decline in popularity. When, in a libidinous geographic parade, Miss Russia, genitalia smothered in ermine but with her backside bare to the winds (and to the customers), could inspire giggles rather than lust, the essential point of these extravaganzas was gone. The satyric gave way to the satiric, so to speak, with the intimate revue increasingly favored by audiences who preferred wit to window dressing. At the Theater Guild's house on Thirty-fifth Street, *The Garrick Gaieties* led the move uptown from *The Grand Street Follies.* Peopled with talented young supernumeraries from the regular Guild companies (Philip Loeb, Romney Brent, Betty Starbuck, Sterling Holloway, Edith Meiser), supplied with a brash, bright score by the unknown Rodgers and Hart (the songs included "Manhattan," "April Fool," "Romantic You and Sentimental Me") and some amusing, irreverent skits, the show, planned for only one Sunday night, was so well received that it was put on for a regular run and inspired a second successful edition the following season.

At the small Belmont Theater, Richard Herndon presented *Americana,* with a title borrowed from H. L. Mencken's scorn-filled column in *The American Mercury* and with sketches by J. P. McEvoy skewering such indigenous institutions as the radio, Hollywood films, the tabloids, and Rotarian after-dinner speakers (the latter uproariously particularized by Charles Butterworth, an impersonation that started the deadpan artist on his career as a specialized comic). These subjects were to become standard lampoon material, to be run into the ground by a generation of successors.

The intimate revue reached its apogee, in my opinion, with the first *Little Show* of 1929, a conglomerate whose contributors included George S. Kaufman, Newman Levy, Howard Dietz, and Fred Allen, the latter also sharing billing and performing honors with Clifton Webb and Libby Holman. "Most of the wit, humor and intelligence that somehow escape the musical stage has settled down pleasantly into *The Little Show,*" was Brooks Atkinson's unequivocal opinion in the New York *Times* the morning after the opening, and the other critics were equally enthusiastic.

"I am Prologue," announced Ernest Sharpe stentoriously at curtain-rise, and was promptly assassinated by a shot from the wings, thus serving notice that the proceedings were to be far from orthodox. Shortly after, we came upon the regimented dancing Tiller Girls at home, doing their household chores with high kicks and, of course, in unison. Later on, in the second act, they appeared again with a justifiable complaint. One drank Coca-Cola; the other smoked Lucky Strike. "So" (*mutinously, in chorus*) "why the hell should we be forced to always work alike?" Then, instead of the usual militarily drilled ensemble, each girl (the fledgling Constance Cummings was one of them) performed her own anarchic solo.

Fred Allen, a nasal young veteran of the vaudeville circuits, whose appearance in several big musicals had attracted scant attention, proved to be a very funny monologist (he knew a man who worked only one day a year — he was a hot-cross-bun designer). Allen was frequently interrupted by his resolutely chipper stage partner (and wife), Portland Hoffa.

The spindly Clifton Webb, hitherto known mainly as a dapper specialty dancer, exhibited a crisp talent for comedy, notably in *The Still Alarm* by George S. Kaufman, in my memory the best revue sketch ever written. Two exceptionally well-bred gentlemen (the other was the deft Romney Brent) are talking quietly in a hotel room when the bellboy arrives with a message that the building is on fire. The news doesn't unduly disturb them. Webb saunters casually to the window and asks Brent to have a look: "It is really quite worth seeing." He peers out and observes that the floors below are almost all burned away. "But it's quite all right up above," he says. When the atmosphere becomes torrid, he picks up the telephone and orders "Ice water in Room _____, please." Soon two firemen, Fred Allen and Harold Moffet, arrive, the latter carrying his violin. He is persuaded to perform and obliges with the number he played so feelingly during the Equitable conflagration. They sit listening, fanning themselves politely, as the room gets hotter and the curtain falls.

The show's topical shafts were aimed at advertisements for How-to-be-popular-in-ten-easy-lessons, at the then-modish history-debunking school of biography, at amateur theatricals, at stock market speculation (two park bums lasciviously reciting Wall Street platitudes, with the reiterated refrain: "Money is much easier today") and, most notably, at movie theme songs, which had reached a *reductio ad absurdum* with "Woman Disputed, I Love You." In this, Hollywood's example was emulated by Big Business, the result being a moving ballad entitled, "Hammacher, Schlemmer, I Love You."

The songs, mostly by Dietz and Arthur Schwartz, were cheerful and one "blues" number with Ralph Rainger's music was stunning. In the first act, the sultry Libby Holman, wearing a strapless red dress, had effectively put over "Can't We Be Friends?" lamenting the termination of a casual love affair. Her tricky contralto, which could hurdle several registers, was not heard again until the end of the second act, when to the accompaniment of some throbbing chords, the curtains parted on a squalid Harlem bedroom, with Libby as a High Yaller sitting on a cot singing the thrilling "Moanin' Low." Then slithering in through the door came her "sweet man" who's "as mean as can be" — Clifton Webb with tan makeup and exaggerated sideburns. They danced around the room in a locked embrace until he suddenly threw her onto the bed, took some money from her and left. The curtains closed on her sobbing refrain, with a high note ending, "He's the kind of man/ Needs the kind of woman li-ike me-e-e!" The vignette provided a vivid climax for the show which, in its perky songs and skimming satire, captured admirably the essence of metropolitan New York.

The year after the first *Little Show,* Max Gordon hired its three leading performers, gathered together the same contributors with the same disrespectful point of view, and produced *Three's A Crowd,* with more elaborate costumes and scenery but with equal success (the progenitors of the original meanwhile put on a *Second Little Show* with completely different performers and a more popular approach but it was a failure).

One of the staples of the big revues was the blackout in which a husband surprised his wife and her lover in bed, and a satire on this staple soon became equally mandatory for every intimate revue. Usually tripartite, these would take a parodic form (a) as written by Eugene O'Neill, (b) as written by Michael Arlen, (c) as written by Noel Coward. *Three's A Crowd* opened familiarly enough with a lover crawling under a wife's bed while the husband kisses her goodbye. But Fred Allen interrupted the scene by calling for the stagehands to remove the bed, saying, "There ain't gonna be no beds." At this revolutionary announcement, the cast appeared, awesomely to repeat the edict and gradually breaking into a spiritual with the theme "There ain't gonna be no beds."

But the show was able to eat its cake and have it too, for the sketch following this principled renunciation dramatized a comparable smutty anecdote, merely substituting a plumbing fixture for the bed (Tamara Geva walks into the wrong bathroom while Clifton Webb is bathing, and after averting her eyes in virginal dismay, stumbles against the tub, looks down at the body of its naked occupant without seeing his face, and exclaims, "Why, if it isn't Bill Smith!").

Encouraged by the success of *Three's A Crowd*, producer Gordon followed it in 1931 with the legendary *Band Wagon*. A canny marriage of brains and beauty, a merger of the satirical topical revue with the seductive, mindless extravaganza, *The Band Wagon* was the dream show of my generation. The cast was headed by Fred and Adele Astaire ("They are like two puppies in a frolic about the stage," Stark Young had written of them); Frank Morgan, the prototypical Polonius, specialist in bumbling character roles; the acidulous Helen Broderick; and a Viennese beauty, the dancer Tilly Losch. The sketches were by Broadway's corrosive farceur, George S. Kaufman, the songs by Arthur Schwartz and Howard Dietz ("Dancing in the Dark" emerged here). Among the show's delights were a musical number, "I Love Louisa," featuring a real, live merry-go-round on the stage, Adele Astaire and Frank Morgan as an ill-matched couple weighing the alternatives and deciding, "I Might As Well Be Miserable with You," Helen Broderick bemoaning in song the fact that "New York's a nice place to visit, but why do they all visit me?," and the emergence of Fred Astaire, hitherto an amiable straight man for sister Adele's clowning, as a skillful comedian in his own right.

8

ALTHOUGH MUSICALS WERE the most fun, my theatergoing was not restricted to that genre. I had my favorite playwrights, who could be counted on for at least one production a season. Since I was most keenly impressed by stylish dialogue, the American list was headed by S. N. Behrman and Philip Barry, the British by Somerset Maugham, Noel Coward and Frederick Lonsdale, the European (with no competition on parochial Broadway) by the Hungarian Ferenc Molnár. I made it a point to see every Behrman play. In spite of or perhaps because of his indigent childhood in Providence, Rhode Island, none of his characters was actually poor, although the subject of poverty was sometimes discussed offhandedly, and most moved in stratospheric social circles ("What's wrong about liking Duchesses? They're as good as other people" is a revelatory line from one of his plays). The wit is civilized, the attitude tolerant and seldom vehement, even when there is considerable justification for anger. In *Rain From Heaven,* when a Nazi sympathizer at an English country weekend taunts the hostess (titled, of course) with the fact that a Jewish refugee to whom he is being inexcusably rude has become her lover, she replies calmly, for a second act curtain line, "Please remember, he is not only my lover, he is also my guest." The dialogue in his plays is sparkling — I still recall a snippet from his first comedy, *The Second Man:* "She's a Tennysonian ingenue with a Freudian patter" — and requires a responding interpretation, which the plays received when the Lunts or Ina Claire headed their casts. Behrman was often accused of sacrificing substance for verbal glitter, but I didn't care — if they wanted substance, they could go to O'Neill.

Philip Barry's plays also concentrated on the overprivileged, the urbanity here being laced with whimsy. Whimsy was his trademark. The bad people, i.e., the four-square, pompous characters, were given stilted dialogue to speak; the good people, who were the fun-loving hedonists, got the quaint speeches and the curtain-line snappers. Barry's message seemed to be, enjoy yourselves now, time to settle down later. Barry is a theatrical descendant of Clyde Fitch — problem plays light-handedly sprinkled with wisecracks.

After the writers of drawing room comedy, I was partial to the distinctive George Kelly, self-professed misogynist (*The Torch Bearers, Craig's Wife, Daisy Mayme*), excelling in character invention (*The Show Off, The Fatal Weakness*). A leading playwright of the 1920s, a Pulitzer Prize winner, held in high critical esteem, it was his fate to end his days known, if at all, mainly as the Philadelphia uncle of Princess Grace of Monaco.

From the early 1920s until the early 1940s, Broadway's invincible playwright was George S. Kaufman. Although *The Butter and Egg Man* was the only solo effort of his to be produced, he was a prolific collaborator, working most successfully with Marc Connelly (*Dulcy*, which established Lynn Fontanne as a comedienne, *To the Ladies*, a propellent for Helen Hayes), Ring Lardner (*June Moon*), Edna Ferber (*The Royal Family, Dinner At Eight*), the Gershwin brothers (*Strike Up the Band, Of Thee I Sing*), and Moss Hart (*Once In A Lifetime, You Can't Take It With You, The Man Who Came To Dinner*). There was seldom a season during the height of his productivity that didn't include a hit play he had helped write, or direct, or had anonymously "doctored" into long life. The opening night of *Once In A Lifetime* was the most exciting I have ever witnessed (sneaking in, as usual with me at that period, and mingling with the standees). Kaufman had of course directed, as he did all his plays, and it had pleased him to appear in it too, casting himself as the embittered Eastern writer spending his days in the limbo of a Hollywood studio reception room, waiting for the studio chief to remember that he had hired him. When the second act curtain rose and Kaufman was "discovered" on stage — is this description still in use in play scripts? — there was a sustained burst of applause, a tribute that must have lasted for several minutes, before the play could proceed.

Kaufman was a meticulous director, with a sure sense of timing, acute in casting his plays with versatile actors who were nimble enough to disguise the glibness of his characters and situations. I watched him once as an uninvited spectator at a *Dinner At Eight* rehearsal, manipulating the action for the final scene, wherein the guests are assembled for cocktails before going in for their ill-fated meal. The actors were to keep moving between three groups and were to simulate a conversational buzz while key snatches of dialogue, rising above the background hum from each group and intended to dovetail, would advance the action. The choreography was complicated, the counterpointing had to be meticulously executed and Kaufman kept the actors at it, occasionally changing their alignments and making suggestions in a low voice. I remember at one point Ann Andrews, playing the shallow hostess, replying to one of his comments by asking, "Is that a direction, George, or a wisecrack?" In performance, the scene was executed with dazzling brio.

Kaufman was by far the most successful playwright of the Twenties and Thirties in America, a sagacious theater carpenter who seldom failed his public. He wrote for the moment, setting up stereotypical characters for his burlesques, which were too broad to be satires (his morose observation that "satire is what closes on Saturday night" has long been a Broadway bromide). A good bit of the fun lay in the audience's foreknowledge and its anticipation of how those cartoon characters would be expected to react in the situations given them. To newer generations of theatergoers, the attitudes and allusions in his plays must seem either quaint or incomprehensible.

The Butter and Egg Man, when revived forty years later, seemed completely lost in the past. The comedy is a show business fable about an innocent from the hinterland — the "butter and egg man" of the title — who is tricked by a Broadway sharpie into investing his small inheritance in a terrible play which unexpectedly turns into a big hit. The scene of the first act is set in the office of Lehmac Productions, Inc. "It is situated in any one of two-score buildings that sprinkle Broadway above Forty-second Street and even just below it. It is the kind of building whose elevators are invariably a trifle too small. They are filled (the elevators) with girls who look exactly alike and men likewise cut to a pattern. One and all are in show business or on the fringe of it, and easy phrases about 'on No. 2 at the Palace' and 'Ain't no call for them short subjects' are shot back and forth. They are mainly given up, these buildings, to the offices of vaudeville and film men, and it is the mark of Joe Lehman's vaudeville training that he has taken an office in one of them. For the established legitimate producer, be it known, is generally to be found in none too opulent quarters over

Alexander Woollcott with playwrights George S. Kaufman and Moss Hart

somebody's theater, or else in a decayed brownstone front in Forty-fifth Street." A world and a time now as remote as Dickens's London.

Joe Lehman, who addresses everyone as "sweetheart," is in part a caricature of A. H. Woods, the colorful producer of bedroom farces and melodramas who made the salutation his trademark. I interviewed Woods for the *Herald-Tribune* in the 1940s, long after he had ceased to be a potent force on Broadway (he was trying for a comeback) and was charmed to be greeted by the legendary cozy epithet. In 1925, he had presented the dramatization of Michael Arlen's *The Green Hat,* which made a star of Katharine Cornell, and he told me that the original script had called for the small roles of a priest and a rabbi, both budgeted at $100 a week. The actor who was wanted for the priest demanded $200. "O.K.," said Woods, "the rabbi goes!" The theater was commonsensical in those days.

The terrible script that producer Lehman is trying to produce is synopsized for the butter and egg man and turns out to be an amalgam of key situations from such past successes as *Within the Law, The Easiest Way, Rain, The Shanghai Gesture,* and *Liliom* — this was Kaufman giving the hilarious recital of the screwy plot a double edge; the original plays are not mentioned but he was secure in knowing that his audience would be aware of them and would share in the joke. Forty years later, they were mostly forgotten history and the laughs engendered by this zany recital were minimal.

Most lacking in the revival, though, was a sense of the style in which the comedy should be played. If it is not performed in the brittle idiom of the period, with each snappy retort delivered as an instant improvisation, the result is more fizzle than crackle. The introspective acting technique in practice since the late 1940s works against this kind of clockwork comedy, which calls for pyrotechnical flash to highlight the farcical situations and distract audience attention from the tick-ticking of the plot.

The subsequent revival of *Dinner At Eight* was even more ineffective, since the British director Tyrone Guthrie had engaged an exceptionally dreary cast for the melodramatic show that required hard-edged brilliance in its playing and staging. When the pedestrian "all star cast" was announced, Paula Laurence summed up the general dismay by saying, "You wouldn't even invite them to a *briss." June Moon,* dealing with the Tin Pan Alley popular song world, fell just as flat for the same reason when it was revived as a TV special in 1974. One of the Kaufman efforts that wore well when resuscitated was his and Moss Hart's Depression comedy, *You Can't Take It With You,* perhaps because characters like its nihilist grandpa and his pixilated daughter — she uses the family cat as a paperweight — are endowed with more humanity than the sharpies and their moronic setups in the other plays. Moreover, the production also benefited from the sensitive staging of Stephen Porter and the playing of the APA repertory company. Another was his and Edna Ferber's *The Royal Family,* directed with a period flair by the former APA head Ellis Rabb. The APA also put on a splendid production of George Kelly's *The Show Off,* which caught the spirit of the original, but it didn't do as well by Philip Barry's *Holiday,* a comedy of manners which requires the kind of artifice seemingly beyond the comprehension of most contemporary directors and performers.

For what gave the theater of the Twenties its exuberance was not so much the playwrights as the players. Eugene O'Neill appears to be the one figure of the period whose reputation — impressive to begin with — has increased rather than diminished. But what has happened to the copious product of Sidney Howard (*They Knew What They Wanted* was made into *The Most Happy Fella,* a successful musical by Frank Loesser some years back, and *The Silver Cord* with its Freudian possessive-mother-and-son theme may still be viable), Elmer Rice (his *Street Scene* likewise was turned into a successful opera by Kurt Weill but the other plays are in limbo) and the even more prolific Maxwell Anderson, the three other most-lauded of the serious playwrights of the decade?

The fact seems to be that plays are brought alive by actors. It was said of the Lunts, at the height of their popularity, that they could recite the telephone book and make it interesting. That of course was show business hyperbole. But seen in the light of today's lack-luster performers, those actors of the earlier period were miraculous. The stage was their métier; their feet were planted firmly on its boards. In a theater functioning lustily, with approximately two hundred and fifty Broadway productions in a season (during Christmas week of 1927, seventeen plays opened, eleven of them on Monday night), with innumerable road companies and stock companies, actors had abundant opportunity to perfect their craft and we of course profited by getting to know their stage habits intimately.

Two or three times a year, their bad luck in having a flop resulting in our good fortune in being able to enjoy them in different roles, we could see stars like the magnificent Alla Nazimova in her Ibsen revivals, or Alice Brady, Fay Bainter, Madge Kennedy and June Walker, or up-and-coming leading ladies like Jean Arthur or Claudette Colbert, or splendid character actors like Walter Connolly, Osgood Perkins, Frank Conroy, John Halliday, or character women like Laura Hope Crews, Chrystal Herne (the original *Craig's Wife*), Josephine Hull, Spring Byington. In the 1930s the majority of them were hired by Hollywood and became the mainstays of the golden age of talking pictures.

The Theater Guild, secure in their position as the intellectuals of Broadway and with a plump subscription list for their five seasonal productions, harbored a glittering company, headed by our most stylish acting couple, Alfred Lunt and the mocking Lynn Fontanne, Dudley Digges, Ernest Cossart, Henry Travers, Glenn Anders, Edward G. Robinson, Eliot Cabot, Philip Loeb, Clare Eames, Margalo Gillmore and pungent Helen Westley, who was also one of the Guild directors (during matinee and evening performances, if she was tired, she would just roll up in a property rug on stage and sleep until time for the next curtain). Ina Claire, twinkling, sparkling, chic, her ironic inflections turning a humdrum line into a gleaming witticism, appeared once a season in a Lonsdale or a Maugham or an adaptation-from-the-French comedy, making sure, even before she learned her role, to sail for Paris to settle the more important problem of her wardrobe. Ruth Gordon, mannered, wily, an impudent hoyden; Jane Cowl, of the velvety tones and the voluptuous, ironic gestures; the ineffable Mrs. Fiske, whom I saw in three indifferent vehicles toward the end of her illustrious career and whose technique was astounding — she would speak with her back to the audience, throw away all but a few key words in a speech and the result was a dazzling comedy performance; Leslie Howard, the most feathery of light comedians; Roland Young, with his puzzled frown, his seeming to have bitten off more than he could comfortably chew; the inflammatory Judith Anderson; the waiflike Pauline Lord; Laurette Taylor, with that little dip of hers and the wheedling, incantatory voice: these are among the most vivid memories of the theater of my youth.

2
Writing

WHEN I WAS twelve years old, I wrote a play, possibly the shortest in the history of the drama. *The Black Cat* was its title, named after the leading character, head of a criminal gang, who went about his occupation masked as a cat — a feline felon. The play was in four acts; scribbled in pencil, it filled about twelve pages of a lined composition book. Assigning myself to be both director and star performer and snaring several schoolmates as subsidiary players, I managed to achieve one open-air rehearsal on the roof of our modest five-story apartment building. After that I ran into casting problems. My actors lost interest, I could enlist no other victims, and the production had to be abandoned. *The Black Cat* remains unproduced.

My only other effort at writing an original play was an unsolic-ited attempt during the early Thirties — I myself was in my early twenties — to construct a comedy for Ruth Gordon, whose per-formances in high farce I greatly admired. This one was called *Flight From Bohemia,* subtitled "a morality play," and it used for its epigraph what had been its inspiration, a quotation from a book review by Herbert Gorman: "the Depression is creating a new Bohemia in this country." The scene was "a duplex apartment in Sutton Place" (the only duplex apartments I had ever seen had been on a stage) and I affixed to the names of the characters such ironically descriptive labels as Knowledge (for a cynical lecher), Experience (what was meant to be Miss Gordon's role, a jaded innocent), Avarice, Everyman, Virtue, Sloth, etc. I have the manuscript in front of me, its originally white pages turned sallow, no doubt as much from mortification as from age. "The audience," I had written on the title page, "is requested to respect the author's whimsies." Whether or not they would have I shall never find out, for after completing the first act I abandoned the project, discovering what most writers who are habituated to prose composition discover, that writing for the theater — my authority is S. N. Behrman, who contributed with distinction to both forms — requires, besides writing ability, a special knack for the pyrotechnics of the stage.

Shortly before the aborted *Flight From Bohemia,* I had come under the spell of Evelyn Waugh's *Vile Bodies,* and thought his mordant comic novel could be made into a play. Since the book was written in staccato, cinematographic scenes and was almost all dialogue, I probably reasoned that the adaptation would flow easily, as indeed it did. Without bothering to find out if the author would agree to having his work gutted (I was of course completely unknown to him and there was no reason why he should entrust the project to me) I broke down the book's episodes, telescoping them so that they could be physically and economically possible for confinement on a stage.

Waugh's glittering London world, of heedless Bright Young Things speeding to their destruction, centers around Lottie Crump's Shepherd's Hotel, a character and a locale based on the legendary Rosa Lewis and her Cavendish hostelry on Jermyn Street. It was here I set the entire first act. When I had it finished, I telephoned Waugh's New York agents, Brandt and Brandt, to ask for his address. Janet Cohn, of the play department, told me that he

Mike de Lisio and I.D. (with hat), aged seventeen, in the days when we were crashing theatrical opening nights

Theatrical press agent Dick Maney referred to me as "a belligerent young man with a crewcut."

JAKE SPENCER

had disappeared into a Catholic retreat somewhere in France (this was 1931, a year after his conversion) and that she didn't know where to reach him. She suggested that I send the manuscript to the care of his London publishers, who would forward it.

So off it went with a covering letter about the impertinence of my trying to dramatize his book and telling him, more or less in detail, that I had telescoped the action for the climactic party scene using "the German (so-called) Impressionistic [I must have meant Expressionistic] method," with a spotlight playing on various groups to cover successive actions. My second act ended with a new version of the gossip columnist's suicide. "It is advisable to have him shoot himself, instead of putting his head into an oven. . . ." I've no doubt I meant for technical rather than esthetic reasons. I must have.

Of course, none of this would have worked too well, and upon rereading the synopsis, what I can see are shadowy stagehands all too visibly putting up set pieces and props on one side of the stage while a spotlight illuminates them as well as the actors in the scene being played on the opposite side.

The script came back a month later, with a letter, not from some secluded retreat, but on the stationery of the hardly monastic Hotel Negresco in Nice. In Waugh's tiny, antlike calligraphy was "I am most grateful to you for sending me the first act of your dramatized version of *Vile Bodies,* which I have read with great delight. I wish I could authorize you to continue with work but, alas: I have already entered into an agreement with Mr. Denis Bradley, whose version is to be produced over here in October, for the American dramatic rights also. I am so sorry that you should have had so much work for nothing. My very best wishes for your future success."* A kind letter from a successful young author of twenty-eight, who in later life was to become noted for his cavalier behavior toward most persons, Americans in particular.

The English dramatization — I seem to remember that Waugh had a hand in it — was put on in London and was a quick failure. So far as I know it was never attempted in America. The brilliance of

---

* Reprinted by permission of A. D. Peters & Company, Ltd.

the characterizations, the callous, brittle world of Bright Young Things, conveyed glancingly in the novel's many scenes, was probably too kaleidoscopic for the stage, where audience reactions are slower and points must be reiterated to make any impact.

Obviously I had neither the talent nor the stamina to write for the theater, or I would have pursued it with the ferocity of the demented. But if I couldn't write *for* the theater, there was no reason why I couldn't write *about* the theater. Starting at the age of fifteen, with contributions to Walter Winchell's "Your Broadway And Mine" column in the *Evening Graphic* and a parody of a press agent's release ("Irving Drutman announces that he plans to produce a musical comedy with book, lyrics and music by Irving Drutman"), which I sent to George S. Kaufman, then compiling drama news for the New York *Times,* and which it amused him to run with a prefatory "Among the more portentous items of the week . . . ," I progressed to publishing an occasional (unpaid) piece for *Variety,* a story with a theater background for the *New York Theater Program* magazine, reviews for a fledgling periodical called *Dance Events* (I wrote of "Fred Astaire's notorious antics with a cane" and was given a lesson in word usage by the editor, who asked, "What do you mean by 'notorious' . . . does he goose people with it?") and articles for the more established *Dance Magazine* and *Stage Magazine.*

I also wrote the first of the personality pieces in which I was later to specialize. The department in *The New Yorker* that most intrigued me was the weekly Profile, informative, detached, never obeisant, usually irreverent toward its celebrated subject, but always in well-mannered prose. I set out to emulate them by attempting a portrait of Winchell, at that time coming to increasing public attention and yet to receive his first tribute as one of the decade's metropolitan *Wunderkinder.* I hadn't the vaguest notion of how to gather material for such an article and it didn't occur to me that the initial step might be to approach my subject and ask for an interview. Also, I stood too much in awe of him to have made such a request. However, Winchell inserted autobiographical bits of information in his column from time to time, usually under the heading

"Portrait of a Man Talking to Himself": he had been reared in East Harlem, close to the neighborhood in which I had spent my childhood and adolescence; he had traveled around the country in vaudeville as part of Gus Edwards's Newsboy act (which also included Eddie Cantor and George Jessel) ; he had started his journalistic career by sending sassy gossip items to *Billboard* and *Vaudeville News*. I pieced these bits of information together, adding to them an account of his frenetic working routine as I had observed it on my daily late afternoon trips to the *Evening Graphic* during my two years as an office boy for Macfadden Publications. When I finished the article I sent it to Barbara Blake, who was then editing the *New York Theater Program* magazine in addition to her regular duties as the writer for the "About the House" section of *The New Yorker*. Several weeks later the article was returned to me with a long regretful letter from Miss Blake, declaring that she liked the piece, had decided to buy it and had put through a voucher for a check to be sent to me, when someone in the business department had suggested that it would be judicious to ask for the Shuberts' approval, since Winchell was on their blacklist and had been banned from all their theaters, which were serviced by the *Program Magazine*. The Shuberts' answer had been that under no circumstances would they permit his name even to be mentioned.

At the time I was devastated but several years later, when there was a proliferation of articles on the Boswell of Broadway, as he came to be termed, I had a sense of deliverance from what I thought of as a fate comparable to damnation: to be caught in an inaccuracy. Winchell, like all autobiographers, had coated some of the events of his life with colors rather prettier than the actuality and a few of the deductions I had made where information was lacking turned out to be wrong. I would have been ruined, at the age of eighteen, with New York's entire editorial community, which of course would have talked of nothing but my journalistic malfeasance.

At Macfadden, I had sometimes ushered in writers come to confer with editors — they were paid a penny a word for their regular contributions to *True Story, True Romance, True Detective* — but I was much more interested in the visitors who stopped by to see Vera Caspary, the editor of *Dance Magazine* (she was later to become known as a writer of mystery stories, in particular *Laura,* from which the movie was made). Our service department was run by a former actor, John Dillon, a florid, heavyset man of middle years who had been with the Theater Guild in its early days and who had retired from the stage for the more certain income to be derived from work in a business office. Some of the visitors to *Dance Magazine* had known him in his former life and they would stop for a theater chat before attending to their business with Vera Caspary. One of these was the wafer-slim Nanette Kutner, at that time the press agent for George White, producer of the *Scandals.* She had just come from a Philadelphia tryout of a new White extravaganza, *Manhattan Mary,* built around the talents of the folksy comedian Ed Wynn, and she was telling of his insatiable lust for advertisement. With a profusion of billboards, posters, window cards and flyers all flaunting his name in large letters above the title of the musical, he had noticed that the show's wardrobe trunks huddled in the stage alley were starkly stenciled MANHATTAN MARY and had refused to perform until "Ed Wynn in" was added as embellishment to each trunk. It remains for me one of the quintessential theater star stories.

When I left Macfadden in 1928 to earn more money as a typist and general office assistant for a small firm of building contractors (during my first week I mistakenly typed "groins" instead of "quoins" on a page of specifications, which my boss pointed out to me as a "pathological error") I did not lose touch with the writing world. My friend Mike de Lisio was employed as an office boy with *The New Yorker,* where he was in a position to meet, and sometimes observe *en déshabillé* when he delivered copy to their apartments, such glamorous figures as Dorothy Parker, Alexander Woollcott, the newly married Lois Long and Peter Arno, and the magazine's dramatic critic, Robert Benchley. Mike also came into daily contact with the celebrated editor Harold Ross and the leading staff stylists, E. B. White, Wolcott Gibbs, and the eccentric James Thurber ("Tell her/him I died of pneumonia," Thurber would command when Mike announced a visitor). Mike carried to extremes the parental admonition not to point. It was frustrating for me to be told, "That's Dorothy Parker," and as I turned quickly to look, see the heel of a woman's shoe disappearing around the corner of the street. Mike had waited a discreet interval to make sure he would not be overheard.

In *The New Yorker*'s early days, contributors were not encouraged to write voluminously. The magazine favored what it called and I think still calls "casuals," a comment, impudent or coltish or satiric, of a thousand words or so on a current foible. Or else it featured the short fiction piece, really an episode rather than a fully worked-out story, sometimes little more than the dissection of a mood. Like many another aspiring writer of my generation, seduced as we were by Ernest Hemingway's stabs of feeling, I dutifully experimented with these exercises in instant trauma, a genre which I callously and defensively described as being about a woman who walks into a room, spits, and walks out again, leaving emotional havoc in her wake. The first one I sent to the magazine came back very quickly but with an encouraging note scribbled on the printed rejection slip: "Almost but not quite . . . do try again. J.M." The initials, I learned from Mike, stood for John Mosher, the first reader, who was also *The New Yorker*'s motion picture critic. In the latter capacity, he was ideal for the periodical and the time. His tone was light, as were most of the films he was called upon to review, and the verbiage was brief. He didn't emit seven columns of gas to ponder on the nonponderable. I still admire his summation of a certain movie as being the kind you can enjoy while eating an apple.

I felt elated by the considerate response from Mosher, almost as set up as if my story had been accepted. In a short time I had written another, sent it off, and again had it returned with some more words of encouragement. A casual I wrote which parodied two regular contributors was kept for several weeks before being returned, this time with a typewritten note on *New Yorker* stationery, not scribbled on the usual rejection slip, saying that they had liked the piece but had finally decided against it because it was felt to be too intramural. With my permission, however, they would like to show it to the gentlemen concerned. I gave my permission.

The antic drama critic George Jean Nathan, an inviolate *enfant terrible,* had started a nose-thumbing monthly literary newspaper called *The American Spectator,* one of whose regular features was a black-bordered oblong enclosing the name of an author whom the editors felt had had his day. Hugh Walpole, John Drinkwater, Will Durant, Giovanni Papini and Thornton Wilder were some of the candidates for these burlesque memorials. I sent a black-bordered oblong with my candidate, George Jean Nathan, to *The New Yorker* and it was returned, with a note from Wolcott Gibbs, "It's a nice idea, though." This uneven exchange, me writing and they rejecting with commendation, went on for some years and I never did manage to achieve acceptance of a by-line piece. They did accept some anecdotes for their Talk of the Town department. I used the four-dollar proceeds from one of them to buy a pair of desperately needed shoes at a Thom McAn store.

The Depression had by then become a firmly entrenched reality. I had been let go by the building contractor and was out of a job. During a short period in the fall, I sold ice cream from a cart in the parks. For a few winter weeks I delivered new telephone directories for the R. H. Donnelly Corporation, rising at 6:30 A.M. to be at the warehouse by 8:00. A truck would take a consignment of us to a chosen district, where with freezing hands we would distribute the directories to subscribers. We were paid, if I remember correctly, one cent for each delivery and two cents for every old book we brought back, to be recycled I suppose.

My friend Frances Smith, the secretary for the advertising manager of the now-defunct *Dance Magazine,* had a new job with *Billboard,* the weekly trade paper which concentrated on carnivals and tent shows but which also devoted small sections to other areas of the entertainment business. In an attempt to gain a foothold in the Broadway theater field, with its lucrative advertising revenue, *Billboard* had begun to publish a separate yearly *Index of the New York Legitimate Stage,* containing casts of the season's productions, actors' who's who's, listings of producers and agents, and names and addresses of the various craft unions.

Frances recommended me for a job as office assistant — running the stenciling machine, distributing the mail, taking over the switchboard during the operator's lunch time — for which I was to receive a small weekly stipend. I was also to have an opportunity to solicit advertising for the second issue of the *Index,* for which I would be paid a commission on any sales I made. My list of possibilities was confined to the performers in "straight" plays, the least likely prospects for this kind of paid publicity; those in the musicals, who frequently were graduates of vaudeville, where self-advertising was a traditional part of professional expenses, were assigned to a saleswoman with long experience in the trade, who had been hired away from *Variety.*

My first week on the job coincided with President Franklin D. Roosevelt's sudden shutdown of the banks. Theaters remained open, accepting checks or I.O.U.'s at the box office in lieu of cash. It seemed not to be the most propitious time to try to sell theatrical advertising. I would leave the office before five on Wednesday and Thursday matinee days, having staked out my theaters in advance. Since most of the matinees ended at the same time, I had to hustle to cover as many as possible. I would enter through the backstage door and ask for the star or featured player, announcing myself as being from *Billboard.* The doorman would either take my name in or more frequently, assuming I was a reporter, just give me the number of the actor's dressing room. I seldom got to talk to a really big star; a secretary or a dresser would appear, ascertain my business, then return with a message that the star was unable to see me.

At the Morosco, I pushed my way through a crowd of excited females in the alley to ask for Francis Lederer, the Continental matinee idol who had been imported to play in *Autumn Crocus.* Lederer imprudently stepped out of his door to see what I wanted and the crowd of women, squealing and giggling, rushed the backstage entrance and propelled him back into his room, waving their programs for him to sign. I fled and never came back, fearing he would remember and blame me for the invasion.

I couldn't get near Ina Claire, then playing in Behrman's *Biography,* but I knocked on the door of her leading man, Earle Larimore, and he listened to my spiel for half an hour as he sat in his dressing gown staring intently at himself in the mirror in full makeup. I suppose he wasn't planning to remove it between performances. Miraculously he said he would take an eighth of a page

(I think it was seventy-five dollars). I gave him a card to sign and he filled it out for himself and his wife, Selena Royle, then playing across the street in another hit, Rachel Crothers's *When Ladies Meet*. He was under contract to the Theater Guild, both he and his wife were popular players, and they certainly didn't need the advertising, so it was kind of him.

I couldn't get in to see Pauline Lord either, then playing in *The Late Christopher Bean*, but I knocked on the dressing room door of Walter Connolly and he also signed for an eighth of a page. So did Moffat Johnston, exuberantly performing a lampooned Jed Harris character in Hecht and MacArthur's *Twentieth Century* at the Broadhurst.

At the Lyceum Theater I succeeded in seeing the legendary George M. Cohan, who was appearing in his own comedy, *Pigeons and People*. The last of the star-managers, Mister Broadway himself, he kept looking quizzically at me while I delivered my sales talk. I think he was amused by my earnestness and perhaps by my youth. I was twenty-two but, short and slight, I appeared to be no more than seventeen or eighteen and I could, when necessary, look awfully sad. "All right, kid," he finally said, and he too took seventy-five dollars' worth.

Alas, those were my only sales. I didn't make much money but I did get a peek into the mysterious backstage theater world and I did get to see and talk to some of the hallowed theatrical figures I had admired for so long.

It was at my next job, a typist at a welfare admissions center, that I first heard about the children's writers' project. Officially entitled the W.P.A. New Reading Materials Program for the Board of Education, it was one of the make-work projects established by the Roosevelt administration during the Depression to provide jobs for needy writers and artists, its function being to create original, illustrated children's stories as supplementary reading for the third and fourth grades. The offices and publishing plant were located on two floors of an old public school building on New York's Lower East Side.

I applied to Miss Ann Bowman, the supervisor, inflating my

meager credentials. I had never written children's stories but since the point of the project was the employment of needy writers and I had brought some of my published work with me, Miss Bowman agreed that I could qualify. I later learned that my attainments were at least on a par with some and superior to others already on the project.

The project's stories were brought out in individual mimeographed booklets, seven inches by eight and one-half inches in size, the drawings hand-colored with stencils. Later on, when more money was allocated, they were printed on a hand press and looked completely professional. We were given a list of five hundred everyday words to use as a basic vocabulary; all others whose combination of letters did not jibe with their pronunciation, and words containing two or more syllables, had to be repeated several times so that the child could become accustomed to them as he read. The prose was not unlike the oversimplification preferred by Gertrude Stein. For example, from my first story, "The Proud Prince," a moral tale in which greed and ostentation get their just deserts: "The prince ordered the cook to prepare a great dinner. The cook was a very good cook. He prepared delicious roasts. He prepared delicious cakes. There were to be fruits, nuts and delicious sweets. . . ."

We must have had twenty or more writers and an equal number of artists on the project, along with typists, clerks who did the color-stenciling, folding and binding, and the printers, all presided over by Ann Bowman, a Southern woman with only one arm, who with exemplary tact, abnegating all personal ego, managed to hold in check and to keep in a state of reasonable contentment the most bumptious and egotistical of her charges. As a vocational class, the illustrators were more accomplished than the writers, the former including one well-known and distinguished graphic artist, Henry Glintenkamp. The writers were a mixture of staid folk and Greenwich Village bohemians, the latter predominating. The most bizarre of these beyond any doubt was Jonathan Lazlo, with the head of a Flemish gargoyle and a witty, malicious tongue so constantly in motion that an exasperated victim once snatched at and held on to it to impede its viperish action.

Another writer, a crony of Jonathan's, was Parker Tyler, who had collaborated on a pornographic novel with Charles Henri Ford, *The Young and Evil,* published in Paris in 1933. Parker, I was told, had also been the subject of a Whither Civilization? editorial in the New York *Times,* occasioned by a poem he had devised which consisted almost solely of definite and indefinite articles arranged in provocative juxtapositions. Parker's androgynous appearance was itself provocative. He had a pretty, girlish face and wore his dark hair very much longer than was the norm in those days of the shorn crewcut. His shirts were topped by what was then known as a John Barrymore collar, wide and tapering into extreme long points. Altogether, with his graceful, languid walk, he gave the effect of being imprisoned in a not very convincing masquerade. Jonathan used to say of him that trucks stopped dead in astonishment when they encountered him walking along the street. His father had been a college classmate of the tough managing editor of the *Evening Sun* and he gave Parker a letter of introduction so that he could apply for a job as a reporter. Parker thought he should make a concession in his appearance for the occasion. He bought a cap, which he placed over his long, flowing locks, to make himself look like a typical newspaperman out of *The Front Page.* Apparently his disguise was penetrated, for he didn't get the job.

He wrote voluminously, turning in a story a week. (The rest of us would average one a month, Jonathan one every two or three months.) Years later, in the mid-1940s, Parker published *Magic and Myth In the Movies* and *The Hollywood Hallucination,* books treating movie stars and plots in terms of Freudian demonolatry. These were original works that influenced future film criticism and gained him a well-deserved, esoteric reputation in an inbred field. When I would see him on the street from time to time, he was no longer the startling truck-stopper but a sedate, somber figure wearing a black homburg.

The poet Mary Carolyn Davies was also a writer on the project, although I never got to know her very well. One woman writer had been the managing editor of a ladies' magazine and told me she used to earn five thousand dollars a year. That was an enviable salary in those days. Another, white-haired, with a gentility so ingrained that any film director would have cast her unhesitatingly for the part of leading small-town dowager, had been a steady contributor of stories to the *Saturday Evening Post*. There was also the ne'er-do-well McMahon, who would often appear, the morning after payday, and boast that he had spent his entire $23.86 weekly paycheck the night before at the Stork Club.

I made a fast friend of one other writer, Jerry Bahr, who had been a sports reporter on various northwestern newspapers. When not fulfilling the minimal demands of his job on the project, he utilized most of his time writing short stories about the robust Polish-Americans in his native countryside, one of which was published in *Story Magazine,* another in *Scribner's.* Jerry and I would spend hours talking about writing. His young wife was a pretty girl with full, voluptuous lips and a blooming complexion, who could have been a model for Renoir and indeed had often posed for an American counterpart, the painter Waldo Peirce, who was married to her eldest sister.

Writers and artists worked at home but were expected to sign in at nine o'clock each weekday morning, following which we could leave for the day. Even this tiny concession to bureaucracy seemed a regrettable nuisance, especially to those of us who were addicted to staying up late. Having been given the privilege of collecting a government subsidy with not too much labor demanded in return, we yet resented the merest infringement on our daily freedom. Many of us were conscientious and would have turned in more children's stories but there was already a sizable backlog which the production departments were unable to keep up with. We therefore had the time and the liberty to do our own creative work. But having to appear at the office each morning broke up the rhythm of the day. After that interruption it was difficult to return home and get into the necessary productive mood.

Once we had signed in, we would stand around and socialize, listening to Jonathan's musical, complaining voice, for though still groggy from lack of sleep, he was incapable of keeping his mouth shut for any length of time. I too found the compulsory early morning appearance a chore, but being with a group so alien to any I had encountered before was a stimulating experience.

The co-workers who interested me most lived in the Village and were bohemian by inclination as well as by environment. Walking through the streets with Jonathan, or at the Saturday night parties given by the artists, I met an array of characters intriguing in their eccentricity. There was a painter who, in contradistinction to the social-realism in vogue at the time, filled his sizable canvases with obsessive delineations of giant roses. There was the designer of women's accessories, a little toad of a man, an opium addict, who beamed when he was told he looked like an Indian. And there was flamboyant Willie Carr, with tactfully dyed blond hair, the first male I ever saw with makeup, wearing, in the early evening, an opera cape with a red satin lining. He would be on his way to dinner at Drossie's basement restaurant, where for fifty cents one could get a well-cooked, nourishing table d'hôte meal. Willie would hang the opera cape on a coatrack, sit down at a table against the wall, and flick out his dinner reading, which was the Communist *Daily Worker*. He lived in a floor-through apartment in a reconstructed old brownstone; every room, including the bathroom and the closet-kitchenette, was embellished with a crystal chandelier. The chairs in the living room were covered in zebra skin and there was a white piano decorated with gold on which he would play smart Noel Coward songs. It was from his portable Liberty phonograph, encased in tan leather, that I first heard English recordings of Gertrude Lawrence singing selections from her Cole Porter show, *Nymph Errant*. The pride of his small library, an alcove also equipped with its own crystal chandelier, was a first edition of every one of the books of Ronald Firbank.

Willie's style of living was sybaritic, and financially many cuts above that of the rest of us. He was mysterious about his means of livelihood and never denied the rumor, which he had probably instigated, that he had a sister in Chicago who was being kept by a millionaire and that she in turn supported Willie. Then one day some busybody discovered Willie's identity and what he did for a living. He was not really Carr but a more plebian Corrigan and he had a soliciting job under that name with the telephone company, inducing ladies in the midtown silk stocking district to exchange their black-coated upright instruments for a chic French-style in pastel colors. The busybody telephoned Willie at his office and said, "Hello, Willie, this is Jack Campbell," and hung up. Willie's secret was pierced. He gave up his apartment and disappeared from the Village. Some said he had gone to London to live, to start afresh. Most of his acquaintances were sorry he had been exposed. The myth had been so amusing and he had done no one any harm. I heard that he returned to New York just before the outbreak of war. I saw him on a bus about twenty years after I had first known him, a shrunken old man, all his panache gone. I wouldn't have recognized him if he hadn't told me his name.

A regular at Drossie's Restaurant, who dined there every night, was the amply proportioned Allan Ross MacDougal, a Scottish poet who had been secretary to Isadora Duncan during the last period of her life in France, who in the Twenties had known most of the Left Bank Americans in Paris, later to become as famous for being expatriates as they were for being writers, and who was currently engaged as secretary to Ben Hecht, then making movies in Astoria, at an enviable salary of fifty dollars a week. Dougie had written a cookbook and had a reputation to keep up as a gourmet and a gourmand. He took a showy delight in being Drossie's star voluptuary. He would buy his own fish and bird and bring it into the restaurant's kitchen for the chef to prepare at his direction. On special occasions he would treat himself to lobster. On one of these lobster evenings, which for some reason, possibly envy, used to bring out the worst in Jonathan, he and Jonathan were having words, each articulating insults across their separate, adjacent tables. "At least I have a job, which is more than you have," said Dougie tauntingly. Jonathan countered with, "Ass-kissing is not a job, it's an attitude," and with a flash of fury he reached across and pulled the red-checked cloth from Dougie's table, sending the lobster in its sauce splattering to the floor. The other diners were shocked into momentary silence, which was broken by George Davis saying, "On the contrary, ass-kissing *is* a full-time job."

3

George Davis

W. H. AUDEN considered him the wittiest person he had ever known. He said so many times in private and repeated it for a multitude of listeners, to whom the name meant nothing, when he was a guest on a Dick Cavett show in 1972. Auden spoke of writing an appreciation of our friend but never got around to it. Janet Flanner did, briefly: in the introduction to her book *Paris Was Yesterday,* she described him as "a sulky, ultra-sensitive, brilliant character and a deadly wit," whom she had first known on the Left Bank about 1929, when he was working on his novel, *The Opening of a Door.*

George Davis was not a public personality, but he was influential in guiding the cultural taste of a generation of Americans. He had an inspired entrepreneurial gift, which manifested itself in the native writers he discovered, encouraged, helped trumpet to fame. As an editor at *Harper's Bazaar* and *Mademoiselle,* he insinuated quality fiction into fashion magazines, bringing to the fore two rococo Southern talents, Carson McCullers and Truman Capote. These were his most notable finds; others, like Richard Wright, he helped sustain with intellectual guidance. Since he was far from being stodgy, his commitment to literature also had its frivolous side. He had a lot of fun molding the distinctive writing career of the striptease star Gypsy Rose Lee (*The G-String Murders, Mother Finds A Body*), to whom he was engaged at the time, the early 1940s. The engagement was broken shortly thereafter, and a good thing. They never would have made it. Gypsy seldom wanted to part with a nickel, and George thought it was a sin to keep one in his pocket for any length of time.

Instead, he married Kurt Weill's widow, Lotte Lenya, a year after Kurt's death in 1950. Since leaving Hitler's Germany seventeen years earlier, Lenya had been unable to get an artistic foothold in this country. It was the wrong place at the wrong period for her. "The screecher," George Gershwin called her, using the Yiddish word *kvitchedicke.* Her singularly harsh style of performing, the brutal, incisive attack on a song, in the cynical cabaret tradition of Berliner *Sprechgesang,* was at odds with the idealistic liberalism to which we were responsive at the time. She was in melancholy retirement, emerging to appear in public only at a memorial concert dedicated to the music of her late husband.

George must have sensed that the decade, begun so ominously with the Korean war, would become increasingly anarchic and that the moment was again ripe for Lenya, as it had been in the Berlin of the Twenties. Kurt Weill had steadfastly refused to consider revivals here of his and Berthold Brecht's most spectacular success, *The Three-Penny Opera,* perhaps recalling a dismal adaptation that had been a Broadway flop years earlier. Writing successfully for the American theater, he wanted to forget his European musical past. But after his death his ardent disciple Marc Blitzstein finished an English-language version remarkably in the spirit of the original. Marc found a director and a management and, with George's help, secured Lenya's consent to an off-Broadway production. George also induced Lenya to appear in her original role of Jenny and then set about building the kind of publicity campaign he had learned from such masters as his French friends Jean Cocteau, Christian ("Bébé") Bérard, and the Paris representative of the *Bazaar,*

George Davis and Lotte Lenya shortly after their marriage

Marie-Louise Bousquet: initial excitement generated through photographs and provocative items in the fashion magazines, compounded by appearances at social functions favored by stylish arts personalities and the chic rich. George knew this world intimately and how to manipulate it, although almost never for his own advantage, since he was incurably self-destructive. Once the success of Lenya and of the *Three-Penny* was assured (the revival ran for five years in New York's small downtown Theater deLys, considerably helped by the Bobby Darin and Louis Armstrong records of "Mack the Knife" and Lenya's emergence as a cult figure), he maneuvered recording contracts for many of Weill's early European works. He was undoubtedly the driving force behind the resurrection and continuing popularity of the Weill oeuvre, and of Lenya as its leading interpreter.

George had arrived in Paris from his boyhood home in Ludington, Michigan, in the late 1920s, when he was barely twenty-three, and had almost immediately ingratiated himself into a select French cultural circle. This was contrary to the pattern set by his fellow expatriates, most of whom were comfortable only when consorting with each other. He spoke the language fluently but judiciously, like an American who had mastered it as a second tongue, not attempting to camouflage the fact that it *was* a second tongue. I remember for instance his idiosyncratically pronouncing *Marseilles* to rhyme with *rails,* as an unschooled foreigner might. It was a subtle display of his independence, for he was sensitive to the nuances of the language, and later translated effectively many of the short works of Cocteau and Colette, two French authors whose writings have not traveled at all well.

Paris was for him, as for a somewhat older generation of Americans, the most sympathetic of environments. He lived in a little hotel in the St.-Germain-des-Prés district where, since there was something irresistibly cozy and appealing in his manner, he became the confidant of the *patronne,* a female extremely tolerant of the sex habits of her lodgers. As George used to say, in reminiscing, "She didn't care *what* you did, just so long as you did it." One lodger was a constant irritation to her, a woman who flounced haughtily past the desk each morning without saying *"bonjour,"* which was taken as a personal affront. One day the *patronne* knocked on George's door and said conspiratorily, "Come with me." She took him down to the next floor, where her husband stood with a ladder in front of one of the rooms. Signaling George to be quiet, she bade him mount the ladder and peek over the transom. He beheld the discourteous woman, the *patronne's bête noire,* in amorous entanglement with a gentleman friend. Two nude bodies in violent and oblivious communion, first on the bed then, in continuation of their ardor, rolling around on the floor. George climbed down the ladder. The *patronne* stood with her arms folded righteously across her bosom. There was a triumphant sneer on her face. "Too proud to say *'bonjour'!"* she said.

Another of George's Paris reminiscences concerned an acquaintance he encountered in a badly battered state. "What happened to you?" asked George. It seemed the acquaintance had been incautious enough to bring two sailors home with him for a nightcap. They proceeded alternately to beat him and bugger him, continuing long after his desire for either exercise had waned. He was a total wreck. "And the worst of it is," he told George with tears in his eyes, "that ten years from now, I'll probably look back on this as one of the happiest times of my life."

Stories like these, which George recounted with such relish, were told not simply as unrelated incidents but to illustrate a humanistic, philosophical point. The comment on fallibility, on corporeal frailty, was what was telling, rather than the swift and snappy rejoinder that is the sole excuse for most anecdotic recitals. He frequently would parody the latter by beginning a sentence with, "Like the one about . . ."

Along with many other young Americans who had emigrated to Paris, George had very little money to live on. Kay Boyle, in her collaborative memoir with Robert McAlmon, *Being Geniuses Together,* recalled a time when George, "on the threshold of the poorhouse . . . unable to pay the rent of his hotel room," was so broke that she, who was almost as destitute but at least had a miserably paid job taking care of Raymond Duncan's weaving shop, took George in, both of them wrapping themselves at night in display tunics, so they could sleep on the floor in the unheated premises. But then he was only a bit worse off than his friend the poet Hart Crane, who rented a tiny room in the apartment of a painter, Eugene MacCown, and whose only access to the bathroom was through the studio, the door of which MacCown sadistically kept locked while he worked. In frustration and retaliation, Crane would put a record on his phonograph and play it over and over at full volume.

Because of his sinuous glide and arrogant demeanor, MacCown was known as The Leopard. During one opulent period he had the studio redecorated. He was wearing a leopard-skin jacket, in keeping with his sobriquet, when he showed off the results to a group of friends. He flung open a door to display the new bathroom. "Shouldn't you have had a sandbox put in instead?" asked George.

With the publication by Harper's in 1931 of his novel, *The Opening of a Door,* George became an instant celebrity. The reviews were laudatory, the sales very good, helped along by a Man Ray photograph on the jacket, of the author looking handsome in a turtleneck sweater, which provoked some lubricious fan mail. When the Harper Fiction Prize for that year was awarded to another novel, George received additional plaudits and sales due to the emphatic opinion expressed by many reviewers that his book had more literary merit than the prizewinner. He was given a $2,000 advance, a large sum at the time, for a second novel, but was unable to complete more than two chapters. He had always been paranoid about his family's attitude toward him, which he held to be patronizing (he would never again speak to one brother he had quarreled with when he was in his teens) and I believe that after the triumphant publication of his book he felt no further urge to prove his talent. In any event, he followed the classic pattern of many gifted young Americans who write brilliant first novels: he never published another. When his money finally ran out — and here my information is sketchy — he returned to this country and in New York became an editor, replacing the departing Clare Boothe at *Vanity Fair,* the general culture magazine that catered to a discriminating cosmopolitan readership.

All this I have pieced together from what George later told me. I first met him in 1935 and he was no longer on the *Vanity Fair* staff, for his chief, Frank Crowninshield, had called his bluff when he threatened to quit unless he was given a rise in salary. He was staying in a small room at the Men's Residence Club on Macdougal Street, a group of tidy brownstones whose interiors had been cut through to form a conglomerate rooming house for respectable gentlemen of modest means. I visited him there once and had the feeling he was living in purgatory, waiting to be shipped out to the heaven of the Upper East Side or the hell of the Bowery. He had of course saved no money from his job, since any he laid his hands on immediately slipped through his fingers. A wealthy, benevolent spinster, who had befriended him, was giving him an allowance of one hundred dollars a month, which was always spent during the first two weeks. He was also selling a bi- or tri-monthly piece to *Vanity Fair* on some sort of agreement with Crowninshield. One, I remember, was about a group of women whose pleasant conversation turned into a violent quarrel over whether or not the moppet Shirley Temple was really a midget.

When the check for the brief *Vanity Fair* contribution would arrive, he would frequently cash it at Drossie's Restaurant in the Village, and it too would soon be frittered away. How he spent money so quickly was a mystery to many of his friends. His rent was minimal; he liked to eat well but did not patronize splendid and expensive restaurants; he was an omnivorous reader of magazines and bought all the more literate weeklies, monthlies and quarterlies, but this could not have accounted for any extraordinary expenditure. He rarely spent much money on clothing. Janet Flanner told me of walking along the Boulevard St. Germain with him in the old days, when he suddenly burst into tears and accused her of being unobserving and heartless, since she had not noticed that he was wearing carpet slippers because he did not own a pair of shoes. She had not noticed because George, even in prosperous years, was clean but negligent in his dress. For some reason, department stores and men's specialty stores intimidated him and he would seldom enter them, preferring to receive castoffs from friends or to buy his clothes in secondhand shops. In these, as well as in cluttered antique shops with their discarded Victorian bric-a-brac, he took a childish delight.

Another idiosyncrasy was his unwillingness to enter banks. Banks made him nervous and I don't believe he went into one in all the years I knew him. He would go to lengths to have his salary checks cashed, either by having a secretary make the transaction for him, or, more often, by patronizing an establishment devoted to the purpose, where he would have to pay a fee. He was suspicious of checks, as if they weren't legal tender and he might be arrested if one were found on him.

George was not exactly a recluse in his Village retreat. His bene-factress would arrange frequent dinner parties for him at her house on Tenth Street. On occasion he would put on the evening clothes he had kept from his *Vanity Fair* days, to go to a formal uptown party. Also on occasion, Ben Hecht's wife Rose would send a chauf-feured car to drive him to dinner at the Hechts' house up the Hud-son in Nyack. Evenings spent there would be discommoding, since George knew he would be expected to perform, with the host ex-pansively introducing him to the other guests as "the funniest man in America." That was enough to make anyone tongue-tied. Charles Lederer, a friend both of the Hechts and of George, interested himself on George's behalf. He invited George to lunch with his aunt, the film star Marion Davies, on one of her infrequent visits to New York. The subject of Harlem, a favorite of nightclub revelers in the Twenties, was broached. The fun-loving Marion, a butterfly whose wings had been clipped by her prudish protector William Randolph Hearst, said wistfully, "Tell me . . . do they still go . . . hot-cha [snapping her fingers in a reminiscent jazz gesture] . . . up there?"

Through his connections with the Hearst organization, Lederer arranged a meeting with Carmel Snow, the indomitable editor of *Harper's Bazaar*. Mrs. Snow read George's book, was impressed, and hired him as fiction editor. Besides ferreting out new story-writing talents, George became an important adjunct to other departments of the magazine. He had a crystal-gazer's prescience in being able to detect which of the forthcoming music, theater, film or literary events could best serve the modish purposes of the *Bazaar,* and soon made himself indispensable at staff meetings. He suggested that he be sent to London on a scouting expedition, where he invaded Bloomsbury, soliciting stories and articles from Virginia Woolf and the Sitwells. He was also on the lookout for the younger intellectuals. He just managed to catch Auden and Christopher Isherwood as they were leaving for China and they agreed to contribute articles about their trip, later published in their collaborative volume, *Journey to a War.* When the young Englishmen, homeward-bound by way of San Francisco, landed in New York, George was on the train platform at Pennsylvania Station to meet them, with what Isherwood later remembered as "lots of money" in payment for their articles. Auden was overwhelmed by the station's Roman vastness and its impressive marble columns. "We ought to be wearing togas," he said.

George moved to an expensive apartment on East Sixtieth Street, continuing his wayward existence, with its irregular, late hours, intermingling friends from the literary, fashion, and nether worlds. He would bring these three factions together at places like Sammy's Saloon on the Bowery, at that time a local hangout still undiscovered by uptown tourists. He had gotten to know the bartenders, the bouncers and the dozen or so raucous female entertainers. At his entrance he would be greeted as if he were a visiting foreign prince. He would buy drinks for the girls, sleazy survivors of lesser vaudeville and burlesque circuits, and they in turn would entertain him with snippets of autobiography told in racy and vivid detail. A scrofulous barfly would be pointed out by one of them as having been her bed partner the previous night. George would be asked what he thought of him. "Well," he would reply cautiously, "if that's the sort of thing you like, I must admit it's the best example of its kind." One of their number had a reputation as a wit, which, as far as George could judge, was based solely on her warning interjection at frequent intervals, "Just don't let me commence!" which would elicit gales of laughter from her companions. "Just don't let me commence!" she would keep repeating. And, as George said in his soft purr, she never did.

He was addicted to low life. Smart ladies he had known in Paris would visit New York and be whisked off to Sammy's or even further downtown on the Bowery to the fetid Silver Dollar. Sedentary professors from the Middle West would be hustled across the river to Brooklyn to be initiated into the crackling Bucket of Blood on Myrtle Avenue, patronized by sailors, whores, stevedores and transvestites. "There's lots of atmosphere and it's very colorful," he told one unsuspecting academician. No sooner had they settled down to their drinks than all hell broke loose. Someone said something that someone else didn't like and in no time at all the place was a shambles. Beer bottles were tossed, shattering the mirror behind the bar, restless fists smashed into nearby jaws, other, uninvolved customers, some innocently bloodied, crashed the front door as they rushed for the haven of the open air. George was transported with delight. "I told you it was colorful," he said complacently to his guest.

He had been a fixture at the *Bazaar* for four years when, one day in 1940, Mrs. Snow called him into her office to protest for the umpteenth time his habitual failure to arrive at his desk much before noon. George explained, as he had explained before, that he did his best work at night and then slept late. The organization had its rules and they could not be flouted continually. In that case, George said, expecting to be coaxed to stay, he had better resign. Unexpectedly she accepted his resignation. He was again out of a job and again, of course, without any savings.

He had to move from the Sixtieth Street apartment and his solution was to lease a three-story brownstone in Brooklyn, in a slightly rundown neighborhood adjacent to but not actually a part of the fashionable Heights district. He turned this into a cerebral commune by renting out two floors to creative friends on a cooperative basis. A housekeeper would be hired to do the cooking and cleaning, and expenses would be shared by all the inmates.

Since George had a penchant for mixing the intellectual species, he implemented his plan with the help of Gypsy Rose Lee, the burlesque stripper who had by now become a Broadway star and whose career George had enhanced with an early article in *Vanity*

Fair. Gypsy's bold good looks, combined with her mixture of shrewdness and naiveté — she was avid for both fiscal and mental advancement — had made her a pet in adventurous literary circles. She provided the initial monthly rent money of $125 and also sent over the black girl who worked for her to serve as part-time housekeeper. With a fine sense of economy (between engagements she was likely to complain, "everything's going out and nothing's coming in") Gypsy was herself living in a cold-water railroad flat on East Fifty-seventh Street for which she paid $25 a month and which, under George's guidance, she had decorated with Victorian furnishings at bargain prices.

The Brooklyn house, at 7 Middagh Street, was to become legendary for the eminent personalities George gathered around him. Among the original settlers was a British contingent, Wystan Auden and Benjamin Britten, the former having recently emigrated to this country. Wystan, with the authority of a school prefect, was delegated to make the monthly expense collections. The foreigners were buttressed by a native galaxy that included at various times Carson McCullers, Paul and Jane Bowles, Richard Wright, the composer Colin McPhee, whom George bullied into writing the classic memoir *A House in Bali,* which is dedicated to him, and the scenic designer Oliver Smith, whose spacious sets for *On the Town,* his first success, were patterned, at George's suggestion, after dime store picture postcards. Everyone invoked his Muse during the day, then met in the basement dining room with his guests (in themselves celebrated) for dinners which would have been historic had anyone thought of recording the conversational goings-on.

Nor was George content to keep the level high-toned. He surrounded himself with a retinue of followers from the borough, for whom he devised varied *noms de cour.* The loyal Victrola, so called because of his gravelly voice, served as unpaid chauffeur, bodyguard and, when necessary, bouncer. The procurer Snaggle-tooth, whose illicit earnings supported an old Italian mother, a sister and an idle brother, was named for the protruding bicuspid that lent geniality to an otherwise unfavorable Neapolitan countenance. Then there was Ginger Ale ("because he sparkles, but it's not champagne"), who by day held some dim job with the railroad but who came into his own at night with a rather startling specialty act. Stripped to the buff, he would sit at the grand piano in George's parlor (the very same piano that Britten had used for his composing) playing ragtime, while a lighted cigarette stuffed in his rear end puffed away in rhythm.

There was a period when the house harbored an actor midget, known as Tallulah's midget because he had appeared in a Bankhead play. For a few months, when the second floor was otherwise unoccupied, George gave it to an animal act he had first met through Gypsy — trainer, wife, two children, a chimpanzee, a monkey and several dogs. George brought an acquaintance down to the basement kitchen one afternoon for a convivial cup of coffee. They heard the toilet flush in the adjoining lavatory and to their astonishment out popped the chimpanzee.

About six months after his departure from *Harper's Bazaar,* George had been hired as feature and fiction editor of *Mademoiselle* magazine, where he was to be an active if frequently disturbing force for the next eight years. He continued his custom of buying high-grade stories and of encouraging new writers (it is here that Capote was first published). For a period of time he also conducted an evening course in creative writing at Columbia University.

Since he had a predilection and talent for intrigue, the fashion magazine was an ideal ambience for him. At *Mademoiselle* one of the telephone operators proved an eager confederate. She listened in to most calls and relayed the gossip to him. In this way he thought he could determine who were his potential rivals and enemies, real or fancied. The cause of his leaving the magazine in 1949 was a vendetta with another editor, whom he had brought in and who was attempting to usurp his functions. One more showdown and one more defeat. By then he had had to give up the Middagh Street house, which was being torn down to make room for the Brooklyn-Queens expressway. He leased a similar seedy brownstone on East Eighty-sixth Street, which again he had to vacate, about the time he lost his *Mademoiselle* job, when it too was assigned to a wrecking crew. The faithful Victor Carl found him a tenement flat on East

Forty-eighth Street ("Oh, he lived in such glorious grubbiness!" said Virgil Thomson), where he moved a few of his most favored possessions: his collection of phonograph records of French music-hall stars, his books, including a cherished set of Balzac, the settee with the frame ingeniously decorated with steer horns, a late Victorian clock, the chromo of Sarah Bernhardt I had once brought him from an auction. He also clung to his pictures by friends from Paris days — the Oberlé watercolor portrait of him as he looked when he first came to France, two line drawings by Cocteau inscribed "à mon cher George," one of which Lenya gave to me after his death and which I in turn gave in his memory to the Museum of Modern Art, the wash drawing by Bérard now hanging on my wall, which George later gave to me, for he loved to give presents.

The ultimate traumatic experience for him was when he was hired, after a year of penury, as managing editor, under the ambitious Fleur Cowles, of a new magazine to be called *Flair*. In retrospect his two previous female executives, among the steeliest of their gender, could not be compared to Mrs. Cowles, wife of the publisher of *Look* magazine, whose arbitrary despotism completely shattered the nerves of her staff. The magazine, a concrete extension of her ego, was meant to combine the cultural sophistication of the old *Vanity Fair* with the slick nuttiness of *Harper's Bazaar,* and George would seem to have been an inspired choice for the accomplishment of its aims. Somehow it turned up his worst side, both editorially and in his relations with his friends. The dictatorial in his nature was allowed free reign. At first he intimidated Mrs. Cowles, who was at home in the prickly fields of advertising and the women's pages of the plebeian *Look,* but could find no firm footing in the more subtly treacherous terrain of high fashion and lofty journalism, even with George as her guide.

I don't know whose idea it was to put a see-through hole in the front cover as a distinctive selling point (I've been told that the notion was lifted from some old *Folies Bergère* souvenir programs that someone showed Fleur Cowles), but it proved to be an open invitation for scatalogical jokes, on the order of one Cowles' executive's, "They put the hole at the wrong end" when he surveyed the contents of the first issue. After the highly perfumed promotion, that first issue was a keen letdown. George and Mrs. Cowles had flown to Europe for a quick look-around at the culture market. Mrs. Margaret Biddle, a social figure who had been hired as the Paris representative for *Flair,* gave a dinner to which George's old friend, the Negro author Richard Wright, had been invited. The dinner service was of gold plate. Wright apparently was bored with the company. "I could see," George later said, "that during the meal Dick was probably thinking that all that gold could be put to much more practical use in his teeth."

At George's instigation, another old friend, Jean Cocteau, was brought to New York on the *Flair* expense account, and turned out *A Letter to Americans,* which was the featured event in the initial issue. Cocteau's intellectual buffoonery had never caught on with American readers and his pallid contribution did nothing to increase his or the new magazine's public. Subsequent issues were no great improvement. As the sense of failure spread, George became more arrogant. His contract was terminated three months before its last issue, for *Flair* had a short, hectic life.

The fact that Mrs. Cowles had been able to get him past the hearty midwestern Cowles executives in the first place was proof of her power, for in appearance and demeanor he was the farthest removed from their idea of what a managing editor should be. He was short and pudgy, with an intelligent, open face and a deceptively folksy manner which someone once described as rocking-chair. As I have said, he was scrupulously clean but his clothes were nondescript and unpressed and made no harmonious ensemble. His voice was soft, the words measured, the tone insinuating. He had enormous charm for the civilized and the uncultivated, but the middle-class business world was his foe and against it he had no protective armor. He was especially vulnerable at Cowles's, where the staff was geared to the lower popular denominator exemplified by the big money-maker *Look,* where the executives resented the publisher's wife and any protégé of hers, and where in any case George's style of life would have been grating, lived as it was in a swirl of melodrama.

I have stressed the fact that he was a wit, but it was not in the sense of making epigrams or delivering slashing remarks. Rather, as Isherwood said, it was a wit of occasion. His lower lip would jut out in a pout, an eyebrow would be raised, the voice with its suggestive inflection would begin to purr. He was a star turn and to quote him without the seduction of the performance is to lose a good deal of the savor of the act. There are of course memorable lines. An acquaintance renowned for his treachery happened in at a stag dinner at a restaurant, with the guests seated at a long table, and snarled, "My word, it's the Last Supper." George silenced him with "Yes, now that Judas has arrived."

When Ernest Hemingway, on safari in Africa, disappeared in his small plane, there was a great commotion on the world's front pages. Obituaries were set to run and I think one actually did. It was such a fitting end for the great romantic literary figure of our time. And then he was found, slightly damaged but alive, his machine having broken down in the jungle. Unreasonably, there was a sense of letdown. "Somehow," George said, "it makes one think less of him as a writer."

During the affluent days, George had a German houseman who seemed to be prospering far beyond the bounds of his monthly wages. Evidence was produced that the employee was kiting grocery and butcher bills to an unconscionable degree and had even taken out an FHA loan using George's furniture as collateral. Asked why he refused to dismiss the pilferer, George said, "But he brings me my orange juice in bed!" Apparently, being coddled meant more to him than being solvent.

When Truman Capote's first novel, *Other Voices, Other Rooms,* appeared, dealing with an odd youngster's growing up in the Gothic South, George tagged it "a perverted Huckleberry Finn." He wasn't impressed with the drawing room comedies of S. N. Behrman, whose dialogue I relished, saying, "He's being witty for the butler." Harold Lang's weak delineation of the title role in a revival of *Pal Joey* elicited the descriptive "more *schlemiel* than heel."

Perhaps I would realize my intention better if I let him speak for himself. He married Lotte Lenya, an old acquaintance although they hadn't theretofore seen much of one another, in 1951, the year after the *Flair* debacle and Kurt Weill's death, his calamity and her tragedy perhaps serving to bring them closer together. George had wheedled Lenya out of her despondent retirement into a triumphant public reemergence. Columbia, with its European affiliate Philips, was anxious for her to make an album in German of her Brecht-Weill songs. Early in 1955 George finally induced her to undertake the dreaded return to Berlin, the city she had fled when Hitler came to power.

In a long letter to me sent a few weeks after their arrival, he wrote that Lenya "is already out of the house, on her way to the East Berlin state library for a few hours of research . . . no use my going on such a trip, since I don't speak German, and what's more, won't, not as long as the little madame is around: this week, for example, I have only one rather unusual word in my vocabulary besides 'bitte' and 'auf wiedersehn' and that's 'spargel' meaning 'asparagus.' . . . Madame does not encourage me in learning — I think she rather enjoys having a language in which 'spargel' makes, let's face it, a feeble retort, and also I have a feeling that she would regard the acquiring of a larger vocabulary as an aggressively pro-German gesture, of which we ain't having any! . . .

"Of course from the moment we arrived I could see that Lenya couldn't rest until she had seen Brecht, and on her first trek to East Berlin she telephoned him and got Helene Weigel, his wife, on the wire, who promptly demanded that Lenya come right over. Which she did; Brecht was sleeping overhead, coming down without any warning that Lenya was there. . . . I am positive that there was real emotion on both sides, and of course both Brecht and Weigel were all for Lenya moving right into their Berliner Ensemble. The following Sunday I went over with her to spend the afternoon with them, preceded by a walk around that part of East Berlin. It is a grim and bleak spectacle, not only for the physical desolation but for the terrible blankness on the faces, a blankness worse than any real display of despair (and this comes over me every time I go there). Brecht and Weigel live in a charmingly furnished house overlooking an old French Huguenot cemetery, and we had coffee with them and delicious Viennese cakes made by Weigel in Lenya's honor. Together Brecht and Weigel look like a pair of shrewd and hardbitten peasants — with at times another atmosphere coming through, of two shady con artists, or a couple that might be running a pawn shop as a blind — and so for me, as you'd guess, overwhelming charm. He has the Stalin Prize, but make no mistake, she's the political power, the schemer, the really dangerous member of the team. Like Mother Goddam she has *survived,* and she wants you to know it. Looks rather like a battered Martha Graham, something of Muriel Draper, with a grindingly harsh voice and the grip of a longshoreman. The visit went well, rather more than that, but it was dark before we started back for West Berlin and on the way to the S-Bahn Lenya announced gaily that she was quite lost and wasn't at all sure what train we should take. At that moment the most convulsive cramps started in my stomach and continued for two days. It has taken her quite a while to realize there is a situation here in which a flutter of Viennese charm wouldn't help. But a few days later we saw *Mutter Courage,* with Weigel in the name part and Brecht directing, and I was completely won over. And last week we saw *Der Kaukasische Kreidekreis* [*The Caucasian Chalk Circle*], not quite as remarkable a production but again achieving things on the stage that I would not have thought possible. I have never seen anything like the poetic intensity brought to the staging, an eye which literally nothing escapes, down to the least detail of gesture and prop. For example, as the peddler's wagon of Mother Courage moves through the play, it deteriorates not in a purely external way but in an incomparably more complex and poetic way — oh hell, let's not go into it. Weigel herself has plainly no natural talent, all is will power and painful study, over and over, and never the sudden instinctive gesture that breaks the heart, but she gets away with what she can do here — and I think would be delighted to have you lined up against a wall and shot if you didn't like it — but I do, I *do!* Needless to say, Madame Lenya doesn't, and isn't in great pains to hide it; and somehow Weigel takes it from her, even to the bitchiest compliment of all from Lenya, 'It's amazing what you've learned.' It was Weigel's job to ask Lenya if she would appear with them in Paris at the Theater Festival — they offered her all the songs, including those of Ernst Busch, the one good singer they have — but Lenya answered, 'It's awfully sweet of you, but I really value my American passport too much for that.' And so it goes. . . . But to finish with Brecht and his theatre: miraculous as it is, in what it reveals of knowledge and consummate taste, after those two performances I've had it. Just when he has won you, when you are captivated as never before, the propaganda begins and from then on never stops; whacking you over the head, making the same point over and over; oh Christ, no thanks! . . ."

The next year he and Lenya were back in Germany for two Weill-Brecht projects to be recorded in Hamburg: (1) *The Seven Deadly Sins,* originally written to be performed in Paris by Balanchine's Ballets '33, with the singing Lenya and the dancing Tilly Losch as alter egos, and (2) the legendary *Mahagonny* opera, during the casting of which George wrote me: "I've had a little heart attack that we knew was coming on — forgive me, Irving, but I knew that if a doctor had a look at me my chance of flying to Hamburg was nil. I was tactful enough, finally, to have it the night after Brecht's death, when Lenya really wanted to fly to Berlin but was afraid of a state funeral — actually the old boy bolloxed them proper, had already written a sealed letter to the East German government that in the event, etc., he wanted no state funeral, no speeches, and burial in that old Huguenot cemetery under his own window — as he had told Aufricht [the original producer of *Dreigroschenoper*] 'I'll get in there — maybe through bribery and corruption, but I'll get in there' — and so he did — Well, that night, the pain was just too tough, I sat up stupid and humble, waiting, and then we called the police doctor, as apparently one must, and the guy came, turned out to be an excellent doctor. Not to go on with this forever, I've had my electrocardiograph, I'm taking shots, pills, slobbing quietly around, trying out the rabbity-old-boy gait for size: the doctor is pleased, and I have only ten, no seven, shots to go for the time being."

He asked if I would airmail him the devastating Truman Capote reportage of the *Porgy and Bess* company's Russian tour, which had just appeared in *The New Yorker.* He and Lenya had seen Truman in Berlin when the company was being briefed at the start of the tour. "Oh, that darling, darling Truman!" George wrote me, in acknowledging receipt of the two installments. "Mind you, not that I'd have the courage now to walk with him from Second Avenue to Madison. . . . By this time I think it an honor indeed to have sprung the little monster [his term of endearment for Truman, of whom he was fond] on the Kürfurstendamm — and to have heard his Southern whine to the Russian interviewer, 'Of course Ah'm a non-political writer. . . .' And when you think how blissfully *safe* all his companions must have felt, how certain they must have been that whatever he wrote would be quaint and fanciful! Surely they don't dare pretend that it isn't true, every damning quoted word."

He and Lenya returned to New York early in 1957 and shortly thereafter he was hospitalized with a heart attack more serious than the first. Once released, he was cautioned to be careful about his movements, to spend a good part of the day reclining. Since that was the position he most favored for his obsessive reading, I remarked that it wouldn't be too much of a departure from his usual routine, to which he replied, "Don't think that hasn't occurred to me, too." He was much subdued during the next few months; all the flare of his temperament seemed to have gone out of him. Lenya was due to leave for Berlin soon to give her approval to a revival of the Kurt Weill opera *Burgschaft,* to attend another revival, of *Mahagonny,* in Darmstadt, and also to make a new, definitive album of *Dreigroschenoper,* which George had been working on with her. His doctor warned him that it wouldn't be prudent for him to make the trip, but he didn't actually forbid it. At any rate George wouldn't be deterred. On one of our frequent brief walks he told me that he had no wish to live anymore (I said, "Oh, George!" as one does, but I could tell he meant it) after he had seen this last project through.

He wrote me on October 29th from the flat they had rented in Berlin, "a bizarre affair, with the walls of the bedroom plastered with big color pinups of Loren, Knef, Elizabeth Taylor, etc., at least a hundred, with smack in the middle a cutout of *one* sport roadster, all very jerk-off, and in a drawer home talent snapshots of our Bulgarian landlord's girl friends, naked and scrawny. Ugly furniture, 1910 Berlin version of Mission style, with its own Sally Bowles charm — that is, by now, with another bed for me sent over by the Aufrichts, and the onanistic shadow of Mr. Kaleff fading away. . . . I have been tottering and creaking and wheezing, with recurring spasms of angina pains; now lessening, thank God, and the last few days I really do get around quite well. . . . In spite of the physical setback, I am happy to be here, the city suits me. . . ."

He was again in the tawdry atmosphere he most enjoyed. The letter ended with "What's going on?" They were the last words I ever had from him, as they had been the first words he spoke during our almost daily telephone chats over such a long period of time. "What's going on?" in that dulcet, insinuating tone. On November 20th, Lenya wrote me that George was in the hospital again with continuous pains in the chest. He asked if I would send him the Truman Capote profile of Marlon Brando that had just appeared in *The New Yorker*. He never received it. Six days later Lenya's cable arrived, saying he had passed away in the night. At the age of fifty-one. It is a tribute to the vividness of his personality that even after all these years, to those who knew him one can still remark, "As George used to say," without there being any question of which "George" is meant. In the lives of so many of us he had been an exceptional presence.

4

Personalities

THE FIRST PERSONALITY piece I ever sold was one on Gypsy Rose Lee and, indirectly, it was George Davis who led me to her. In the mid-Twenties, literary commentators on a slumming trip, notably Edmund Wilson and Gilbert Seldes, had used burlesque shows as a theme for somewhat condescending critical essays. Totally unaware of such esthetic trailblazers, I was familiarizing myself with these hearty entertainments at about the same time, when I was in the eighth grade at P.S. 30 on East Eighty-eighth Street. One of my classmates, Fat Brody, whose given name I don't now remember, had a weekly pass to the Hurtig & Seamon burlesque house in Yorkville, which his father received in exchange for exhibiting a placard in the window of his nearby candy store. The pass admitted two and I was frequently favored to accompany my school companion.

Billy Watson and his Beef Trust was a staple on the circuit that booked the house, the Beef Trust of course consisting of a line of overweight chorus girls. Others were Mollie Williams, who headed her own show, and a star comic, "Bozo" Snyder, whom I remember

Gypsy Rose Lee in full panoply (and about to remove it)

only because of his cozy sobriquet. Burlesque was then considered to be a robust but permissible family diversion and there was nothing untoward about finding two twelve-year-olds, without an accompanying adult, at a weekday matinee. When hard times began to affect the box office, in the early days of the Depression, the sketches became inescapably lewd and the strippers were added, in an effort to stimulate business. Gypsy was one of the earliest of these, and since she performed with humor, divesting herself of her garments in a conspiratorial you-know-I'm-only-kidding manner that nevertheless proved provocative, she was soon recognized as an outstanding personality with a sound box-office value.

At this point I was snobbish in my entertainment preferences and disdained burlesque shows as elementary and not worth my bother. But George Davis kept describing the different striptease stylists at the Irving Place Theater in such an amusing way that I was intrigued and went back to see for myself. The first two soloists on the bill were as a rule colorless and could be readily dismissed. As the show progressed, the girls with less perfunctory routines began to stand out as individuals. The featured strippers were known to the customers for their specialties. One — was it the Countess Nadja? — appeared wearing a Russian costume with a high neckline, long sleeves and a full skirt that covered her to her ankles. She would sing "Ha-cha-chon-ya" soulfully, to the accompaniment of groans from the audience. When the groans accelerated and became wails of derision, she would suddenly swoop down and lift her skirt high about her head, revealing her unclothed lower torso. Another specialist, Carrie Finnell, could rotate her pendulous breasts in opposite directions simultaneously. My favorite stripper was red-haired Georgia Sothern, who wasted no time in teasing. To the accompaniment of a heated Ellington composition, she would glide to stage center, tear off her outer garment with one quick motion, and go into her frenetic dance, shimmying, shaking, bumping, grinding, jerking her head between her legs in orgiastic spasms, stalking purposefully to the proscenium arch and using its edge as an accessory in simulated copulation. It was a most erotic performance. During off hours Georgia wrote romantic poems, which she later committed to a published volume.

Gypsy's performance was far less incendiary. Tall and handsome, a tomboy unsuitably bedecked in female finery, she gave her act a mock-decorous air. She would pace the stage with an athletic stride rather than the sinuous glide considered *de rigueur*. Where her sister strippers exhaled a standard pop song before embarking on their libidinous gyrations, Gypsy had had the enterprise to find special material, sophisticated, leering recitatives, implicit rather than explicit in their narrated obscenities. They were the songs of Dwight Fiske, a performer in smart uptown nightclubs, and Gypsy had simply lifted them from his recordings, without bothering to obtain permission. As a general rule the men in the audience listened politely if uncomprehendingly to this polysyllabic jargon, waiting for her to start disrobing and interrupting only occasionally with shouts of "Come on, Gyps, take it off, we know ya!" Fiske told me sometime later (I wrote an article on him called "Pixie") that Otis Chatfield-Taylor, a social friend of his who had seen Gypsy in her act and had become acquainted with her, first informed him of the abrasion of his copyright and had brought him down to the Irving Place to hear for himself. Chatfield-Taylor had then taken him backstage and introduced him under a pseudonym. "Where did you find that amusing song?" asked Fiske. "Oh," said Gypsy, with a noncommittal wave of her hand, "It just came to me." Fiske thought it would be fun to lure Gypsy to a party at the house of one of his friends and get her to sing the purloined material. The night of the affair, he was licking his lips in anticipation of the shaming denouement, but he was to be frustrated. When he arrived at the party, Gypsy had already discovered his identity and was irate about the trick he was planning to play on her. She greeted him with an unequivocal "You son-of-a-bitch!" He was so delighted with her brazenness that he gave her permission to continue to use his material.

Gypsy designed and sewed her own stage clothes. She would face the audience in a maidenly frock, looking freshly scrubbed and in blooming health. While she was talking her suggestive song she would unfasten a pin from a fold in her dress and toss it insouciantly into the orchestra pit, the drummer emphasizing its landing with an exaggerated thump. Gypsy continued to unfasten pins, making a great play about discovering yet another, and another, to be flung mockingly on the drum, until the garment was entirely free of its fastenings. She would then slowly drop it from her shoulders to reveal her breasts and quickly exit. Applause and reappearance, with the dress held loosely across the lower half of her body. Gypsy would caress one bare breast and admit to the gents out front, "Mmm, I'm getting to like this myself." More byplay with the dress, another exit, another teasing re-entrance, with the implicative "You really shouldn't ask a lady to do this," and then a seeming revelation of the entire frame naked except for an obligatory G-string. But Gypsy never really showed it all. At the last moment, with the sleight-of-hand of a practiced magician, she would manage to drape her garment becomingly and enticingly over one hip and, bare-assed and bare-breasted, her modesty would somehow still be preserved. "They come to hear me sing," she would claim.

I had written some song lyrics for submission to various Broadway revue producers and it occurred to me, after seeing Gypsy's performance several times, that she might undertake to use them in her act. One night after the show I went backstage and asked for her. She came out in a dressing gown and when I told her that I had some special numbers that might suit her and left them in an envelope with her, she made an appointment for me to appear at her Irving Place apartment up the street after the next day's matinee. She lived on the roof of her building, in a commodious penthouse overlooking Gramercy Park. The social life of the apartment obviously centered around a small barroom, one wall of which was papered with billboard posters of the burlesque shows in which she had appeared, the others being decorated with signed photographs of strippers, movie actors, and players from the legitimate stage. When I arrived the chromium bar was populated by Georgia Sothern and two other girls from the Irving Place show. Gypsy sat on a stool pouring drinks and speaking vivaciously and almost continuously in her husky contralto. The chatter was all shoptalk, the diction unrestrained. I might have been a familiar of many years' standing. One of the girls had just signed a disadvantageous contract and was down in the mouth about it. "What could I do?" she explained. "They gave me nine shots of rye, and I was ready to sign anything." Gypsy was scornful. "Honey," she said, "they pulled that on me too, but I brought along Mother and a few friends and they didn't get away with anything. I go where the dough is." She told of having refused an offer from Leon and Eddie's, an important night spot, because the salary was less than she had been getting in burlesque, which she claimed was $900 a week. Gypsy could get very animated talking about contracts. In this she reminded me of the dancer I was once told about who would sit on the lap of a fat, rich old man at a party and say, "Money makes me passionate."

I was fascinated by my unaccustomed surroundings, fascinated by the cameraderie, fascinated by Gypsy in animation, constantly hitching up the skirt that hampered her, reminiscing in her piquant locution about her nights as a "white zombie," a mute showgirl on parade at the Casino de Paree. She told me she liked my song lyrics but that they weren't right for her at the Irving Place (they weren't). On the inspiration of the moment, I blurted out, "I'd like to write an article about you." Suddenly, the atmosphere at the bar changed. Now I was on the other side of the show business tracks, "the press," and the informality quickly evaporated. Gypsy said that *The New Yorker* some months ago had assigned Meyer Berger, the leading crime reporter of the New York *Times,* to do a Profile of her, but nothing much had come of it. Since Berger's two previous Profiles had been of a Broadway chiseler and a Brooklyn waterfront moll, Gypsy's cooperation had been less than enthusiastic. She made a date for me to return several days later and I left the apartment in high anticipation.

In contrast with the exuberance of my first meeting with her, the interview for the article was a letdown. Gypsy was on her good "being-interviewed" behavior. The raffish hoyden of a few days ago was not to be resuscitated (she hadn't yet learned, as eventually she did, that candor could make interesting copy). She was circumspect about almost everything, speaking guardedly about "a certain actress," "a well-known comedian," as if she were a gossip columnist. She did say one thing that I could have used maliciously — when I asked what kind of books she liked to read, she answered airily, "Anything skintillating" — but I felt it wouldn't be gentlemanly to do so. I thought what a fool I had been to tell her so soon that I wanted to write about her.

I wrote the article, using Gypsy's laundered biography, as she told it to me, for background, and, for color, an abstract of what I had heard and observed that first time sitting around the bar. I submitted it to *Stage* magazine, which rejected it on the grounds that she wasn't well enough known, but then I sold it to a new publication called *Globe*.

About six years later, I interviewed Gypsy's sister, June Havoc, in Hollywood and had a glorious time, with June giving me an unvarnished and uproarious rendition of their life in vaudeville with their grasping mother Rose. It would have made a good story when I was in quest of information at the Irving Place penthouse. It made a good story when Gypsy cleaned it up considerably and used it in her memoir *Gypsy*. And it made a dandy musical comedy under the same name.

Cue magazine, the weekly New York entertainment guide, was my first regular source of writing assignments. In 1936 the fledgling magazine's editor, Jesse Zunser, bought a short-short story I had sent him. Then, as now, *Cue* was primarily a service publication whose raison d'être was its complete listings of movie house programs in the city and the surrounding suburbs. For additional reader interest each issue also featured a brief piece dealing with a personality, or a theatrical reminiscence, and frequently the kind of short "mood" story that was associated mainly with *The New Yorker*. Because of the latter's finicky requirements *Cue,* although it paid only $10, later $15, and then $25, was sometimes able to publish stories by well-known writers that the more-established magazine had obviously rejected and that didn't suit any other market.

Jesse and his two associate editors, Brailsford Felder and Orville Prescott — Prescott was later to hold down the job of daily book reviewer for the New York *Times* for many years — liked the way I wrote and I soon became a favored contributor. From June through December of 1936 they bought seven of my stories, most of them, as the titles will indicate, having theater or film people for their main characters or points of reference. The first one, "Celluloid Man," dealt with a drunken movie star on location and was based on a bit of gossip I had heard on my initial trip to Hollywood. The others were "No Casting" (the middle-aged female playwright envious of a pretty ingenue), "Hollywood Idyll" (a producer gives an old friend the brushoff), "Rehearsal" (a star and her director have a set-to about her first entrance), "The Barrymores of Fortieth Street" (a silly woman boasts of having the esteemed Ethel Barrymore as a neighbor), "'The Comeback" (a former opera star's manager quietly cancels an opening night party because he knows her return performance will be disastrous), and "The Crisis" (two quarreling women friends at an art gallery settle their differences by being spiteful about the exhibiting artist's wife).

That year I also sold *Cue* ten articles dealing with personalities, beginning with Big John, who had served as elevator operator and doorman at the old Empire Theater since its opening forty-three years earlier. Big John was an easy piece to do, sentiment interspersed with anecdote. "Tell us, John, about the Golden Age. Tell us, John, about Maude Adams. About Charles Frohman, about John Drew, and William Gillette, and all the rest. . . . Those were great days, sir. Big John grins wistfully."

Martha Graham had become an illustrious figure in the confined world of modern dance since I had seen her in the first year of her solo recitals a decade earlier. Using the most gifted of her pupils, she had developed a performing company of gymnastic marvels, who could contort their bodies to their demanding choreographer's will. She was a striking, original figure in the world of art and I suggested to the *Cue* editor that she would be worth an assessment. An "appreciation" is what they termed it when the article was printed under the title "High Priestess of the Dance," a label used reverently by her relatively small, ardent public, and sneeringly by her detractors, who, as I wrote in my opening paragraph, associated her with such "crackpots" as Pablo Picasso and Gertrude Stein.

From the late *Vanity Fair* I reprinted some dialogue that had served to caption one of caricaturist Miguel Covarrubias's "Impossible Interviews," between Martha and the fan dancer Sally Rand:

Martha: I don't think we have anything in common.
Sally: Forget it, kid, we're in the same racket, ain't we. Just a couple of girls trying to wriggle along. . . . You take the women's clubs, and I'll take the men.
Martha: (Enviously) For plenty.

Originally, when the *Vanity Fair* issue had appeared, Sally Rand (or more likely her press agent) had sent an indignant letter to the newspapers saying she held Miss Graham in high esteem and had even, in her youth, been a student in one of her instruction classes. She admired art but a girl had to make her living. Martha of course didn't rise to the bait. She had thought the travesty amusing.

I interviewed her in her studio on lower Fifth Avenue, above the film theater near Thirteenth Street. I found a woman in repose, with none of the electric nervous energy of her stage presence. She was articulate and lucid about her complex works. Although she had inspired pretentiousness in the cult that had sprung around her, there was not the slightest trace of the *précieuse* about her. Nor in the relaxed, low-keyed talk I listened to for several hours was there any hint of the termagant I knew she could be. She was a knowledgeable showwoman.

I had gone to her manager, Frances Hawkins, for background on Martha (the use of her first name rather than a more formal designation came about as naturally to anyone who had spent the least bit of time with her as "Isadora" must have to her revolutionary predecessor). Frances was also at that time handling the Austrian dancer Harald Kreutzberg, and Lincoln Kirstein and George Balanchine's infant American Ballet company, chrysalis of the resplendent present-day New York City Ballet. Frances was a rabid enthusiast for her clients and although she had no trouble in booking Kreutzberg, who was a popular concert draw, it was much more difficult to find engagements for her two other attractions, modern dance and ballet both being box-office problems throughout the country. I had met Lincoln Kirstein through Paul Magriel, who was then working in the year-old ballet company's office over an Irish dance hall on the corner of Madison Avenue and Fifty-ninth Street, and thought he would be a good subject for an article. Kirstein had become obsessed with the ballet as a child in Boston, when he saw Pavlova dance, and felt frustrated when his mother refused to take him to see Nijinsky in *L'Après-midi d'un faune,* which was erotic and a scandal. As an undergraduate at Harvard, he and Edward M. M. Warburg, son of the banker Felix, had formed the Harvard Society of Contemporary Arts, giving startled Boston its first view of cubist Picassos, surrealist Mirós, and the early sculpture of Alexander Calder. They had sent a truck to Calder's studio to transport the exhibit, which as it turned out consisted only of a coil of wire, since Calder intended to shape his wire figures on the spot at the gallery. At Harvard, Kirstein had also written and had published a young man's obligatory novel and had founded and funded, through his father, who was vice-president of Filene's Department Store in Boston and Bloomingdale's in New York, an intellectual quarterly of the arts, *Hound and Horn,* based on T. S. Eliot's London *Criterion.* His enduring passion was for ballet, however, and when he had met Balanchine in Paris in 1933, he had urged him to come to America to organize a native ballet company, for which he induced Warburg to supply the backing.

All this had been accomplished by the time Kirstein was twenty-nine. I called my piece "Balletmaniac" (I was even younger than he) and dubbed him "America's No. 1 aesthete-under-thirty," amplifying the impudent qualification with a genuinely admiring sketch of the 6'2" prodigy. Lincoln — he has been an on-and-off intimate ever since — is brilliant, intense, so erratic and volatile that he can be depended upon to create a scene without bothering about provocation. Childlike, he is addicted to sudden violent and generally short-lived enthusiasms. His temper is lightning-quick, his nerve ends so exposed that the most ordinary daily contact with him can suddenly become an inflammable misadventure. "I've known him for years," an acquaintance of his once told me, "and I wouldn't dream of saying 'hello' to him first." His vendetta list is a long one, and in rational moments he will admit that in many cases he has no idea what black moment sparked the original quarrel. His wife Fidelma has said, "Lincoln needs his enemies."

Having set the stage, so to speak, with two pieces on the dance, I continued with articles on Charles Weidman, Angna Enters, and the Hindu Uday Shan-Kar (he was en route with his troupe from India and not due to arrive in New York until the day before his opening performance; to meet my deadline I had to write the piece from clippings and information from the Hurok office, and never did get to interview him). I also did a piece called "Ex-Fancy Amateur Dancer," about a different kind of artist, the pathologically egocentric painter Louis Eilshemius. I took the title from a remarkable business-and-personal calling card of his in which, following his name, he listed his achievements and talents: painter, essayist, poet, playwright, composer, pianist, scientist, inventor and — the last bewildering item — ex-fancy amateur dancer. I never got him to explain the singular nature of his accomplishment.

So far as his belated, grudging acceptance into the pantheon of art history went, Eilshemius was the American counterpart of Henri Rousseau. He began painting in early youth but his poetic landscapes, enhanced with primitive female nude figures, were ridiculed or ignored by critics, museums and picture dealers. He had to wait until he was sixty-two, in 1926, before being favored with a one-man show. At that time Murdock Pemberton, *The New Yorker*'s art reviewer, wrote that the dealer Valentine Dudensing must have had "his tongue in both cheeks" when sponsoring the exhibit; other reviewers were equally condescending or downright vituperative. Only Marcel Duchamp and Henry McBride, the astute critic of the New York *Sun,* were champions of his work.

Their proselytizing, which made note of the early neglect of Ryder and Rousseau, was so effective that by the time of Dudensing's second Eilshemius exhibit five years later, the critics were more respectful. The imposing French house of Durand-Ruel gave

Louis Eilshemius in his bed-sitting room

him a Paris showing, and he received the benediction of Matisse; the Luxembourg Museum purchased one of his pictures. The Whitney had already purchased another, *The Flying Dutchman*, and the Metropolitan followed, acquiring *Lake, Delaware Water Gap*. But he had waited too long for these triumphs. In a pamphlet of excoriating poems he published at the time — signed "Mahatma Louis M. Eilshemius, M.A., etc., Mightiest Mind, Supreme Parnassian and Grand Transcendant Eagle," he chastised "These Conceited Millionairesses" (Marie Harriman and Mrs. Harry Payne Whitney — "Are ye Americans? For six decades long, you have ignored America's marvel in Art and Song. Shame!"), "Those Worthless Art Magazines," "The Metropolitan Art Antique Shop," and "These Modern Stupid Critics" ("their brains could not fathom my work superior . . ."). He had painted for forty years, for several decades more he had tried to compel attention to his work, and now that he had received belated recognition, no amount of fame could eradicate his bitterness.

By the time of his fourth New York show, in 1936, he was well established and his pictures were enjoying a brisk market. He had stopped painting in 1922, but he had a backlog of five thousand paintings, he told me when I went to see him in the brownstone house on East Fifty-seventh Street, since torn down, which he and his brother owned and on the third floor of which he had secluded himself. Until 1931, he had been a familiar obtrusive figure in the city's art galleries. A medium-sized man with a trim white mustache and beard and long white locks strung back from a very high forehead, dressed in an old suit stuffed with newspapers to keep out the cold, he would enter a gallery and loudly denounce each picture to any viewer who happened to be present.

His shabby appearance was never the result of economic necessity. He came from a wealthy family, was listed in the *Social Register,* and had always had a more than comfortable income. The brownstone had been in his family since the 1880s. When I went there, my appointment arranged by Dudensing, a housekeeper sent me up to the third floor. The walls of all the rooms I could see appeared to be covered with Eilshemius paintings, looking down on once-opulent, now dingy Victorian furnishings. On the second floor, in a spacious dining room, was his brother, mumbling curses at me as I passed. The brothers, both bachelors, had not spoken to each other in years. On the third floor the painter sat in his bed-sitting room, wearing a dark, discolored smock, with a steamer rug thrown across his lap.

He had been hit by an automobile five years earlier, which had torn
a ligament in his leg, and he had been confined ever since.

He had very few visitors, he told me. Most of those who did come
were students, asking for a gift of a painting. Members of his own
craft did not bother with him. He attributed this to jealousy. "Why
don't the great men, the big names, come to visit me?" he asked.
"I'm the best painter in the world. They have time to go to cabarets
for girls and drinks, what's the matter with coming to see me? I'm
just as good as any damn girl!"

By his own count, he had written two hundred fifty books, of
prose and poetry, the majority of which he himself had published
and distributed from his house. He had stopped writing, however,
because "you can only write poetry when you're young. I'm the
greatest poet about girls . . . as big as Heine and Bobbie Burns.
But what's left when you're old? No girls . . . I can't write poetry
about men." From his *Sixty Sonnets*, "all written in the classical
manner," which he showed me, I copied one example, "The Sweetest, Shortest Sonnet," "written," he said, "in the *new* classical manner":

> Dove!
> Bliss
> Is
> Love.
> Prove
> This?
> Kiss,
> Love?
> Life
> Seems
> Sweet:
> To Meet
> Wife —
> Dreams!

As I thumbed through the rest of the small book, I noted that this
was not an unfair example of his poetry as a whole.

He also, he said, stood high as "a musical composer of a classical quality. I'm the best composer since Beethoven — his feelings were the same as mine, so it stands to reason I'm as good as he was." His unabashed praise of himself, his denunciations of all who tried to temper this self-assessment, had antagonized even his well-wishers. A terribly lonely, terribly bitter old man, he lived out his last years fretfully. He died in 1941. Recognition had come too late.

Since the three *Cue* editors were amenable to almost every article suggestion I gave them, I had a wide range of people in the arts and allied entertainment fields to choose from. I would do a personality sketch of a nightclub performer, Dwight Fiske, who numbered among his admirers Marie Dressler, Tallulah Bankhead, Eugene O'Neill and the evangelist Aimee Semple McPherson. His frisky songs had titles like "Ida, the Wayward Sturgeon," and his sly, steamy lyrics bordered on the pornographic (Paul to Virginia at a nudist camp: "Don't look now, but I think I'm falling in love with you"). Fiske had a genial leer, like the movies' Eric Blore, whom he somewhat resembled. He played his recordings for me and shrieked with laughter at all the funny lines, repeating with reckless insistence, "That's good, isn't it?"

Sol Hurok had been preeminent as a manager of star concert attractions since the early Twenties. For a world-renowned impresario, he was unimpressive in appearance, full-faced, pink-cheeked, bald, dressed inconspicuously. He could have been one of hundreds of Seventh Avenue garment manufacturers or workers of the period. He was a shrewd personality, sympathetic to talk with about his performers, evasive when the talk turned to business matters. But, although ruthless in his contract dealings, he was no mere money grubber; he still retained traces of the idol-worship from his gallery days at the Metropolitan Opera as a fourteen-year-old Jewish immigrant from Russia. He was paternally boastful of his artists and tolerant of their idiosyncrasies. All artists must have temperament, he asserted with pride. His attitude was a contrast to the dulled cynicism of other art-worn managers.

He remembered Richard Strauss chiefly as an inveterate poker player, who always demanded his concert money in advance of the performance. Isadora Duncan confined her pre-concert demands to champagne, but had a bad habit of signing checks unsecured by a banking account, the checks inevitably bounding back to Hurok. Glazounov was "the kindest man I ever met," ready to endorse his own name to the works of hungry composers, to facilitate a sale. Chaliapin, notoriously difficult to handle, was indulged by Hurok for years. He fraternized with him, once dressing as a tramp so the two could sleep in a Bowery flophouse, Chaliapin being eager for the experience. They spent many nights in Turkish baths, to which the basso was addicted. "Here," he would say, "is the true democracy. For rich and poor alike — the same water." Pavlova was naive about financial matters. "She never discussed money with me all the years I know her," said Hurok.

Although he had been in the United States since 1904, he had never been able to master the language, which remained a sensitive spot with him. In my article I described him as speaking "a blatantly deformed English, full of hacksawed idioms," which the editor toned down by excising the latter half of the statement.

Several months after the article appeared, I saw him standing in the rear of the auditorium of Carnegie Hall as I was arriving for a concert. I greeted him and shook his hand. He didn't seem particularly pleased to see me. "Tell me," he suddenly blurted out, "who speaks perfect English? No one. Just one man I know. President Woodrow Wilson." And he nodded his head to emphasize his point.

I also wrote articles on the Spanish classical guitarist Andrés Segovia, then the painter Paul Cadmus, who had recently become celebrated for his Hogarthian depictions of unbuttoned New York City life, then a piece on Tony Soma, proprietor of Tony's, favorite speakeasy haunt of the affluent writers and actors of Prohibition days. In "Dowling, Shakespeare & Co." I described how Eddie Dowling, a musical comedy star of such plebian diversions as *Sally, Irene and Mary, Honeymoon Lane, The Sidewalks of New York,* had come to be involved as a producer of Maurice Evans's *King Richard II*. When I asked him about it, Dowling, a fourth-grade grammar school dropout but a pious dispenser of bromides, said,

"Well, you see, I have always loved Shakespeare." The truth, as I found out and published, was that the production had come to him as a package and the billing was part of his reward for booking it into the St. James Theater, of which he was the lessee. Then — and no doubt now — you didn't necessarily have to produce to become a Broadway producer.

Then, for a short-lived magazine called *New York Woman*, I wrote about Mrs. Louise Hellstrom, under the title "Professional Horror." I first heard about Louise as a holdover from the gin-drinking Twenties, an obstreperous female who had made a career out of being horrible. An unprepared meeting with her, I had been told, was a challenge to the nervous system. Seemingly, she was completely uninhibited, going to great lengths to attract attention. She had been known to throw herself upon the floor at a crowded art gallery opening, kick her legs high into the air, and bellow her appreciation of a picture that had pleased her. At a charity auction, she would leer at a prosperous-looking stranger and shout, "What are you sitting there for? Why don't you *buy* something." With Louise, there never was any question of understatement.

What attracted me to her as a subject was her background and her intimate acquaintance among the celebrated and the notorious. Born in Philadelphia of solid Dutch Quaker parents (she never did reveal her maiden name to me), she had run away from home at the age of sixteen to become a chorus girl with a touring musical comedy. Eventually the troupe reached San Francisco shortly after the turn of the century and Louise decided to make the city her home. On the day of the 1906 earthquake she was going horseback riding with her current beau when the first earth rumblings were heard. The next two days were full of nightmare and panic for the rest of the citizenry, but Louise had a grand time. She and her friend, on hastily requisitioned horses, followed the fire fighters, watching as miles of city blocks were dynamited. Their only nourishment for forty-eight hours was two raw eggs and a whole case of champagne.

She left the destroyed city shortly thereafter, to set herself up in New York, where she remained for four years. "She had accumulated enough money not to have to work for a while," I wrote, with no further explanation, since she had been vague about the source of her subsidy. She then went to live in Paris, where she studied painting at the Ecole Moderne. In 1912 she was back in New York looking for a job. She had a flair for clothes and began designing dresses for Hickson, the smartest of the town's prewar dress shops, and was so successful at it that she made it her vocation. In 1919, on one of her frequent fashion trips to Paris, she met and married a Scandinavian novelist, Gustaf Hellstrom, "The Swedish Dostoevski," and returned with him to the States, where they rented a summer cottage in the new artists' colony Hervey White had established in Woodstock, New York. The marriage was of short duration. Hellstrom, who preferred a peaceful existence to bedlam with Louise, soon went back to Sweden. Meanwhile, in Woodstock, Louise had met the many-faceted Robert Winthrop Chanler, onetime cowboy and sheriff, now artist and millionaire playboy, who was just as exhibitionistic as she was. "Bob and I could always make more noise than a roomful of people," she told me matter-of-factly. She became his mistress and they went through the Twenties together at a boisterous pitch until his death in 1930. She compared their friendship with that of Horace Walpole for Mme. du Deffand, and if you could imagine Walpole kicking his dear correspondent down a flight of stairs, shouting, "Bitch of bitches!" after her, I suppose she had some sort of point.

Chanler and Louise seem to have been well-matched. Each detested polite society, each enjoyed violent quarrels and raucous public display, and each was a prodigious guzzler, with Louise having the edge since she could drink all night and work all day with very little sleep, a feat beyond the endurance of her partner.

At his twin houses on East Nineteenth Street, and in Woodstock, Chanler gave large parties attended by an amazingly heterogeneous group of people. Actors, artists, Upper East Side dowagers, models, prizefighters and royalty rubbed elbows and dodged glassware. Two of his most noteworthy shindigs were given for Edward, then Prince of Wales, and King Albert of Belgium. Louise also entertained at her apartment in 9 East Twelfth Street. "Cutie, I had a

salon that was famous," she said to me. There were seldom fewer
than fifty people for cocktails and more than a hundred for larger
evening affairs. If she found the guests enervating she would demand
that they all get out, or else she herself would leave to go to some
other party which she thought might be more amusing.

Louise's social manner was, to put it mildly, unbridled, and
Chanler was never content to be a mere spectator. A dinner for
sixteen people would be progressing nicely when Louise would say
something that displeased him. Whatever course the meal had
reached was almost certain to be flung at Louise's head. During one
dinner party, not at all atypical, a platter of lobsters was brought in
at the unfortunate moment when Louise was proclaiming her desire
to crack someone's skull. Chanler, presiding at the other end of the
table, picked up a lobster and threw it at her. She ducked. He threw
another and another until the platter was empty. Louise had the
last word. She looked at him calmly and said, "You bore me."

Chanler had been dead six years when I first heard about Louise.
Apparently a vital part of her life went with him, for I was given to
understand that she had since calmed down somewhat, and was
spending most of her time at her house in Woodstock, in rather
straitened circumstances. I sent a note to her there, telling her I was
interested in writing an article about her and she wrote asking me
to come up the following weekend. She said I could stay overnight
at her house on Friday but that I would have to spend Saturday
night at the local inn, since Marcel Duchamp, an old friend, would
be visiting her then and she had only one guest room. She was
planning a cocktail party for him, to which I was invited.

Meanwhile in New York I interviewed people who had known
her in her heyday. I saw Duchamp, who with spare, dry humor
recounted Louise's hectic existence with Chanler and gave me numerous examples of her anarchic behavior. He had known her for
twenty years. Another old friend who talked understandingly about
her and without priggishness was Marian Bouché, wife of the
painter Louis Bouché. By the time I left for Woodstock I was well
primed with information.

Louise's house was in a pretty, woodsy area a short distance from

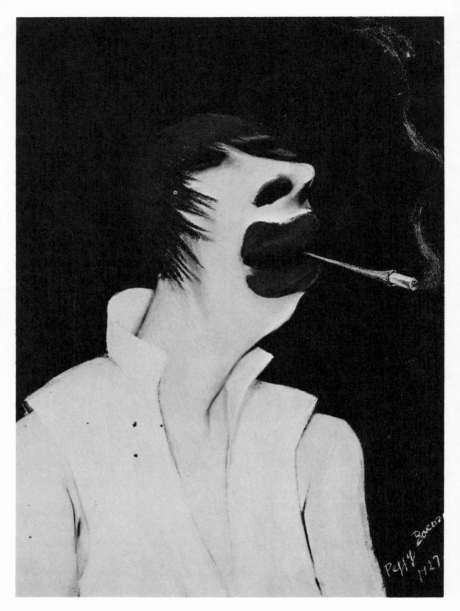

The extraordinary Louise Hellstrom as painted by Peggy Bacon

the town. The interior was comfortably furnished, the spacious living room being enlivened by a variety of plants and many paintings, some by her friends, some, surprisingly conventional and unremarkable, by Louise. Dominating them was a large portrait by Chanler, dated 1927, showing her wearing a striped dress and looking rather edgy in what must have been a rare moment of imposed calm. The pride of the room was a large, many-paneled screen, also by Chanler, elaborately painted, gessoed and gilded in an intricate pattern of lush foliage. These screens had been his special contribution to the art of his day; they were what his somewhat esoteric reputation was based on.

Louise was about fifty when I encountered her and she looked a bit spent, although she must have been exceptionally hardy, for she was to live on for a great many more years. She was slightly built, with long slim legs and very thin arms which she kept waving histrionically as a further adjunct to articulation, I guessed, since she frequently interrupted her hoarse chatter with an interjected series of incomprehensible noises which sounded like *wuz wuz wuz wuz wuz.*

Her appearance could quite accurately be called striking. She had bright orange hair, closely cropped, with a fringe of bangs covering her forehead; her gray eyes were framed with purple shadow; her thick lips were painted a bright magenta and her complexion had a greenish tinge. As a madcap around town, she had been a character in several contemporary novels of the Twenties. In Max Ewing's *Going Somewhere* (printed elegantly by Knopf on tinted paper) she is Lenore Lanslide, a sculptress, forty-nine of whose models are poisoned by her lethal gin. Carl van Vechten's *Parties* pictures her as Simone Fly, "A cross between a poster by Cheret and a caricature by Toulouse-Lautrec . . . she resembled a gay Death." The painting by Peggy Bacon, from the collection of Alfred Steiglitz, which the magazine used to illustrate my article, gives her the look of a chic anthropoid, moodily smoking a cigarette through a long holder. I also have a crayon sketch by Peggy Bacon that Louise gave me, which depicts her, again with a cigarette, for she was a chain smoker, in angled animation, a contortive virago.

She told me many stories, seeming to relive again the enjoyment she had derived from her outré behavior. I had heard of her interest in witchcraft and asked her about her studies in black magic. If she quarreled with a friend who the next day happened to sprain an ankle, she would say, "You see, I put the curse on you." A Woodstock neighbor once found her pacing the floor of her house, muttering to herself. "Which way is New York?" she asked. The neighbor pointed southward. "My God," said Louise, "I'm putting the curse on someone in New York and I'm facing the wrong way. Now I'll have to do it all over again."

My purpose in bringing up the witchcraft was to verify a startling claim she had been making for years. In 1927, Bob Chanler was in Paris, living next door to Isadora Duncan's quarters in the Parnasse Studios. "She was being a goddess all over the place," said Louise. "I don't understand that business. I'm not mystical." Louise had been unable to accompany Chanler but he wrote to her almost every day. At first his letters made passing references of Isadora, then her name began to be mentioned more often. Finally the letters stopped altogether and Louise received a cable from Walter Shaw, a close friend of the dancer's. "I think Isadora has won," it read. Louise became panicky and cabled Chanler, "What does Walter mean he thinks Isadora has won?" She found her answer in the next day's newspapers, which announced Isadora's engagement to Chanler.

Louise was then living at the Brevoort Hotel. When she read the announcement she left her workshop and retreated to the hotel. All day long she would see no one. She paced up and down in her room, muttering incantations. This went on all night. When, the following afternoon, she read the headline proclaiming Isadora's sudden death, she sent another, a triumphant, cable to Chanler: "Tell Walter that Louise has won." "She was in my way," Louise said to me. "I had to get rid of her. Her death may have been a coincidence; you can take it or leave it." Chanler was delighted with her message. He went to Isadora's funeral with the cable, and waved it in the faces of her friends and admirers. Louise's eyes lit up when she remembered this. "It must have been a terribly dramatic scene," she said. "God, I wish I'd been there!"

New York Woman would not publish my article until I got a release from Louise, since they wanted to guard against the possibility of a libel suit. I had to send the article to her in Woodstock to get her consent and she sent back a letter of suggestions and corrections. She didn't object to the "Professional Horror" title or to my recounting of her robustious pattern of behavior. "I do not like about everyone visiting me wishing they had not had so much to drink, etc.," she wrote. "It is not true and sounds as if my parties were an awful bore. In fact you do not make it definite any place that my parties are the gayest and best organized of any parties up here — or in N.Y. for that matter — and that is why everybody always came — but the way you have expressed it — no one — not knowing me — could ever imagine why anyone ever wanted to come at all. Born in Phila. fifty years ago will not do at all, might as well make it eighty and be done with it — about forty is all I will stand for — we gals being so sensitive — I do not mind particularly about friends but I do about strangers. . . . In the George Gershwin story, when Eva [Gautier] comes down to the footlights and asks if he is in the house, I said, 'No — he is not — but his mother is' which is much funnier. . . . I do not like the 'Court Clown' — it sounds condescending and it was Bob who was the clown not I. . . . Why do you say I only felt at home in N.Y. and San Francisco when I felt very much at home in Paris. I lived there six years and knew as many famous artists as I did here. The people my husband and I knew were Picasso, Kisling, Modiglino [sic], Marcel Duchamp and Brancusi was my very best friend. . . . You did the [Blanche] Yurka and Fanny Ward stories superbly only don't forget that Texas [Guinan] arrived in her Rolls Royce. . . . I don't think these changes will be difficult — and think there are very many amusing things in it."

I made a few alterations in the manuscript, then telephoned Louise to make an appointment to come up to Woodstock with a staff photographer. She was photographed seated in front of the Chanler portrait, wearing a becoming garment with a brocaded top and in her lap a favorite Persian cat. "Mrs. Hellstrom at home, in a rare moment of repose" read the caption; Louise had her crayoned eyelids lowered and both she and the cat seem to be thinking up some deviltry.

I never saw Louise again. Some years later I heard that she had hired out to cook for a family in Woodstock (the verbal disorder of her existence didn't carry over to her physical surroundings; she was a good Quaker housekeeper). The last mention I had of her was in a letter from Marcel Duchamp. I had written him for some information about a lithograph I had bought of his Coffee Mill painting and had noted our long-ago meeting at Louise's. In his reply he asked if I knew of her whereabouts. He was trying to find some posters he had designed and which he had given her some forty years earlier. No one seemed to have a notion of how, after all this time, she could be traced.

5

Two Disparate Wits

Oscar Levant

S. N. Behrman

Oscar Levant

THROUGHOUT THE LATE THIRTIES and into the Forties, one of our most popular adult radio programs was *Information Please,* a question-and-answer show for which Clifton Fadiman served as quiz master. Fadiman's queries were aimed at a panel of "experts" that included one celebrated guest (changeable for each show) and three regulars, Franklin P. Adams (the columnist F.P.A.), John Kieran, the erudite nature writer for the New York *Times,* and a brash, impudent, irrepressible songwriter, pianist, musical know-it-all and Broadway wiseacre named Oscar Levant. Oscar's circle of intimates included S. N. Behrman, George S. and Beatrice Kaufman, Ira and Leonore Gershwin, Moss Hart, Harpo Marx, and Alexander Woollcott, who had dubbed him a "wit's wit" and had once complained querulously that arguing with him was like fighting a man with three hands.

Oscar, the only *Information Please* panelist unknown to the general public at the show's inception, had been the surprise hit of the program and his reputation solidified when he published a saucy collection of gossip, reminiscence and opinions called *A Smat-tering of Ignorance,* which became a best-seller. Indicative of the book's tone and contents was the dedication to the musicologist-editor who had helped him put it together, Irving Kolodin:

> With whose considerable aid
> I have augmented my influence
> **and**
> diminished the circle of
> my acquaintances

The acknowledgment embraced both Oscar's aspirations to be well-considered in New York and Hollywood's accepted cultural circles and his obsessive urge to test his relationships in those circles to the breaking point.

In the introduction, S. N. Behrman eulogized what he called "the spiked embrace of his friendship": "To say that Oscar is provocative would be putting it too mildly; he is practically a compulsion. As you can't always take him and you can never leave him, many of his friends find themselves for a long period in a state of uncomfortable abeyance like Dante's Limbo, until they finally decide that the tranquillity of an Oscarless life has only a negative compensation."

The tranquillity of my Oscarless life was broken when I tele-phoned him one day to say that I was writing an article about him for *Cosmopolitan* magazine and would like to arrange a meeting. I had suggested the piece through my agent for a series called Cosmop-olite of the Month and the editors had signified their interest. His first words, after the initial "Hello," were a characteristically belli-cose, "Why did they choose you?" to which I could only answer feebly, "I suppose because they thought I was good." Since Oscar had established, as was his custom, an immediate intimacy, I con-tinued with, "I've been seeing some of your friends for anecdotal material." "And what did you find out?" he asked combatively. Sink or swim; one *enfant terrible* deserved another. "I found out that you were a baby." His curiosity piqued by this matching of impudence, he said, "All right, I'll meet you in my building lobby in half an hour."

At the Paramount studio. Oscar Levant playing for me and the still photographer

Before tackling Oscar, I had begun by interviewing Ken McCormick and Charles Gorham, editor and publicity man for his book's publishers, Doubleday. Both of them were quick to confess that they treated him warily. I had also been to see Beatrice Kaufman, wife of the playwright and *grand dame* of the circle known generically as the Algonquin Round Table. She was one of Oscar's closest and most forbearing woman friends, good at psychological diagnosis and with an instinct for the illustrative anecdote. Most of the best material in my article came from her. She had put up with him during all his years as a disgruntled Peck's Bad Boy in the midst of a glitteringly successful group of journalists, show composers and playwrights and she could now view with maternal equanimity his recent elevation to the ranks of the celebrated.

In the days of his penury, it had been Oscar's habit to telephone his better-heeled friends to ask about their plans for the evening. He would then select the engagement that most appealed to him and brazenly turn up, uninvited but demanding. Frequently at a restaurant, after a dinner party that he had crashed, he would say impatiently to the host, "Come on, pay the check and let's go." Mrs. Kaufman recalled one such meal at the restaurant "21" where she and Edna Ferber had Oscar as an impromptu guest. While he was eating the spaghetti he had ordered, Miss Ferber remarked politely that it looked good. "Here, try some," said Oscar, winding a heaping portion around his fork and pushing it at her. Miss Ferber was germ-conscious and fastidious in her eating habits. To touch a utensil that was being used by someone else was far from appealing. However, wishing to be polite, she nibbled at the spaghetti, trying not to have her lips touch Oscar's fork. The feat accomplished, she handed it back to him so he could continue eating. "Waiter," called Oscar, equally germ-conscious, "bring me another fork." As a correlative, when I reminded Miss Ferber, a lifelong spinster, of the incident some months later, she added indignantly, "And *he* had a social disease at the time, too!"

Oscar could be unrelenting on the subject of his friends — of Beatrice Kaufman he once ungallantly told me, "She's the sort of woman who thinks there's nothing she couldn't do if she set her mind to it; unfortunately, her mind won't collaborate." There was also a much quoted remark about another close friend, Moss Hart. Moss, although he frequently escorted numerous young ladies around town, showed signs of becoming a perennial bachelor. Finally he seemed to have settled on a single candidate, an actress, as a matrimonial partner, and their engagement was widely rumored. The pair walked into Lindy's Restaurant one night while Oscar was sitting at a table with some cronies. "Here comes Moss Hart," proclaimed Oscar, "with the future Paula Laurence." Actually, a few years later, having responded to a well-publicized psychoanalysis, Moss did marry the singer Kitty Carlisle.

Nor did Oscar spare himself. His first marriage had endured for only six or seven months; when a reporter observed that it hadn't lasted long, Oscar said, "The hell it didn't — did you ever spend an hour with me?" The reason he gave for the divorce was incompatibility, adding, "Besides, we hated each other." In *A Smattering of Ignorance* he admitted that "my usual exercises consisted of groveling, brooding and mulling." He was not arrogant, nor was he boastful; in fact he tended to underrate any achievement of his. His boyhood passion had been music (he reputedly had ten thousand compositions at his fingertips) and he had become a good concert pianist, but he did not blind himself to the fact that his popularity as a soloist was based on the notoriety that had accrued to him as a radio smart-aleck. He knew that he would never be another Rubinstein or Horowitz, and to be less than that was to settle for second-best. It was not good enough. When his success on *Information Please* had made him a national figure, he said to his mother, "Now are you satisfied? I'm famous. It's not what I wanted to be, but I'm famous."

Beatrice Kaufman had told me that Oscar formed instantaneous likes and dislikes to people and I was apprehensive about having a snarling initial encounter with him. However, at our first meeting he was completely affable and I was beguiled by his considerable charm, the quality which enabled his friends to condone the frequent periods of bumptiousness which had made him a Broadway and then a national legend. He appeared to take to me and an intimacy of sorts developed rapidly. He generally rose at about 1:00 in the afternoon and went to his analyst. I would telephone him, or sometimes he would telephone me, at about 2:30 or 3:00 to ask what was doing. He seldom made definite plans in advance; outside of business engagements, he disliked having to commit himself to a social schedule.

Our usual procedure was to meet in his apartment on West Fifty-eighth Street, where I would have a few words with his second wife if she was available — he had married a very pretty, modest girl called June Gale and they were expecting their first child — and then Oscar would be ready for his promenade. He almost always wore a dark blue suit, not too scrupulously valeted, frequently enlivened by a favorite Charvet tie, food-spotted, which had a pattern of big red apples. I particularly remember the tie as one I could not afford but had admired in the window of Charvet's shop on East Fifty-third Street. I think it had been a gift to him from Moss Hart. We would walk down Seventh Avenue, with Oscar being greeted on every block by songwriters, actors, sportsmen, plainclothes detectives, musicians — a complete roster, in fact, of Runyonesque characters. This was Oscar's enclave, and he was on chatting terms with a good many of its inhabitants.

Frequently we would stop off at the downtown Lindy's on Broadway near Forty-ninth Street for some coffee — he was a caffeine addict with an average intake of fifteen to twenty cups a day. In that indigenous eatery, where custom had set aside distinct occupational areas, we would be seated at a table on the street level, the turf of the horse-players and pop music figures; movie people transacted their gossip and business affairs on the restaurant's second floor.

At his apartment Oscar sometimes played me some Gershwin songs, on which he was an expert, in the original arrangements. The illuminating chapter in his book called "My Life, or The Story of George Gershwin" is a most remarkable account of a master-disciple relationship, in which Oscar detailed his hero worship without sparing himself or his idol. (In the drawing room of a train taking them to a concert in Pittsburgh, George commandeered the lower berth as his prerogative, leaving the less accessible one to Oscar, with the unselfconscious statement, "Lower berth — upper berth. That's the difference between talent and genius." On another occasion Oscar had asked the composer, "Tell me, George, if you had to do it all over, would you fall in love with yourself again?" Both these remarks were widely disseminated at the time of the book's appearance and have since become part of the Gershwin iconolatry.) Moss Hart gave me an example of what a jealous and violently possessive disciple Oscar could be after he had become an almost daily fixture in the Gershwin menage. Each newcomer was looked upon as a possible rival and when Moss was brought to a party at the house after the success of his first play, Oscar took it upon himself to attend to the introductions. "This is Moss Hart," he would announce with distaste. "He wrote *Once In A Lifetime,* and that's all." After Gershwin's untimely death in 1937, Oscar had been in great demand to play the composer's music at concerts and he had resented having to make a living as his late friend's shadow. But since his emergence as a public personality the resentment had abated and he could speak of the relationship with some detachment.

The article I wrote was candid about his frailties as well as his virtues, and *Cosmopolitan* was so pleased with it they planned it for an early issue. Oscar complimented me on the article and we continued our usual afternoon walking routine, varying it occasionally, as when he invited me to a screening of a film he had recently made in Hollywood in which he was the comic feed for Bing Crosby and Mary Martin (was it called *Rhythm on the River?* All I remember about it is Mary Martin singing a song, "Ain't It a Shame About Mame").

As an example of a typical encounter with Oscar, recorded by me at the time: I was walking along Fifth Avenue after lunch one afternoon when Oscar accosted me and said, "Hello." We chatted for a while, then he said, "Come and have some coffee with me." I agreed, and we hadn't gone two steps when he said, "You know, I didn't have to stop to say hello to you." I said, why shouldn't he want to, and he said I was too angular — meaning of course my personality. I said, but so are you Oscar, and he replied, "I know, that's why we shouldn't see each other too often." We had a nice talk over coffee, then when we were parting he said again that he didn't like to see me too often because I was impertinent. I suppose I'd got to the point where I was bullying him as he bullied his other friends. At any rate, we parted on good terms.

The Levants had bought a house in Westport, I think because they were expecting their first child "around World Series time," with Oscar claiming June was already poisoning the child's mind by writing nasty little notes about him and swallowing them. I was invited up for the day and experienced Oscar as a country squire, an unlikely and uncomfortable role for him. After the child, the first of three daughters, was born, he asked me to go to the hospital with him to visit June one afternoon. The delivery had been a difficult one and Oscar must have been under a good deal of tension, which erupted in a bickering argument with June, who was still weak from her confinement. The argument ended in a quarrel of such intensity that I had to leave the room in embarrassment. Although I had been told of Oscar's temper tantrums, it was the first time I had experienced one.

I continued to have a good rapport with him for some years, for when he was in the mood he could be an amusing and rewarding companion. When later I became a friend of the Ira Gershwins I would see even more of him, for he was very close to Lee Gershwin and she was his staunchest defender. The break, when it did come, was my response to what I felt was a failure of friendship on his part.

I had been writing some songs with Jack Lawrence, a successful songwriter with whom at one point Oscar had also collaborated (he claimed that Lawrence wrote indifferently with him and then went home and concocted his hit songs by himself). When I had the required number of published and performed songs to make me eligible for membership in ASCAP, the collection agency for the profession, I filled out an application blank, which also called for the signatures of two member sponsors. As a sentimental gesture, I asked the two I was most fond of, Ira Gershwin and Oscar. Ira signed without hesitation, but when I telephoned Levant, he hedged, as if I were asking a great favor, and said, "I dunno; let me think about it." I was irritated and hurt. The sponsorship was merely a matter of form and implied no recommendation as to my ability; it would have meant nothing to his integrity even if he didn't like the songs I had written, which incidentally he had not heard. Ira was then working with Arthur Schwartz on a George S. Kaufman–Nunnally Johnson musical, *Park Avenue,* and when I told him about it, he said, "Oh, for God's sake," and turned to Arthur, whom I was then meeting for the first time, and asked if he would co-sponsor me, which he readily agreed to do. I thought Oscar's procrastination so picayune and so indicative of the lack of generosity in his nature than I could never really like him again. Some few weeks later, when we were all sitting around in the Gershwins' suite at the old Madison Hotel, Oscar said to me conversationally, without aggressive intent, in response to some provocative remark I had made, "You know, you can be awfully rude sometimes." The pot calling the kettle, I thought, and, still smarting at what I felt had been his defection, I turned to Lee Gershwin and said, "You know, I'm Oscar's Oscar Levant." Oscar was furious. The wits' wit didn't like to be challenged.

S. N. Behrman

s. n. (for samuel nathaniel) Behrman was a writer I very much admired and wished I could emulate. He was unique as a creator of drawing room comedy, a genre that has completely disappeared, along with the actors who could accommodate themselves to that exotic form of stage life. The felicities of his theater dialogue, the grace of his prose pieces, were to be cherished and envied.

Behrman was preoccupied with the world of the rich, treating his millionaires as sympathetic characters, contrary to their traditional theatrical role as despoilers of the poor, the class from which he had

risen. "Even his bums are well-heeled," said Hiram Sherman, who
had performed one of his affluent social truants and who claimed
he was the bull in Behrman's china shop because he had never been
in a drawing room. When the playwright, a frequent hostage to
Hollywood, was working on the screenplay for *Quo Vadis?* it was
predicted that every Christian in his script would have a private
source of income. Behrman was piqued by the implications em-
bodied in these comments. "All great playwrights have written
about rich people, not through snobbery but because the rich are
free," he once told me in an interview. "The playwright can express
aristocratic ideas only through using aristocratics as a medium. The
rich can be critical and independent about the life around us. The
facts of the poor are too overwhelming; they are always intellec-
tually submerged."

Town and Country seemed the ideal setting for a portrait of this
Boswell of the overprivileged, as I called him, and the editors
agreed. "He writes like a silk herring," Fanny Brice had said in
admiration of a style that glittered and yet, she felt, contained
sustenance. I found the simile so expressive that I titled my piece
"The Silk Herring." Behrman, I wrote, portrayed his subjects as
having minds and hearts as well as stocks and bonds. They were
gifted with instincts of purest gold and they were platinum-tongued
as well. His drawing rooms were peopled with indefatigable conver-
sationalists, never at a loss for the perfect phrase, humorously
turned. "It's like a little boy's glamorized version of the rich,"
complained one of his more literal-minded directors. Captious reviewers agreed that nobody this side of Heaven talked like that. As
I discovered immediately upon meeting him, Behrman was a living
refutation of this criticism, for he himself spoke with the wit and
urbanity of the dialogue in his plays.

Beatrice Kaufman had warned me that he was "as elusive as a
mosquito" and I found it was not easy to pin him down to a
meeting. He was supposed to be in Philadelphia, where the Lunts
were trying out his new play, *The Pirate,* preparatory to a New
York opening. But he was a slippery dramatist. A point being
discussed during rehearsals would need an arbitrator. "Let's ask

S. N. Behrman

Sam," the director would suggest, turning to the darkened auditorium. "Sam, don't you think . . . Sam . . . Sam!" But Sam,
who disliked embroilment ("It leads to unpleasantness") had already disappeared. At the Playwrights' Company, his producing
organization, he was the only one of the five dramatist-founders —
the others being Robert E. Sherwood, Elmer Rice, Maxwell Anderson and Sidney Howard — to have his name in gold letters on the
boardroom door. This was in ironic tribute to the fact that he had
almost never attended any meetings and indeed had seldom even
stepped into the company's offices.

Bill Fields, the scholarly publicity man for the Playwrights',
finally was able to get Sam to consent to an interview. I took the
train to Philadelphia and met him at his hotel. Like everyone else, I
was immediately enchanted. Warmth emanated from him; he took
you without question into his company of the culturally elect. He
was short, round and bald, a seemingly stolid, unimpressive figure.
Philip Moeller, who directed his early plays, had called him Mouse-
in-the-Mist. It was difficult to reconcile his appearance with one's
mental image of what our wittiest and most urbane theater writer
should look like. His old friend George Gershwin had continued to
be puzzled even after Behrman became securely established, saying,
"Somehow, you could never imagine that such a plodder could ever
get to be a famous playwright." The last word on the subject was
delivered by a forthright English dowager who swooped down on
Sam and his producer at the highly successful London opening of
The Second Man, with Noel Coward in the leading role. She was
sure that a comedy so brilliant must be a pseudonymous work by
dear Noel. "Indeed not," said the producer. "This is the author."
The lady looked at Behrman and looked away. "I don't believe it!"
she said.

Sam was a highly gifted raconteur and he delighted in telling me
the above story, also another in which a robust English girl had said
to her companion just after Behrman had left them, but within his
hearing, "I adore cads like that." He was also delighted with the
personages he met during the *Second Man* engagement. One night
in Noel Coward's dressing room backstage, he was presented to the

Duke of Connaught. Connaught happened to be talking about his childhood and told an anecdote of his school days, when his eldest brother had written their mother, Queen Victoria, for some money and she had written back that he must learn to live on his regular allowance. To which the Prince of Wales replied, "Thank you, I don't need the money now, because I sold your letter for seven pounds." When he left, Coward turned to Behrman and asked how he had liked the Duke. "He seems to be very well connected," said Sam.

The oddities of human behavior fascinated Behrman; he found a rich lode in Hollywood, where he began working as a peripatetic scriptwriter in the early Thirties. He was one of the first to practice deicide on the movie czars. Deluded by his geniality and by the uproarious laughter that would greet his anecdotes around a dinner table, they felt he was bestowing upon them a new kind of importance. They would ask him to repeat the same ludicrous tales about themselves over and over again, "Sam, tell the one about where I said . . ."

A prime target was Sol Wurzel, an executive producer at Fox Studios. Wurzel's outstanding characteristic was bluntness. "I know how he can make those instantaneous decisions," said Sam. "It's because he is never deflected by thought." Asked for his opinion on one of Behrman's plays, Wurzel replied, "It stinks!" "Ah," said Sam, "I see you have a gift for innuendo." Harry Cohn, the foul-talking head of Columbia Pictures, was also a leading figure in the Behrman repertory. On a visit to London, Cohn and an assistant were being shown around the Gaumont Studios by a dignified functionary. Cohn was unimpressed by the British film company's equipment. "Why don't you get such-and-such; it's the latest," said Cohn. "Because it's too expensive," said the official. Cohn's assistant snickered derisively. "Listen to this son-of-a-bitch," he said. "Won't get new equipment because it costs too much." The official was outraged by the folksy expletive. "Really, Mr. Cohn!" he said. Cohn hastened to make amends. Patting him on the arm, he said placatingly, "Call me Harry." Or there was Louis B. Mayer, who, when it was suggested that Toscanini be hired to conduct an M.G.M.

operetta, said, "Don't tell me what he's done; just tell me one thing — does he know melody?" Then there was my favorite, about Samuel Goldwyn in New York, going off to make a speech at Princeton and pressing Sam to accompany him to the train. Sam was touched and wanted to know why. "Because," said Goldwyn, "I like to have an author with me up to the last minute."

Behrman's facility as a storyteller was widely appreciated, but he was no conversational hero to his brother-in-law, Jascha Heifetz. Indeed, one of his wry family anecdotes concerned the violinist, who had once telephoned his sister, Behrman's wife, to say he was coming for dinner, "but I've got a bit of a headache so will you tell your husband not to talk." Behrman had been entranced by the mother of the siblings, whose admirable detachment he had found awesome. When he telephoned Mama Heifetz to tell her he had eloped with her daughter Elza, her answer had been, "Show me the license and I'll give you my blessing." Of another daughter, she had remarked enviously, "What wouldn't I give to be stupid like this girl!" He had taken her to a performance of Maurice Evans in *Richard II*. Their seats were well down in front; Evans covered these choice spectators with a fine spray while raving and ranting as the hapless Richard. "I have no sympathy for him," she said as she kept wiping the spittle from her face.

The friends and associates whom I might query about Sam made an impressive group. My notes list Supreme Court Justice Felix Frankfurter, Theresa Helburn and Philip Moeller of the Theater Guild, Samuel Chotzinoff, Frank Crowninshield, Oscar Levant, Guthrie McClintic, Herman Shumlin, Richard Maney, and Rudolph Kommer, the mysterious general factotum for Max Reinhardt (he was noted for surrounding himself with lovely and famous women; when I saw him in his suite at the Ambassador Hotel, the walls were covered with framed, inscribed photographs of Lady Diana Manners, Lili Darvas, Ina Claire, Tilly Losch, Greta Garbo, Princess Matchabelli, Lillian Gish . . . a who's who of the world's most publicized beauties. I was grateful to have one more legend confirmed). Sam had a unique relationship with Kommer. He would send him the manuscript of each of his new plays; if Kommer disliked the play, Sam felt he had prospects of a hit; if the verdict was enthusiastic, a flop seemed to be in order.

Still another but less pleasant confirmation came with my brief and only experience of the waspish Alexander Woollcott, who had appeared in two of Sam's comedies and was, besides, an old friend. I telephoned him at the Gotham, and told him I was writing a piece on Sam. "I have nothing of interest to say on that subject," he snapped out, and banged the receiver. When I informed Sam of the incident, he was not surprised. He and Woollcott had recently had a falling out; Sam had injudiciously given Woollcott as a social reference for an apartment he wanted to move into; Woollcott, addicted to practical jokes, had answered that Behrman gave wild parties all night long, was vague about paying bills, etc., none of which was true; the upshot was that the reclusive Behrmans were turned down as undesirable tenants. Sam had sent Woollcott an irritable note. Woollcott had returned it, scribbling "Kiss my ass" across it, to which message Sam had replied, "In a Christian world, it is a pleasure to receive such a noble gift — will you send it express or by mail, etc." Although Sam had dismissed the episode from his mind, apparently the vindictive Woollcott had not. As an example of Woollcott's reckless dispension of venom, Sam told me of the guest book kept by Mary, the Lunts' housekeeper on their Wisconsin farm, in which he had seen inscribed, "Dear Mary, It gave me a great pleasure to see your smiling, beaming face in the morning. Edna Ferber," while underneath was another message from the next visitor, "Dear Edna Ferber, You turn my stomach. Alexander Woollcott."

Gottfried Reinhardt recalled to me Anton Kuh, termed by him the wittiest man in Europe, a "coffeehouse writer" who expended his talent in brilliant café monologues. Kuh was known as a *schnurrer*, a beggar existing on handouts from friends. Alexander Korda, the film producer, put him under contract at a good salary, on condition that he borrow no money from anyone. After a short period of abstinence, Kuh gave up the job to come to America, where he knew he could get along because *"schnurrers* they need everywhere." Sam wanted to be of help in getting him started in this country. He proposed writing a profile of Kuh for *The New Yorker,* for which he would get $1,000, top price at the time, which he would split with his subject. Kuh rejected the offer, his reasoning being that his clients would find out and then he couldn't get any more money from them.

The friendship with Sam that started with my *Town and Country* article was to last for thirty years, until Sam's death in 1973. I interviewed him quite often for the *Herald-Tribune* and I was pleased that he thought of me and referred to me as "an old shoe." In between times we communicated, mostly by letter. He was wary of the telephone, because "once you lift the receiver to answer it, you're trapped." He advocated that people should write to make an appointment saying at what time they wished to phone.

The last few times I actually saw him he had become frail. This was in 1968 when the Ira Gershwins were in town for the tribute to George and Ira at the Museum of the City of New York. Mrs. Gershwin's sister Emily Paley and I called for him in a taxi to take him to the opening of the museum exhibition. When we left to escort him home again — he had only emerged from his apartment because of his great fondness for the Gershwins — a modishly hirsute young man approached, an acquaintance of Emily's, whom she introduced as John Guare, the playwright. He was stimulated by meeting Sam. "Kendall Frayne!" he sprung out to the startled Behrman. I quickly explained, since it was one of the vivid memories of my adolescence, that Mrs. Frayne was one of the four characters in his first produced play, *The Second Man,* which the Theater Guild had put on over forty years ago. Sam had completely forgotten the name he had given to his creation, who had been played by Lynn Fontanne.

I saw him again shortly thereafter when he came to dine with the Gershwins at their hotel. The Century Club, of which he was a member, was brought into the conversation and I said I had never been there; Sam offered to remedy that lapse. He took me to lunch at the club several days later. I was impressed by the turn-of-the-century surroundings and especially by the ancient waiter who, when I ordered a vodka and bitters, brought me the vodka in a small glass, with a large tumbler of English bitter on the side.

Sam seldom left his apartment after that spree. The following spring I invited him to lunch. He wrote to say, "I have been ill practically all winter and now I feel depleted. It is a great effort for me to do almost anything. It is an effort for me to go out to lunch. I haven't been to the theater in years." Soon he was unable to perambulate on his own. He said in a note that he had been "locked in for months with a 'walker' which I push around from room to room. It is all quite discouraging." From time to time I would send him a "news" letter with stories about acquaintances. "There are two people I can always count on — you and the ineffable Emily Paley" was in answer to one of these. "I have not been feeling very well, but your letter is a placebo."

Sam's eyesight had gradually been failing and I learned from Emily Paley that he could no longer read, which for such a voracious consumer of the printed word meant the end of any reason for living. A month or so before he died at the age of eighty, he sent me a parting gift, an anecdote, through Emily. She had just come from seeing him; he told her he had happened to think of it that morning and knew it would amuse me.

The remembrance, from a prince of raconteurs, was of something that had taken place in the mid-1930s. Noel Coward was dictating a telegram over the phone, to be sent to Gertrude Lawrence. He told the Western Union operator to sign it Fiorello LaGuardia. "Are you Mayor LaGuardia?" she asked. "No, I am not." "In that case, you can't sign his name." "Oh, well," said Coward, "sign it Noel Coward." "Are you Mr. Coward?" "Yes, I am." "Oh," said the operator, "in that case, you can sign any name you want to."

Sam delighted in enigmatic stories. I pass on this last gift from him, in the hope that you will share this delight.

6
Scratch an Actor

"SCRATCH AN ACTOR," said Monty Woolley, "and you'll find an actress." The bearded Woolley, bearded in a day when to wear one was a distinct novelty, was my first interview subject for the New York *Herald-Tribune*. I began to write for their Sunday drama section on a free-lance basis in the fall of 1939.

Woolley was about to open in the most eagerly anticipated comedy of the season, *The Man Who Came To Dinner* by Moss Hart and George S. Kaufman. The character he was playing was based on the irascible Alexander Woollcott, then at the height of his celebrity as radio's Town Crier, dispensing a popular mixture of bile and treacle on his Sunday evening program. Woolley was a celebrity in his own right, a former professor of drama at Yale, who had influenced, among other pupils, Stephen Vincent Benét, Douglas Moore, Philip Barry, Thornton Wilder and Dwight Deere Wiman, who became a Broadway theatrical producer and who lured him away from scholarship to the stage as a performer in *On Your Toes*.

Woolley knew his way around in the conventions of eccentricity and was as adept as Woollcott at the withering mot juste. I did not use the "Scratch an actor" epigram in my article because it would not have passed by Arthur Folwell, the editor of the theater section of the then-staid *Tribune*. But it came to mind often in the years that followed, when I interviewed hundreds of performers and found the vanity of the males exceeding that of the females by a wide margin.

I asked one juvenile how old he was and he said, "I'm eighteen, but please don't publish it." Why not, I asked, puzzled, since he looked no older and was just the right age for the role he was playing. His answer was, "Because when I'm twenty-eight ten years from now, people might remember." I interviewed Philip Merivale, who as a young man had played with Beerbohm Tree and the tempestuous Mrs. Patrick Campbell in *Pygmalion,* whose stage credits in *Who's Who in the Theater* filled three columns of small type, and who superciliously — an Englishman dealing with the American press — recited those credits throughout an exasperating two-hour lunch at Sardi's, and couldn't think of one anecdote, one noteworthy reminiscence of anything that had happened during that long career. I told the play's press agent, Sam Friedman, that I had no material for my article. He said he would interview Merivale himself and see if he could inveigle him into something I could use. I got two pages of Merivale's talk recorded verbatim, and I pieced together some sort of account. I met Sam on Broadway shortly after the article had appeared. "What did Merivale think of it?" I asked. He told me Merivale had been outraged, saying, "Why, that fellow misquoted me!"

When I was preparing the Monty Woolley piece, I followed the procedure that was customary for my magazine articles. I not only interviewed the subject but also a few of his friends and associates, to try for a rounded picture. That took time and care, and I was gratified to see the article in print within a week after I had delivered it. It was given a three-column spread on the first page of the section, with a two-column carryover. At the *Tribune*'s space rates, the check I received was for $16.67. The paper also sent out feature material through its syndicate, and Ben Kornzweig, the show's press agent, subsequently showed me clippings from newspapers all over the country that had picked up the article. I was of course not paid anything extra for this additional use.

For my next piece, on Howard Lindsay, chief actor and half-author of *Life With Father,* I received $15.95. The low point was $5.00 for a piece about Cole Porter which ran four columns across but only an inch and a half deep. I had written my usual eight hundred or so words but most of them had been cut for space and of course I was only paid for what was used. Thereafter I didn't bother seeing friends and associates but interviewed only my subject and made sure to fill the piece with as many play titles as possible for added increment, as in "The next season he appeared in *Thisand-That* and *SoandSo* and *Whatsitsname*; he has since been seen in *Hamlet, Macbeth, Tobacco Road,*" etc. Cutting was done arbitrarily on the *Tribune,* whenever advertising was unexpectedly heavy or when Folwell decided to use more pictures for the week's openings. Sometimes a chunk would be just snipped off the last part of an article and readers often must have been puzzled to find themselves without the tag line of an anecdote.

The Sunday *Tribune* entertainment section featured on its front page second-thoughts columns by Richard Watts, its drama reviewer, and Howard Barnes, who criticized films, a giddy interview by the staff playboy, Lucius Beebe (the city editor, Stanley Walker, said he wrote in "basic pidgin"), and, depending on how much space was taken up by the pictorial layout (which in turn depended on the number of theatrical openings for the coming week), an interview by one of the free-lance contributors. Helen Ormsbee covered the female stars every Sunday, which she had been doing since the early Thirties. As a newcomer and therefore low man on the list, I still managed to get in a piece about twice a month. Since Beebe was assigned most of the male stars who were appearing in new plays, I searched out interesting secondary players and vintage character actors. I found them more rewarding than the young leads, to whom very little had yet happened (mostly it amounted to the cat who had walked onstage during their big scene in summer stock), or seasoned stars, who had been interviewed so often that nothing fresh about them could possibly be recorded. I would bring along with me four sheets of copy paper, folded in half to make a booklet. I wrote very quickly, meticulously inscribing every quotable remark exactly as spoken so I could get the flavor of the subject. This was of course before the emergence of the tape recorder as an interviewing prop. When I finished writing on the first eight half-pages, I would reverse them to the unused side to form a second book. Once that was covered, I knew I was in the clear; I would have enough material for my article. Many times an actor would come prepared with little speeches concerning the character he was playing. This was regrettable, since the verbal interpretations were almost always banal. I would listen patiently until he had gotten that off his chest, then ask questions about his start in the theater. In going over this professional background, I could often extract some anecdotes which I felt would make amusing reading.

The heads given to my *Tribune* pieces were synopses in capsule of the story to follow. PLAYS IN ONE LIFE, RECALLS ANOTHER. That was John Drew Devereaux, grandson of the famous matinee idol of the turn of the century, and nephew of the three Barrymores. He was playing Clarence Day, Jr., in *Life With Father*. The other life he was recalling, at my prompting, was that of John Drew. He showed me the autograph album Drew had prepared for him on his first birthday . . . sentiments and signatures of George M. Cohan, Minnie Maddern Fiske, Yvette Guilbert, the French prizefighter Georges Carpentier, the tennis champ Bill Tilden, P. G. Wodehouse; Ellen Terry, George Arliss. "Imitation is the sincerest form of Cecelia Loftus," wrote that impersonating genius. "Early to bed and early to rise and you will meet very few prominent people," wrote the humorist George Ade. Under this was a reproach: "It depends on what you call prominent — you would be able to meet me, for instance!" signed by the fractious Lady Astor.

Young Devereaux told me of a demolishing remark made by his Aunt Ethel Barrymore when he was playing with her in *The Ghost of Yankee Doodle*. John Barrymore, in his declining years, had married an aspiring, youthful actress considered by his family and friends to be much beneath him. This May-December romance had received wide tabloid publicity because of endearments released to the press in which the aging bridegroom had referred to himself as Caliban to his inamorata's Ariel. Devereaux was passing by the patrician Ethel's dressing room after one evening's performance when she summoned him inside. There stood a sheepish-looking John and his lavishly caparisoned bride. "Say hello to your Uncle Jack," said Ethel, "and this," she added, pausing to let the vivid picture sink in, "this is your Auntie Ariel."

A LODGE SPEAKS TO HOLLYWOOD ON HIS WAY TO BROADWAY ROLE. John Davis Lodge, of the Boston Cabots and Lodges, later our ambassador to Spain. After a lackluster term with Paramount Pictures, he had come to Broadway and was then playing in Lillian Hellman's *The Watch on the Rhine*. One of the subheads in this article was "In the Hay With Marlene." He had a scene in *The Scarlet Empress* in which he and Dietrich were lying on a haystack; it required sixty-two retakes because he was afflicted with hay fever and kept sneezing.

ALAS POOR HIRAM! HE IS BACK ON THE OLD STRAW-HAT CIRCUIT. Hiram (Chubby) Sherman, one of the joys of my life, on and off the stage. An incomparable light comedian, who could engender more audience laughter with a bland facade and a deprecating stare than could many actors with a bagful of hypothetically funny lines. The most noted Shakespearean clown of his generation, he could even charge those burdensome beasts with amusement. Wolcott Gibbs declared that he despaired of being able to describe his flawless technique.

He was the kind of actor who got notices even when he was not part of the performance. On a memorable occasion, Walter Kerr wrote: "During one of the intermissions of last night's *Taming of the Shrew* at the Phoenix, the management sent Mr. Hiram Sherman before the footlights to say a few words on behalf of the American Shakespeare Festival Theater of Connecticut. This may have been a serious mistake. For Mr. Sherman has a naturally funny mind, and he cannot mention the summer route to our local Stratford without pointing out that it is 'not to be confused with spurious Stratfords in other countries' any more than he can touch on Shakespeare himself without turning him into an all-American-family entertainment boy. I'm not doing justice to Mr. Sherman's wry irreverence here, but the upshot of the whole interlude is that Mr. Sherman gets more laughs in three minutes than a company of twenty-nine does in two and a half hours. He reminds you, scoundrel that he is, what a really big guffaw is — and the contrast is embarrassing. . . . Because the balance of the company, unlike Mr. Sherman, has no secret amusement, no personal humor, no aimed-at comic image stored away at the back of its collective mind."

Chubby spent much of his long career, before retiring in his early sixties, turning down parts. He was constantly rejecting play manuscripts, bringing them back early in the morning so he wouldn't have to face the producers who had sent them. He once contemplated, but never seriously, writing his memoirs with the title *My Thirty Years Off Broadway*.

VETERAN OF 164 ROLES IMPARTS STATURE TO TEN-MINUTE SCENE. The marvelous, irrepressible Joseph Buloff. Trained in the Yiddish theaters of central Europe, Buloff's insatiable appetite for scene-stealing and his dazzling efforts to satisfy his craving have made him a legend in the profession. Stella Adler was once offered a tempting role in which her vis-à-vis was to be Buloff. Absolutely not, she said. But there is a big scene for you in which Joe just sits there and says nothing. Especially if he says nothing, absolutely no, said Stella. She was finally persuaded, against her better judgment. Rehearsals were uneventful. Opening night arrived. Stella got to her big scene, her big speech. Out of the corner of her eye she could see Buloff. He had a handful of Indian nuts in his hand. He kept popping them into his mouth, cracking them, and spitting out the shells. The fascinated audience couldn't even *see* Stella, much less listen to what she was saying.

Hiram Sherman was with him in a summer stock production of Molnár's *The Play's the Thing*. The barn theater had a small stage which a maladroit scenic designer had crammed full of furniture, including a grand piano. Sherman thought, "Even Joe won't be able to pull one of his stunts here, it's too crowded." Buloff came on for his first scene, leaped deftly onto the piano and played from there.

A PERENNIAL FIRST GRAVEDIGGER TELLS OF THREE DECADES OF ACTING. Dear Whitford Kane of the mellifluous north-of-Ireland speech. He had been First Gravedigger for twenty-three different Hamlets, including Osmund Tearle, Walter Hampden, William Mollison, John Barrymore, Godfrey Tearle and Maurice Evans, but the one that stuck in his memory was the most ludicrous, Mrs. Bandmann-Palmer, in whose English repertory company he had played early in the century. She was known as the Lady Hamlet, and in spite of the many actors he had seen in the role, his mental picture of the Dane remained that of "a fat little woman in high heels." Whitford was a personification of The Old Actor, his entire world bounded by the stage. He had a long noteworthy career, especially in the plays of Shakespeare, whose lines he knew by heart and would recite at random moments, in spurts. I once took him to a press screening of a Spencer Tracy film, Tracy having played with him on the stage before he became a movie star. Breaking through the audience silence, Whitford's distinctive voice could be heard, exclaiming with delight, "Look at old Spence up there . . . *acting!*" He was very happy that Spence had at last learned to do it. He was on the road with Katharine Hepburn in *As You Like It* when his old friend Sara Allgood died in Hollywood. As soon as the tour reached Los Angeles, he went to the cemetery where she was buried. The attendant couldn't at first recall the name of Allgood, then suddenly remembered, "Oh yes, they had Barry Fitzgerald as a pallbearer." In telling of this experience, Whitford shook his head sadly. "Poor Sally, couldn't even get star billing at her own funeral." Toward the end of his life he was offered the part of the Irish father in a revival of *Abie's Irish Rose,* which he turned down, saying, "I'm not going to my grave with *that* on my conscience."

JOHN LUND GOT FIRST BIG ROLE BY MAKING PRODUCERS CURIOUS. He was enjoying a theater success in *The Hasty Heart,* which brought him to Hollywood, where he had a career as a leading man in the 1950s. He is memorable to me for an offstage remark he made to a pathologically vain actor in the company. "I've been reading about you." "Where?" "In Krafft-Ebing."

OLSEN SAYS IT'S NOT THE JOKE THAT COUNTS, BUT THE NARRATOR.

Ole Olsen, of the vaudeville knockabout team of Olsen and John- son. They had hit it big with a boisterous evening of gags and practical jokes, played on their fellow actors and on the audience, called *Hellzapoppin'*, which had been sneered at by most of the critics but which Walter Winchell trumpeted into popularity. I was as fastidiously disdainful of them as were the professional reviewers and did not suggest them as subjects; it was an assignment given me by the *Tribune*. I had asked the press agent to arrange a lunch interview in a quiet place (with Olsen; Johnson lived in the coun- try and commuted only for performances). Olsen chose the Adver- tising Club. Here is how I described the interview, one of the most embarrassing in my journalistic experience: "Three decades of pro- fessional rectitude, during which neither of the Olsen and Johnson team has ever missed a performance, is not an event to be celebrated in seclusion. Nor can the dining room of the Advertising Club be called a hushed solarium. 'The quiet luncheon,' it turned out, was to be eaten in company with some five hundred of the membership, gathered in jovial conclave to participate in a raffle stunt called 'The Advertorium.' Between endless fraternal greetings Olsen di- vested himself of his memoirs and his credo. 'I talked to the fellows here recently,' he said, 'about the business side of laughs. The public doesn't know the careful analysis, study and preparation that go into a show.' " Etc., etc.

Olsen was a dyed-in-the-wool Rotarian surrounded by five hun- dred of his bumptious fellows. My resentment at being forced into the midst of them quadrupled when over the loudspeaker came a demand for silence, followed by an announcement: "Our member Ole Olsen is here, being interviewed by Irving Drutman of the *Herald-Tribune*." Olsen then rose and made a speech introducing me to the assemblage. If I'd had a gun on me and knew how to use it . . .

BOBBY CLARK ON THE DAYS WHEN BURLESQUE WAS IN FLOWER. A comic horse of quite another color. One of my favorite comedians. He was hilarious in revue sketches and uproarious in classics like *The Rivals* and *The Would-Be Gentleman*. In his burlesque days, the character he assumed was that of an aristocratic bum, with the painted-on spectacles, a cane and a trick cigar as his chief props (he retained these for the rest of his career). One day, he told me, he was standing outside the stage door in Kansas City, Missouri, in full makeup when a genuine hobo carrying a cigar and a cane walked by him. As the hobo passed, he flipped his cigar, twirled his cane, and looking genially at Clark, said, "Not many of us left now." Then he walked grandly on.

AN ACTOR WHO KNEW GANGSTERS ENJOYS CHANCE TO PLAY ONE. This was David Burns in an underestimated musical, *Billion Dollar Baby*, by Betty Comden and Adolph Green. It remains a favorite memory of mine for the wit of its book — a cynical rather than sentimental re-creation of the bootleg Twenties — and the stylish period costumes of Irene Sharaff, laced with parody, a brilliant comment in themselves (I remember especially the chic widow's weeds for the mobster's funeral). Where the show failed was in the uninteresting score by Morton Gould, bland where it should have been sharp. Burns was directed to play his hoodlum as a mug, in the safe tradition of *Broadway* and *Little Caesar,* but he protested to me that in doing so he was betraying not only history but his own memory. "They were mostly pretty smooth guys," I quoted him as saying. "They used good English, for one thing. Take Larry Fay, the milk racketeer, for instance — one critic claimed the character was based on him. I knew Fay; used to see him and talk to him when I was playing vaudeville with Lou Holtz. Fay was always well dressed. He'd never handle a gun or even have one on him. He was the kind of fellow who, if someone pulled a gat on him, would push it away and say, 'Whyn't you put that waterpistol down — you might get wet.'

"I remember talking to Fay once — he was sitting in a dinner jacket at Dinty Moore's. Benny Baker and I were with Gus Edwards then. 'What are you kids doing now?' Fay asked, and we told him, 'We're making a hundred and twenty-five a week but we'd like to get more.' Fay said, 'Tell Gus I said to give you more.' We thought it was a joke, but we went to Edwards and he raised us to $175."

"STARTLE 'EM!" ACTRESS ADVISES. Leonora Corbett from London, playing the ghostly Elvira in Noel Coward's *Blithe Spirit*. A delight.

Hiram ("Chubby") Sherman

Chubby and Whitford Kane in **The Shoemaker's Holiday**

> *Whit: Did you read the reviews*
> *Chub: What did they say?*
> *Whit: They said you're a droll.*

Stella Adler in **He Who Gets**
Slapped

Joseph Buloff (r.) with Leslie Banks in **To Quito and Back**

I was by no means the only one to be bowled over; she had been a great favorite of Bernard Shaw, T. E. Lawrence, A. A. Milne. She had gotten the idea for her ghost makeup from Ingres' gray Odalisque in the Metropolitan Museum of Art. I asked her what was the real color of her hair under the makeup. "Light marmalade," she replied.

LION TAMER'S ROLE TOO TAME FOR MISS ADLER. Stella, in a revival of *He Who Gets Slapped*. The heart-shaped face of a very pretty child, hungry for experience. The opulent voice, the florid figures of speech. She and her brother Luther are the gifted acting offspring of two famous Yiddish actors. Teddy Thomas, himself the son of a famous Yiddish actor, Boris Thomashefsky, used to define the Adler family's way of talking as "British Yiddish." I was first brought to meet her about 1942. Stella is statuesque. I am more humbly proportioned. Her splendid bosom, not really hidden by her dress, met me at eye level. Flustered, I looked up at Stella's face; she approved my approval of such a treasurable asset.

I am fond of Stella. She is a sympathetic person; she has wit and perception. But I am sometimes put off, as I am by Leonard Bernstein, by the Oriental luxuriance of the verbiage. The Stella Adler School for Acting is possibly the best-known in its field. She is more indulgent with the young men pupils than with the young women. I heard this complaint, of course, only from one of the young women. During a lesson one day, Stella told the students to march around the room. "Do we start with the right or the left foot?" asked my female friend. Stella can be impatient.

"Just march," she snapped out. "Don't try to intellectualize."

Stella was one of the early members of the Group Theater, which promulgated the Russian director Stanislavsky's teachings in this country (myself, I believe that, like chop suey, the Group's Stanislavsky method was more native than foreign). I don't know how true it is, and I wouldn't dare ask her, that in the 1930s, when she went to the Soviet Union to meet the Master, she told him that the Group was following his precepts, thinking only of the character they were playing, and not of the audience. "But Madame," he is reputed to have replied, "I *always* think of the audience first." In

1964 Stella arranged to have four leading members of the Moscow Art Theater come to this country to talk about Stanislavsky's theories. The sponsorship was impressive: the Institute of International Education, with the cooperation of the American Council of Learned Societies and our Department of State. The three sessions of the first series were held in the Aalto-designed conference room at the New York headquarters of the Institute, across from the United Nations Plaza. I had been asked by the editor of the *Times*'s Sunday drama section to cover the meetings and write a piece about them. Thirty top-brass United States practitioners of The Method had received special invitations to attend. I'm afraid I was there with a skeptical rather than a free mind, as may be seen from the opening of my article, which was captioned RUSSIAN METHOD-ISTS MEET THE AMERICAN:

"Shelley Winters was there, horn-rimmed eyeglasses mitigating the frivolity of her perky poodle hairdo. Uta Hagen was there, in a sober brown shirt and sober beige blouse. Harold Clurman was there, and Robert Lewis, and Cheryl Crawford and Herbert Berghof and Rip Torn and Gene Frankel and Madeleine Sherwood. Hal Holbrook and Paul Mann of the Lincoln Center Repertory were there, and Paula Strasberg of the Actors' Studio hierachy. It was Stella Adler's project, and she was, of course, there, in the formal attire of a chairlady instead of her customary engaging decolletage."

The sessions droned on, all morning long, three mornings in a row. Two of the four Russians were academics and spoke (as translated for our earphones) in pedantic gobbledegook — "the super objective," "the super super objective," "Stanislavsky was a High Priest of Art," etc. The two actors, Vasily Toporkov and Angelina Stepanova, both of whom had studied with the High Priest, were fascinating; they had vibrant personalities and were adept at demonstrating the practicalities of memory transference, which apparently is the basic tenet of The Method. Mme. Stepanova admitted, humorously, that sometimes it backfired, giving as an example a classroom exercise in which the actors were told to imagine that the bank has failed. All but one simulated agitation, the renegade's reason for remaining calm being "My money's in another bank." It reminded me somehow of the one Group Theater session that Hiram Sherman had attended, in which he was asked to imagine that he was in a forest and was approached by a bear, what would he do? "Run like hell" was his logical but un-Method-like answer. In summing up at the end of the three sessions, one of the academics stated that Stanislavsky had attempted to base his method on emotion-memory, i.e., the actor used his stored experiences to create a role. He said he couldn't understand the confusion it had caused in this country. Stella, as chairlady, then said with finality, "If it isn't clear now, it never will be. We will go on emphasizing emotional memory. The other group will go on emphasizing the use of the circumstance" (meaning the literal action as laid down by the playwright). A question and answer period was scheduled to follow. Shelley Winters created a slight diversion, rising ostensibly to ask a question but actually, it turned out, to launch into a bit of autobiography. She spoke of the acting problems she had encountered while making the film *An American Tragedy* ("I try to cry but I can't, I just keep talking slowly and do the scene that way: when the picture comes out, every woman in the audience cries") and of her successful attempts to use emotional memory on the stage, while playing *A Hatful of Rain* ("Stella helped show me where my life and the character's coincided"). By now, however, Stella, saying, "We are here to learn from them, not from you," had left the room in irritation. The Russians protested that they would like to hear about the Americans' experiences, too, but by then the allotted time had expired.

I seized on this incident as a comic high point of the sessions. I then telephoned some of the auditors to ask if the seminar had achieved its purpose — the clarification of Stanislavsky's teachings to actors and directors here — and quoted their equivocal answers. I ended the piece with a dialogue between myself and Robert Lewis, who was running his own Method-inspired acting school. Lewis felt that while the seminar didn't contribute "anything novel, it did help clear up existing misconceptions." "Of course," he said, "Stanislavsky got his method from observing and studying Salvini and Duse." I baited him with "And where did they get their method?"

He hesitated and fell. "Well, I guess from their own genius." (Lewis directed Anita Loos's version of the Colette novel *Chéri;* he wanted Marlene Dietrich for the leading role. She turned it down, saying, "I know just how it will be — when Bobby reads it to the cast, he'll use up two boxes of Kleenex crying.")

After the article was published, Stella telephoned me. She was very disturbed. She thought that I had treated the affair frivolously — as indeed I had, out of my own feeling that the American Method-ists had turned the disciplined craft of acting into an improvisational gambit and that some of its practitioners were merely opportunistic. What could she do to get her own point across? I advised her to write a letter to the drama editor, explaining her position and refuting the validity of mine. Don't make it too lengthy, I cautioned, about a page and a half at most. "Why don't you write it for me?" she asked. I said, "Stella, I can't write a letter complaining about myself." She apparently didn't see the logic of this. I don't think she ever sent the letter, for the *Times* would have been glad to publish it and it never appeared.

FROM BOTTOM, THE WEAVER, TO CHEKHOV, WITH STOPS BETWEEN. Dennis King, a versatile actor, who could shift readily from Shakespeare to operetta to Ibsen and Chekhov to musical comedy. I interviewed him at The Players' and told him I had just come from a run-through of a drama directed by an old associate of his, who was a lesbian. She was also playing the leading role in the drama, that of the Mother Superior in a Dutch convent. I described one of the early scenes to him. A super comes running in, looks her straight in the eye and says, "The dykes are gone!" King said, "It's not possible." Why was he doubting me? "It's not possible," he repeated, "to look her straight in the eye."

VIVIENNE SEGAL AT CREST OF SECOND CAREER. The delectable singing comedienne of *Pal Joey*. She was then playing in a revival of the Rodgers-Hart show *A Connecticut Yankee,* and we had supper right after the evening performance. She dutifully submitted to the interview, giving me the name of the first show in which she had appeared when she was sixteen, but balked at naming the second. I couldn't understand why, since it was a matter of record. She giggled and said she would tell me if I promised not to use it. The show was *Miss 1917;* the date would have revealed her age. Gentlemanly, I refrained from mentioning the title, referring to it in my piece as "Dillingham and Ziegfeld's new show at the Century Theater." When I had finished taking notes, she leaned back in her chair, relaxed, and said, "Now, let's dish." And we did.

HARRY CAREY RECALLS THE CROSS-OVER BEARD. Some more reminiscences, by one of the last of the old-time Western movie stars. He was returning to the stage, where he had started his career, in a play I remember nothing about called *But Not Good-bye.* He had startled me by suddenly asking, "Did you ever hear of a crossover beard?" When I confessed ignorance, he explained that his first job on the stage was with a repertory company that played "all the jerkwater end-of-the-trolley towns in the East. Sometimes we got a theater, but often we had to play in halls with stages that had very little depth. To get any acting room at all the backdrop had to be set up flat against the rear wall. Well, if an actor had to exit left and re-enter right in the same act, there was no space to do it backstage. How we made out was to disguise ourselves. We changed our coats, put on a beard, and walked across in full view of the audience.

"It made no difference what kind of scene was being used. If it was outdoors, no one thought an explanation to the audience was necessary. We just left them to assume that it was a passer-by. But if it was an interior, say in the middle of a love scene, some new lines were improvised. The leading lady would suddenly look up startled and say, 'Who is that man?' and the leading man would answer, 'I dunno,' and then return to the author's lines."

By this time the intruder was out of sight on the other side of the stage and it was hoped that the audience would be so interested in the scene being played that they would overlook him. In the profession, the device was known as the crossover beard and it was used by all small-time touring companies.

"That kind of improvisation was necessary in those days," said Carey. "For one play we used a trapdoor, and I remember once an actor dropped through and didn't come back for the rest of the show. No one had time to look for him, so we had to cut him out of the play at a minute's notice. When it came time for him to reappear, a character would say, 'Where's So-and-so?' and the other person would answer, 'Haven't seen him,' and interpolate the part into his own. After the show we found out the trapdoor led to a coal bin and the actor had just dropped into that and couldn't get out."

Carey also recalled seeing a touring musical comedy, "large cast — straight from New York," which consisted of twelve people: a leading man, leading woman, Irish comic, the heavy, and eight chorus girls. The rest of the chorus girls were painted on the backdrop.

The interviews usually took place at lunch in a restaurant, arranged and paid for by the show's press agent. The theatrical hangout, Sardi's, was a favorite choice, so the actor could be seen, but there were so many friends and acquaintances around that it was difficult for either of us to concentrate on the work at hand. To the consternation of the actor, I would usually ask for a table at the back. (When I had a social lunch engagement at Sardi's, I naturally wanted, like everyone else, to be seated in the preferred area in front.) The press agent Richard Maney, a witty, practical Irishman who during most of his career handled a good many of the leading Broadway managements and stars, never went out for lunch, confining his midday caloric intake to the munching of a chocolate bar in his office. He resented these excursions on the part of anyone else. I interviewed Larry Hugo, a juvenile in a show he was handling, on the eve of Hugo's departure for military service. Hugo, mindful that he wouldn't have many such opportunities in the army, gorged himself on oysters and lobster and I went along with the same fare. The bill for all this gluttony was something like $6.50, which I presented for payment to Maney, as was customary (the *Tribune* didn't provide me with expense money). Maney sent me a check with a note which read, "Dear Sir and Brother: The orgy engaged in by you and Hugo at the Blue Ribbon [a modestly priced restaurant at best] must go down in history as 'The Clash of the

Trenchermen' — a gustatory debauch, something to lift the scalp of Brillat-Savarin! Scorned the blue plate special, eh?" Not content with this salvo, he sent me another salute in the mail a few days later, this one addressed to Irving Brillat Drutman. Enclosed was a newspaper clipping headed EIGHT-COURSE MEAL FITS IN SOLDIER'S VEST POCKET. The story dealt with a new $5\frac{1}{2}''$ emergency ration packet developed to meet the needs of paratroopers dropped behind enemy lines. Below this, Dick had typed, "I've arranged a deal with G.H.Q., whereby I'll be able to equip you with one of the above named each time you venture forth to harry an actor."

Dick had an individualistic way of being abusive without using coarse words, of which he disapproved. "He's the prince of dunderheads!" might be his version of another man's "stupid sonofabitch!" When an article I had written on one of his shows didn't appear within the first couple of weeks, he labeled me "King of the Overset," the newspaper term for feature material not immediately newsworthy but put up in type for random insertion. He was more celebrated than many of his clients and a favorite with editors for his candor and his original prose style, in which he toyed amusingly with alliteration. Helen Hayes, Gertrude Lawrence, Tallulah Bankhead were, he wrote, "madonnas of the marquees. My survey of these sorceresses was cautious, perhaps craven."

He handled the early producing career of Billy Rose, making that short-statured showman memorable with phrases like "the Mighty Midget," "the Bantam Barnum," "the Basement Belasco." "The sorcerer I served [Rose] was no man to split a spotlight." When Rose's spectacular Aquacade opened in Cleveland, he sent Maney a telegram complaining of the lack of publicity and ending, "I'm getting tired of the Maney legend." Dick, who had created the Rose myth, replied, "I'll match my legend with yours."

Wolcott Gibbs wrote a Profile of him for *The New Yorker* which was headed "The Customer Is Always Wrong." He was certainly not inclined to coddle his employers. When the boy impresario Alexander Cohen hired him to promote one of his shows, Dick advised him to retire from the field. To the somewhat chagrined Cohen, he genially explained, "You lack two things that make a good producer — talent and taste." Gilbert Miller once composed an opening release for a play he was presenting and handed it proudly to Maney, to show, apparently, that anyone could write that kind of thing if he put his mind to it. Maney read it through and handed it back. "It's not English," he said. Tallulah Bankhead insisted that he be hired for every production in which she appeared. When she played for the Theater Guild, which had its own press department, one of her stipulations was that they hire Maney to handle her publicity. She brought the contract to his office and pointed out the unprecedented clause. "Now," she said boastfully, "who's your favorite actress?" Answered the ingrate, "Helen Hayes!"

7

Worldly Ladies

Tallulah Means Terrible

*Mae West: Pardon Me for
Loving and Running*

*A New Year's Card from
Polly Adler*

Tallulah being doused for a scene in Lifeboat

Tallulah Means Terrible

I AM LOOKING OVER notes I made more than thirty years ago for an article on Tallulah Bankhead, an article I was not able to finish. In part the fault was the reticence of the language allowable in the journalism of the day. A typical Bankhead anecdote depended for its point on the kind of ripe expletive that no newspaper or magazine was then prepared to print. Her vocabulary had to be watered down by substituting dashes, asterisks, or euphemisms. Also, in spite of her hedonistic, devil-may-care life-style, I found that her vulnerability deterred me from presenting a truly candid portrait. Her squalls of temperament could become cyclonic when faced with an unabashed picture of herself. In any event, to put my notes in chronological order:

Tallulah was fifteen, an ornamental native of Huntsville, Alabama, when she arrived in New York in 1917 to make her way on the stage ("She's not worth a damn for anything but acting," said the family of the troublesome child). From her mother, Ada Sledge, who died shortly after her birth, Tallulah had inherited striking good looks. Her truculence, her capriciousness, her disregard for public opinion, were also gifts from the maternal branch. The Sledge women were beautiful and dashing and the Sledge males might easily have served as models for that swashbuckling fictional creation Rhett Butler. From the paternal side (Grandfather Bankhead had been the last Confederate veteran in the Senate; Uncle John was in the current Senate, and Tallulah's father Will was shortly to become the very popular Speaker of the House) she acquired her professional southernism, her considerable charm and her absurdly romantic first name. She had been brought up to believe that Tallulah was the Indian word for love maiden. Later, when she was busily maintaining her reputation as one of the most uninhibited females of her time, it pleased her to discover that the family etymologist had been mistaken. Tallulah, it fortuitously turned out, means terrible. The amended definition seemed more in keeping with the notoriety on which she was to feed for the rest of her life.

Although her first years in New York were punctuated with brief appearances in a few plays, it was not until she got to London in 1923 that her career gained impetus. Playing opposite the matinee idol Sir Gerald du Maurier in a piece called *The Dancers,* she was an immediate success, titillating audiences with her tomboy swagger. The British, whose theater deities personified either ornaments of the upper class or caricatures of the lower, considered her a heaven-sent — and typically American — amalgam of their two favorite types. From the beginning she began acquiring her army of "gallery girls," consisting not only of young Cockney women but also of women approaching middle age, who formed long queues at the box office, who surrounded her nightly at the stage door (after one premiere, a crowd of two thousand had to be dispersed by the police) , and who were to be the mainstay of her public during her eight spectacular years in the English theater. Her hairdo was copied, her idiosyncratic growl imitated. After she played the heedless Iris March in *The Green Hat,* green felts became the rage, worn slanted insouciantly, Tallulah-style, over an eye. Her *La Dame aux Camélias,* slammed by the critics, still brought forth tears enough to flood the Thames. She was one of two celebrities (Steve Donohue, the famous jockey, was the other) immediately identifiable by their first names. The day after each of her openings, news vendors' placards would announce, "Tallulah Is Back."

She had arrived in London at a time of postwar moral anarchy, when the Bright Young Things of the upper middle class were setting a rollicking pace. Her social acceptance among the smart fast set was assured when, making her initial appearance in a Mayfair drawing room, she turned a handspring and announced, "I'm Tallulah Bankhead; I do what I like and I say what I like." Doing what she liked included appearing completely naked in front of rather proper people ("Pardon the décolleté," she would caution), and saying what she liked included her chronic use, before the same kinds of people, of Anglo-Saxon epithets that came to be known as Tallulah's "short" words.

Her need to shock was incessant. When Prime Minister Ramsay Macdonald brought his spinsterish sister backstage to see her, Tallulah introduced a doctor who was also visiting and said, "Darling, you must remember his name, he's wonderful at abortions." Adoring schoolboys down from Eton and Harrow would be pressed into service as performers in carefully arranged tableaus: staid callers were to discover them seated casually around a room in her house on Farm Street with their penises exposed. When she rented a country place near Eton, the headmaster, it was rumored, posted a notice declaring Tallulah out of bounds.

Her audacious doings and sayings provided almost daily luncheon and dinner table gossip and were chronicled insistently in the penny press. Such a household bogey-word was she, Kenneth Carten told her, that when his nurse had asked what, if he had one wish, that wish would be, and he had answered, "To fly the Atlantic with Tallulah," the nurse had clucked reprovingly, "Now, is that *quite* nice?" The Edwardian theater star Mrs. Patrick Campbell, herself no stranger to unbridled behavior, readily pinpointed the reason for the Bankhead *réclame*. "She's always skating on thin ice," declared the specialist, "and the British public wants to be there in case the ice breaks."

Tallulah claimed that she was introduced to intoxicants when her daddy came to see her off on the boat to England. He had ordered champagne, saying, "It'll either kill you or cure you." Although intrigued by extremes, she was not destined to face either alternative. Throughout her life her capacity for alcoholic consumption was to astonish even the most confirmed tosspot (she died in 1968 of pneumonia, at the age of sixty-six). Soon after that trial imbibition she discovered brandy, which she learned to swallow neat, with champagne as a chaser. She must have had an iron constitution, for she could drink steadily all week long, staying up most nights with very little sleep, and still perform in the theater — her attendance record throughout her career was exemplary — with the audience unaware of her condition. Hosts and hostesses, however, were only too conscious of having a problem on their hands. At parties, after she had reached a certain point, she was just as likely as not to slap anyone within slapping distance, accompanying the action with a simultaneous stream of billingsgate ("Hit me in the belly, don't hit me in the face," she would say to anyone who attempted to strike back in self-defense). An exhausted escort summed up her usual condition with, "I don't know what to do with her — she can't stand up and she *won't* sit down."

Although her coital adventures with assorted males were freely — and specifically — discussed by her, she must have yearned for a glamorous sanctified union, for she put on a lengthy, eventually unsuccessful campaign for Lord Napier Alington and even became engaged — but not married — to Count Anthony de Bosdari. Her ambivalence in sexual preferences also became part of her legend. A schoolgirl, seeing her getting out of her Bentley, asked, "Are you Tallulah Bankhead?" Said Tallulah, mischief overriding decorum, "How dare you mistake me for that awful lesbian?" "I hear she's an Elizabethan," a confused matron was overheard confiding to her companion at a Bankhead matinee. After one evening performance, when Tallulah announced to a backstage visitor that she was having supper with the Earl of Lathom and Gladys Cooper, he dampened her enthusiasm. "They'll be no good to you," he warned. "One's got consumption and the other's got a matinee."

Aimee Semple McPherson, making a sensational appearance at the Albert Hall, was taken up by Tallulah and Beatrice Lillie, who tried to overcome the evangelist's vow of temperance by getting her drunk. When she resisted, they felt she needed to be punished. Miss Lillie was leaving for America and Tallulah asked Aimee to come along for the drive to Southampton to see her off. Somehow the car broke down, the party got lost and were all night on the road. Journalism was ready for a made-to-order situation. AIMEE LOST IN FOG WITH TALLULAH ran an insinuating headline.

Tallulah's dissolute London life, which included drug usage ("Cocaine's not addictive," she would argue, giving as proof "I've been taking it for years"), came to an end in 1931, quite possibly at the suggestion of the increasingly censorious British authorities. It was about this time that Frank Crowninshield, editor of *Vanity Fair* and a sucker for a pretty face, published his panegyric: "You are the little threads of red that run through the dull gray pattern of a Persian rug. You are the figure of Pierrot amid a company of tragic muses."

Whether or not her departure from England was at the instigation of the Home Secretary has never been made public. Ostensibly she left to take up a new career in American films. Paramount had signed her to a contract on the assumption that she would prove a rival to M.G.M.'s Greta Garbo. Arriving in New York in January of 1931, she was introduced to Walter Winchell, who said, "I've heard a great deal about you." "It's all true!" snapped Tallulah, and undoubtedly much of it was.

After making three pictures at the studio in Astoria, Long Island, she was transported by Paramount to the West Coast. Hollywood dutifully greeted her as the Exotic of the Exotics. Not given to procrastination, she started in immediately to set the tone for her stay there. She had rented William Haines's house, with its lovingly furnished period pieces and its collection of antique glassware, which was prized by the owner. At parties she gave, she would take the glasses off the shelves and smash them, simply to enjoy the noise (the bill for damages was phenomenal). Garbo was taken there for dinner one evening and left early, saying, "That's a girl to keep away from." Tallulah had always been terrified of being alone, even in the toilet. Kenneth Carten, her houseguest, seeing her squatting primordially one morning with the door ajar, sneered in passing, "Exotic of the exotics!" "I suppose you think Garbo craps orchids," said Tallulah, ever the realist.

She made six films in two years, all unsuccessful critically and financially. Their titles are the key to their artistry: *Tarnished Lady, My Sin, The Cheat, Thunder Below, The Devil and the Deep, Faithless*. Nor was she able to transcend her material, as Garbo did. She was soon chafing at the relentless studio schedule (awakened for work at dawn, at which time in London she hadn't even started to go to bed) and the ridiculous social existence, an unintentional travesty of high living (invited to an informal dinner by Joan Crawford, she arrived wearing slacks, to be greeted by her hostess in an elaborately tasseled gown and to be seated at a table for six — one of the guests was the child actor Jackie Cooper — adorned with place cards and individual menus) .

Her unsheathed vocabulary and her penchant for disrobing in public — an act simplified by her aversion to underpants — were again features of local gossip. While these idiosyncrasies were kept within the confines of the movie colony they could be dismissed as flamboyant but forgivable personality embellishments. However, boredom and frustration over the low quality of her films led her to go one step beyond the acceptable. In an audacious girl-to-girl interview with a veteran journalist, Gladys Hall, she confided (as later published in *Motion Picture* magazine) I WANT A MAN! SAYS TALLULAH. "I haven't had one for six months — do you know what that means?" "Of course," added Miss Hall, suddenly prim for the occasion, "I can't use the language that Tallulah used in telling me this, etc. . . ." In that heyday of the fan magazine, the story achieved wide circulation and attracted the kind of attention frightening to the film industry, then in the dichotomous position of trying to keep its product lascivious and still appease the powerful church groups. The industry's self-censoring Motion Picture Producers' Association met to consider adding "verbal" to the moral turpitude clause in its contracts with players. What was more serious to Tallulah, Daddy was so disturbed over the commotion she had caused — and the possible political effect on his electorate — that he telephoned long-distance from Washington, an unusual occurrence since he disapproved of the expense.

When Tallulah first arrived at Paramount, the studio had prepared an introductory trailer headed, "We gave you Dietrich, now we give you Tallulah." When Tallulah objected to the debutante classification, saying that she was already well known, her producer had facetiously suggested, "How about 'We give you *back* Tallulah'?" Which now was exactly what they did. Since her films had failed to be popular, her employers released her to the theater. She returned to New York in 1933 to prepare for her first Broadway appearance since her London glorification. "Has time tempered Tallulah, smudged her luster?" asked press agent Richard Maney in the New York *Times* — rhetorically, as it turned out. Time hadn't even made a dent in her behavior patterns.

She was tempestuous as ever, her invective as scatalogical, her strip scenes as compulsive. And she talked continuously, a diarrhetic affliction she couldn't control (she referred to herself as "a conversation piece"). "A day away from Tallulah," said Howard Dietz, out of hearing-reach for twenty-four hours, "is like a month in the country."

Her opening night in *Forsaking All Others* brought out a crowd of predetermined idolators who laughed and applauded indiscriminately. The theater critics were more restrained; while admitting that she had an electric stage personality, they were willing to wait until they saw her in a worthier showpiece before making a full commitment. They were to wait six years while she stalked restlessly through such shallow plays as *Dark Victory, Something Gay, Reflected Glory,* and even made a disastrous attempt at Shakespeare's difficult *Antony and Cleopatra* ("Last night Miss Bankhead barged down the Nile and sank" was John Mason Brown's ungallant and much-quoted summation).

Meanwhile she continued her merry pranks, both in and out of the theater. She stopped a rehearsal of *Something Gay,* saying she was not in the mood. "Well, what would you like to do?" asked the exasperated director. "I'd like two bottles of champagne, a big double bed and [pointing to her handsome English leading man] Hugh Sinclair." In London she had lost the coveted part of Sadie Thompson in *Rain* because she had offended Somerset Maugham. The play was revived for her in New York to a disconcerting lack of acclaim. "She seems too self-reliant," wrote Heywood Broun. "One feels that even without the assistance of the Marines, she might down the Reverend Mr. Davidson with a good right hook to the jaw." The actor playing the Reverend was a shy man; Tallulah goaded him mercilessly. The climax to the second act has him rushing offstage after he has yielded to the temptation of the prostitute Sadie. Tallulah would be in the wings waiting for him, posed in the kind of tableau she used to arrange in London to confound the conventional: her dress up around her neck, legs spread wide apart, and her maid nearby holding a condom on a tray. "What are your views on love?" asked a young girl reporter from the Middle West during a mass interview. "I don't understand what you mean, my dear," said Tallulah. "Do you mean fucking?"

Even under what might be considered inviolable circumstances her instinct for self-mockery could override prudence. At the White House, where she was taken by Daddy to be presented to Eleanor Roosevelt, the First Lady arrived a bit late, explaining she had been held up visiting a Home for Wayward Girls. "You should have taken me along," said Tallulah, "because I'm the most wayward girl you'll ever meet." At a point when even Tallulah's resistant consititution betrayed her, she was confined to a New York hospital for several months with a serious internal disorder. On the day she was finally released, as she was being wheeled down the corridor to be taken home, she turned to her doctor and shouted, "Don't think for one moment that this has taught me a lesson!"

The turning point in her American career was her triumphant appearance in Lillian Hellman's *The Little Foxes*. As the sulphurous Regina Giddens, a termagant unleashed, she gave the kind of performance that used to bring down the house in the days of Modjeska and Bernhardt. After the string of failures which had threatened her professional existence, she had at last justified her

London reputation. The combustive demands of the part were of course made to order for her, but she could have squandered her effects by her congenital lack of discipline if she had not been held in line by playwright Hellman and the producer-director Herman Shumlin. At one of the very first rehearsals, when she started to disrobe in front of the company, Shumlin said firmly, "Now Tallulah, I don't want any more of that." Tallulah's demands that some of the lines be changed were ignored by Miss Hellman, a lady with a mind of her own. She did manage to drain a bottle of bourbon during the opening performance in Baltimore, and at an after-theater gathering in the hotel, she created what could have led (in 1939 and in that sensitive city) to a lynching situation by thrusting herself invitingly against the Negro waiter, a criminally thoughtless act for a white female born and bred in the South.

Her ecstatic reviews after the New York opening assured her a reputation as a powerful actress. However, once settled in for a long run, the old habits of carelessness reasserted themselves. She would be a magnificent virago one night, a lackluster performer the next. And her offstage peccadilloes no longer amused people; the shock technique was worn out. After one of Tallulah's interminable monologues colored with the usual gutter linguistics, a moment of quiet was broken by Dorothy Parker asking plaintively, "Has Whistler's mother finished?"

Tallulah followed her *Little Foxes* success with the part of Sabina in Thornton Wilder's *The Skin of Our Teeth,* in which she was again acclaimed for her performance. Heretofore she had squandered her large earnings (she was generous, even profligate, with friends, acquaintances and strangers — "She would give you the shirt off her back even if you didn't want it," the merciless Mrs. Parker told me). For the first time she invested in annuities and bought what became after extensive alterations a ten-room, four-bathroom house she named Windows, situated on fifteen acres of land in Bedford Village, New York (another house she had previously bought in Rockland County burned down before she could move in). She had been a slovenly and frequently destructive tenant of hotel apartments most of her adult life, much of the carnage having been caused by her addiction to pets, including a lion cub who chewed up the furniture at the Boston Ritz and a golden marmoset named Senegas, after Sarah Bernhardt's hair-dresser, who, like his mistress, was neurotic about being left alone and would pee on her in protest whenever she was dressed to go out. Now as chatelaine of her own establishment she became a domestic tyrant, demanding spotless housekeeping of her servants and guests.

It was here that I met her for the first time. She had just returned from Hollywood, where she had completed shooting of the leading role in Alfred Hitchcock's wartime melodrama, *Lifeboat*. It had been a chance for a movie comeback and she had been more or less on good behavior during the production (although she had found time on an off-Sunday to appear at a garden party at George Cukor's wearing nothing but a bunch of violets as a crotch-decoration). When *Lifeboat* was released early in the following year, she was given an award by the New York film critics for the "best performance by an actress in 1944."

I was sure I could do an entertaining piece on Tallulah for *Town and Country*. My editor, Harry Bull, although warning me that in the long run I would find her a boring woman, told me to go ahead. I thought he was being excessively jaded; how could such an amoral, irrepressible glamour girl be boring?

An acquaintance of mine in the publicity department of 20th Century–Fox, which was releasing *Lifeboat,* made an appointment for me to go out to her country place. When I arrived about noon, having taken a train to Bedford Village and a taxi to the house, Tallulah was on the lawn to greet me. She apologized for not having sent the chauffeur-butler Eli to the station but explained that she was short of help and he was busy preparing lunch for us. Dogs were yelping all around her; she had five of them, a Pekingese, a sheep dog, a wire-haired terrier, a Sealyham and a mongrel.

We went into a large, abundantly fenestrated living room (hence "Windows"). The furnishings were those she had had in her London house, chosen, she told me, by the era's most fashionable decorator, Syrie Maugham. Prominent on one wall was the haunting El Greco-esque painting of her, full-length, a wraith in pale pink, by Augustus John (apparently her proudest possession — "She carries it around on her back wherever she goes," said her actor friend, the sardonic Glenn Anders) .

Tallulah asked Eli to fix a Scotch for me and a Coke for herself, explaining that she had been on the wagon ever since the fall of Dunkirk and had vowed not to touch alcohol again until that defeat was avenged. She had previously foresworn spirits as a penance so that the gods would favor the New York Giants baseball team, of which she was a rabid booster, in that year's World Series. They had lost.

From the moment the taxi had delivered me on to her front lawn, she had not stopped talking except for the few occasions when I interrupted to ask a question. In fact, "talks incessantly" is one of the first items in the notes I made at the time. Another is "can't keep her mind on one subject." The virtuoso monologue, with her favorite "divine"s and "darling"s escalloping every other sentence, skittered over her recent California experience, over her past and over her present.

An imprecise reconstruction strung together from my notes would go something like "I didn't have a dog in Hollywood, I almost went mad, darling, I cannot get up at 6:30 in the morning I never miss anybody I know divine people everywhere but few of them intimately how's your drink darling I won't be rude to people in their own homes if they want to meet me in a restaurant it's their own damn fault I dislike bad manners I consider I've committed a mortal sin if I've been unmannerly — without provocation. I'm good at timing it's a typical American thing it's not so much that I'm witty I hate witty people I've let Dottie Parker be witty occasionally because I knew I couldn't top her the only witty thing I've ever said was when Alec Woollcott took me to a Maeterlinck play it was very pretentious and I said, 'There's less in this than meets the eye' am I talking too much darling when I first went to England someone in the gallery shouted 'Speak up' and for eight years I had laryngitis from shouting I've had a violent temper ever since I was a child I used to throw divine fits and they would have to throw cold water on me my grandmother would say, 'Well, what do you want me to do with her, I can't kill her' I was a bad girl in school but I never enjoyed being bad I was an innocent child but darling I was never naive and don't forget I was brought up like a lady and I always behave like a lady . . ."

Here I couldn't help interjecting, "Now Tallulah, you know I'm going to have to mention that you use naughty words occasionally." "You mean like 'fuck'?" she said, covering her mouth in mock horror. "Don't you dare! I'll call your editor and I'll cry and carry on . . ." She was being amusing about this, but I couldn't help remembering how absolutely furious she had been with Mike Mok because his interview in the New York *Post* had started with a direct quote: "Daddy's coming up for re-election this year and I want no goddam swearing in this piece."

Eli came in several times to offer me another drink and to bring Tallulah a fresh Coke (I was told later that she had the Cokes spiked with aspirin or ammonia, which presumably provided the necessary stimulation she would have derived from alcohol; whether or not this was true, she certainly seemed to be getting more exhilarated) .

At about 1:30 we were joined by her permanent house guest, the actress Estelle Winwood, whom Tallulah had known since her early days in New York and whose dry wit was legendary in the theatrical profession (when the chairlady of a suburban drama group had referred slightingly to actors as "they," Miss Winwood ever so firmly reminded her, *"We* are no more *they* than *you* are") . At about the same time, Eli announced lunch. We went in to an attractive, sunny dining room and sat down, Tallulah still doing most of the talking. At one point, I recall, she was telling her house guest that for the forthcoming weekend she had hired a Harlem waiter who was going to serve all the meals in drag and Miss Winwood with a grimace said, "Oh dear, all those feathers getting into the soup." The lunch was commendable and Tallulah was a considerate hostess, taking pains to see that I had second portions and that my wine glass was refilled. Later she showed me around the property. Eli had telephoned for a taxi and when it arrived I said I would like to see her again after I had interviewed some of her friends and associates. She asked if I would show her the article before I turned it in. I said no, that wasn't ever a good idea, but I would go over some of the notes with her to check on facts. As she stood there waving good-bye, the dogs barking and running playfully around her, Tallulah made a pretty picture of a contented country gentle-woman. I was certain I had the beginnings for an illuminating article.

Those friends and acquaintances who had known her longest and were still seeing her (a dwindling number) told me when I got in touch with them that she had no illusions about herself, that she was the least counterfeit person they had ever come across, were unanimous about her generosity ("although if she gets mad at you, she'll ask for the presents back"), and then gave examples of her willful, irresponsible behavior in London, Hollywood and New York. Dorothy Parker started off gently as was her habit and gradu-ally warmed to her subject. Tallulah would be much easier to write about, she murmured, if one had invented her. Tallulah's great quality was her resilience; she could snap back quickly from any catastrophe (she walked into Tony's nightclub after her disastrous reviews in *Antony and Cleopatra,* and on the heels of Orson Welles's triumphant *Julius Caesar,* gallantly announcing, "My head is bloody but unbowed"). Tallulah had once been picturesque but she had now gotten dowdy. At Antibes some years before, she had appeared, flamboyantly beautiful, well groomed — but with a corn plaster adhering to one painted toe. That, to Mrs. Parker, summed up Tallulah's character. In conclusion, Tallulah was a person of the "utmost vulgarity."

Tallulah, others told me, was pathological about Communists ("They want to come and take my fur coats away"). Although not too clear about the Soviets' political philosophy, she did know that Communists were her natural enemies. She would use the term indiscriminately as an epithet, sometimes under wildly inappropri-ate circumstances. At the New York opening of *Gone With The Wind,* she could growl, "shut up, you Communist!" to a talkative spectator seated behind her without bothering to find out that it was the eminently Republican Jock Whitney.

Just before the New York opening of *Lifeboat,* Tallulah officiated at a mass interview attended by twenty-five reporters. When she was introduced to the representative from the newspaper *PM* (I believe it was young Shana Ager on her first newspaper job) Tallulah's smile disappeared. As reported: "She drew a deep breath, lowered her head, drew her eyebrows together, hunched her shoulders and clenched her fists on the arm of her chair. 'Of all the filthy, rotten, Communist rags,' she began, speaking between clenched teeth and a rising inflection that brought the word *rags* out in a kind of upper register snarl, 'that . . . is . . . the . . . most . . . *vicious . . . dangerous . . . hating* paper that's ever . . . been . . . published.' Then the man from *Collier's* leaned forward. 'For God's sake, Tallulah,' he said, 'what kind of talk is that? I thought you were a liberal. That's what *PM* is. I don't see . . .' 'Liberal, my *eye,*' she yelled. 'It's a dirty Communist sheet. I loathe it. *Loathe* it. It hurts everyone's feelings. It . . . I don't want you to mention my name in your lousy paper. And if I ever get my hands on that Bob Rice [Robert Rice had written a forthright but not particularly damaging piece on Tallulah that appeared in *PM* in 1942] I'll . . .' What Miss Bankhead said she would do to Mr. Rice, she could not have meant and we omit it. The reporters shifted uncomfortably in their chairs. 'I don't get it,' one of them said. 'Compared to the profile *Life* did of you, the Rice piece . . .' 'Darling,' said Tallulah, 'the *Life* piece was just *dull,* that's all. It wasn't vicious and cheap and disgusting and *foul.'* 'Neither was the *PM* piece,' said someone. 'Now I tell you, Miss Bankhead,' said a plump reporter, 'I don't like *PM* either and never read it, but I know lots of people who work there and they all go to church on Sunday. Now Communists . . .' 'Darling,' said Miss Bankhead, who was beginning to calm down, 'I'm sure there are perfectly *lovely* people working there.' . . . She turned back to us. 'You know, you look just like a dear friend of mine' . . . She paused reflectively, then added, 'She committed suicide.' "

I had interviewed more than a dozen people, some of whom Tallulah had suggested that I see, and had also gone through her clippings at the *Herald-Tribune* and *Time.* When I had collected enough material to cover fifteen sheets of typed notes (longer than I had planned the article would be) I telephoned her and made an appointment for the next afternoon at the hotel she stayed in on days when she came to town from the country. In her hotel room, I sat in an armchair and Tallulah sat, legs crossed yoga style, on the bed. I told her that the main purpose of this visit was to check on facts and to have her elaborate on certain incidents of which I had only a sketchy account. I glanced at my notes and didn't know where I could begin. The early events of her life, as I have recorded them here, were as she had related them to me, and there was no point in my going over those. She did confess, endearingly I thought, that she frequently lied about her age but, being a timid liar, she lied by only one year. Most of the information I had obtained subsequently was of so intimate a nature or so gamey that I was embarrassed to relay it to her. At one time she had said, "I was alway a very maligned young lady . . . that's not quite true. I've done practically everything I'm supposed to have done, but not at the time and place I'm supposed to have done them." But since her periods of candor were often followed by periods when she glossed over her behavioral excesses, and since she was currently bent on producing a bland picture of herself, I felt she would disqualify any item in the least unflattering.

I started with such innocuous notes as "You have a retentive memory; you can read a book in an hour and remember it in detail for a long time?" Yes darling, gabble, gabble, gabble. . . . A harmless anecdote that Dick Maney, her press agent, had told me, about Tallulah getting the New York Giants' baseball uniforms mixed up with that of the opposing team and rooting for the enemy instead, drew the first fire. No, of course not, she would never get confused about which team was which, where did I hear such a story? I put an X mark in the margin. A guest appearance on the Kate Smith radio show: the hostess had told her when to come on, and Tallulah had reportedly said, "You big tub of lard, are you going to tell me how to make an entrance?" No, no, I wouldn't do anything like that, I'm a lady. A penciled X next to that story. Once when Tallulah had vowed to cleanse her language, she had dressed chastely in white to attend a theater opening. Someone accidentally stepped on her train and she let out a good old Alabama swear word. Oh, why do you have to put in things like that, I don't remember any such incident, darling. So it went, with Tallulah either denying as untrue any anecdote having to do with her rambunctiousness (and I didn't dare question her about the most outrageous ones) or asking me why I had to drag up all *that* stuff (such as the Gladys Hall fan magazine article, which was a matter of public record). Finally I brought up a story about a woman with whom she had quarreled. Her face darkened, she leaned forward and, protestations of gentility forgotten, said savagely, "That woman is a cunt!" (Later I repeated the remark to "that woman," who said wryly, "Well, I suppose it's the mot juste.")

For the next week or so I tried working on the piece. I could get no further than the first two paragraphs. I had what I thought was a good title — "Tallulah Means Terrible" — but with each new lead I found the tone, against any conscious intention on my part, getting more and more unpleasant. Once, Tallulah telephoned me on the pretext that she had forgotten to tell me the name of the decorator of her country house. She then asked casually how I was getting on, and did I have enough material? I told her I had started work and would let her know if I needed any more information. I had the feeling that she was apprehensive about what tack I would take. It puzzled me that, after all her don't-give-a-damn years, she should suddenly begin to worry about her public image. I could only think it was because she had just started a promising new film career with *Lifeboat,* and didn't want it sabotaged with printed recollections of former high jinks.

Finally, I told Harry Bull that she had intimidated me so with her claims to refinement that I couldn't finish the article. When I spoke to him again about another piece, he said Tallulah had telephoned him to find out if I had turned in anything and he had informed her candidly that I had abandoned the article, and why.

I was eating lunch in a small Italian restaurant next to the Martin Beck Theater about a month later when Tallulah walked in with her leading man. She had signed for a new Philip Barry play,

Foolish Notion, and this must be the rehearsal break. Our eyes met and as I half rose in greeting, she introduced her companion. "This is Donald Cook," she said, "and *this,*" she told Cook lightly, "is the son-of-a-bitch who couldn't write an article on me because he found I was too much of a lady."

Mae West:
Pardon Me for Loving and Running

WHAT IMAGE OF UNRUFFLED sin has persisted longer than that of Mae West? Eroticism, to paraphrase one of her own skittish lines, had nothing to do with it. Her irreverent approach to a sacred subject originally manifested itself in *Sex,* her first "legitimate" play, in which, as actress-author, she titillated the gullible but was ignored by the sophisticated. She was then (1926) ludicrously over-weight and it was difficult to believe in a gluttonous Circe. Two years later, considerably slimmed down to an hour-glass shape, she found her métier in *Diamond Lil,* an impudent pastiche of turn-of-the-century melodrama, which brought her fame in the theater and in films when it was turned into *She Done Him Wrong.* Lust could not be treated with equanimity in any entertainment form ever after.

I interviewed her for the *Herald-Tribune* in 1944, when she returned to the stage after twelve fat years in Hollywood. Her movie career was at a standstill and she was trying to resuscitate it with a theater vehicle she had fashioned for herself called *Catherine Was Great.* She kept referring to the libidinous Russian ruler, with a reverence tinged perhaps with envy, as the Empress. The Empress, she wanted me to believe, was not merely a meaty stage role; she was a crusade. Miss West (I discovered that very few people, old associates included, ever called her by her given name) had a theory that the Empress's boudoir exploits were a means rather than an

Mae West with some of the diamonds goodness had nothing to do with

end; that her one vital interest was in affairs of state. To substantiate this, a line from Catherine's diary had been quoted in the play: "I need men to inspire me so that I may inspire them."

The play had taken her longer to write than any of her other works (*The Drag, The Constant Sinner,* etc.). She explained that this was because she had stuck fairly close to historical facts. When the idea had first come to her five years earlier, she had read all the books she could find on the subject, including two which she paid to have translated since she was only conversant with French, Spanish and German, she told me. She did most of her writing in bed, jotting down notes on any odd scraps that were handy, including wrapping paper and pieces of cardboard. The final version was then dictated to two secretaries working in shifts from 1:00 P.M. to 2:30 A.M.

"Of course, I tried to write in as many legitimate laughs as possible," she said. "But I mostly stuck close to the spirit of the character. I didn't want to put in too much comedy because then you cheapen the thing. Naturally, when you've led the public to expect a certain characterization, it's a little hard at first to feed them something different. But I think the audience would resent it if I'd made a satire out of Catherine. And anyway, she's like the character I've been playing all along — except on a higher plane, of course. Her psychology is the psychology of Diamond Lil. You know, I've played wicked ladies of history before. In Shubert revues I've been Cleopatra and Lucrezia Borgia. And I had a terrific scene in one of their shows as Circe."

I recorded all this deadpan, and the *Tribune* followed suit by captioning the piece "Catherine Is Diamond Lil on Higher Plane." Miss West was a woman to be admired, a professional giving a professional interview. Our meeting had taken place in her rented apartment at the old Marguery Hotel. She had had me wait five minutes — no more — after my arrival so that she could make a proper entrance wearing a fluffy, baby-blue negligee. If her given birthdate — 1892 — was to be believed, she was then in her early fifties and she looked twenty years younger. Her chin line was firm, her skin smooth as an adolescent's and almost as unlined, but without the tightly stretched look that is the result of cosmetic surgery. She especially delighted me because nothing she said was wasteful, every statement, even the patently fanciful, was quotable.

Catherine Was Great had many scenes, all of them strikingly similar. Mostly these consisted of interviews: the Empress interrogating an officer while she looked him up and down meaningfully, with an especially protracted gaze at his crotch; the Empress questioning a footman, a guard, a peasant, all chosen for their pulchritude and the bulge of their genitals. Colin McPhee accurately described the performance as being like the Chinese theater, in that one could walk in or walk out at any point without missing a thing. The play was not a hit and Miss West didn't realize her objective, which had been to fashion a stage property successful enough to be turned into a film.

Two seasons later she made another attempt with a play called *Ring Twice Tonight,* which she tried out on the road. Her screen career was definitely in abeyance and she was a woman who liked to keep working. Not out of financial necessity, since she was reputed to be quite wealthy, nor even entirely out of greed, although she was exceptionally canny in business arrangements, but most probably out of vanity and habit — she had been performing since the age of six.

At the time, I was collaborating on songs with Jack Lawrence. We had sold several of our efforts to films, a piece called "Twilight Song" for a program picture, "The Bachelor's Daughters" with Adolph Menjou ("I hear a nightingale at twilight," it began, neither of us New York City boys having ever heard any such sound), and a lively waltz of the bal musette type, "My Bel-Ami," that was used as the recurring theme for a movie version of de Maupassant's mordant story, with George Sanders and Angela Lansbury. Jack was acquainted with Al Rosen, Mae West's company manager, who told him that he was negotiating a recording contract for her with Columbia Records and that she was looking for special numbers. She was appearing in Philadelphia in the closing weeks of *Ring Twice Tonight,* which had been unsuccessful on the road and was not to be brought to Broadway. Al suggested to

Jack that we meet in Philadelphia to discuss what sort of material she would like. We drove down in midweek to have dinner with her before a performance. Al brought us up to her hotel suite and introduced us to his star. I reminded her of our previous meeting, which she pretended to remember although she obviously didn't. There was little reason why she should have, since newspaper interviewers were certainly no exceptional event in her life.

Conversation was awkward; she obviously had no flair for small talk. I had the feeling that she was sizing us up, speculating on how much use we could be to her. We went down in the elevator and out to her limousine, the door held open by her bodyguard-chauffeur, who, we were later told by Al, carried a gun as part of his livery. In the car, palaver remaining at a standstill, I attempted a pleasantry. "That's a nice hat," I said. It was indeed an imposing edifice. "Yeah," she said, patting the back of her head reassuringly, "I like it; it gives me heighth."

We drew up to Lew Tendler's, the local steak house patronized by theatrical and sports figures. A small group was gathered on the sidewalk to see which celebrity would emerge from the limousine. The chauffeur-bodyguard held the door open. Al stepped out first, then waited for the lady to emerge. She didn't budge. I got out, then Jack got out, and when all four males were lined up, Miss West allowed herself to be helped out. We were no longer friends or associates; we had become an entourage. She gave the spectators a good show as we trailed her into the restaurant.

After a drink (I don't think she had one) and during dinner, we were all more relaxed. I asked her about *My Little Chickadee,* the film she had made with W. C. Fields. "Yeah," she said contemplatively, "they wanted to co-star me. . . ." I waited for the denouement, since her mood seemed to have darkened, but there was none; she and Fields had indeed been forced to share top billing. I told her a delightful story I had heard from one of the Boston film critics, a group of females who were notable drinkers. Two of them, old friends of Fields from his vaudeville and revue days, had been on a visit to Hollywood, where the comedian invited them to his house. They were impressed with a room at one end, with shelves from floor to ceiling, which seemed to hold all varieties of liquor. The tour continued; at the extreme other end was an identical room, equally well-stocked. Fields explained the seeming redundancy. "Never know when one wing of the house might burn down," he said.

This brought on a reminiscence of her own. During the *Little Chickadee* filming, she had delegated one studio employee to watch Fields to see that he didn't slip out for a few nips at the bottle between scenes. Although kept under diligent guard, he still seemed to get increasingly plastered as the day wore on. The source of his supply was finally discovered. Before filming had started, he had emptied the water cooler in his dressing room and filled it with gin.

I told Miss West that I had seen her on the stage as Diamond Lil and how much I had enjoyed the performance. She nodded in agreement. "Yeah," she said. "I coulda won the Pulitzer Prize for that. . . ." I waited with bated breath for a fuller explanation. ". . . but I dunno," she continued, "I was busy, and . . ." her voice trailed off.

She was coming to New York in two weeks and we agreed that we would be in touch with Al about the songs. We wrote two of them for her, keeping in mind her locker-room style of sly double entendre. One was "My Man Friday," which ticked off the days, each day being reserved for a different lover with varied accomplishments ("My Tuesday's man is asbestos lined, My Wednesday's and my Thursday's got a brand new grind, But my man Friday, He can hypnotize me, really mesmerize me, I mean he satisfies me"). The other was "Pardon Me for Loving and Running" and there was no mistaking its message either ("It's hard on you, it's hard on me, but pardon me for loving and running").

We decided to invite Miss West to dinner in Jack's penthouse apartment on Washington Square, where the atmosphere would be less strained than in a restaurant and where Jack could play and sing the songs for her after the meal — he was an effective demonstrator. The invitation was accepted. Jack's houseman, who was to cook, was wildly excited. On the appointed evening, he brought a friend from Harlem with him ostensibly "to help with the washing-up" but actually of course to get a glimpse of the celestial. He had also brought napery he thought more suitable for a Presence than any his employer possessed — an elaborate lace tablecloth with napkins to match.

Miss West was taken up in the elevator with her chauffeur-body-guard as escort. Having delivered his precious charge, he was then told to call for her at ten-thirty. Divested of her hat and coat and in a simple little pastel dress, she was smaller than I had remembered; her figure was also trimmer, the S shape formed by her bosom and bottom not so pronounced as they were in her professional appearances. I had the feeling that she padded for those occasions.

She refused a drink of hard liquor but accepted a glass of sherry, mostly out of sociability, since she kept sipping at it tentatively. Alcohol was apparently not one of her pleasures. Earl Wilson, the New York *Post* entertainment columnist, had that day published an item in connection with her. "Did you read what Oiel wrote about my grandmother?" she asked, keeping her native Brooklyn diphthongs intact. "That she had three, uh, breasts?" There she primly sat, on the edge of the chair, lowering her head like a cloistered maiden at the word "breasts." Suddenly I thought of my interview with her two years earlier, when I had told her about seeing "Mae West" in a dictionary to denote the slang term for inflated life preserver vests issued to aviators during World War II. She had been proud of that, saying, "Yeah, I'm part of the language." Although she was a worldwide synonym for ribaldry, her diction in social situations was schoolmarm proper. In the times I was in her presence I didn't hear her utter one Rabelaisian word.

During dinner, with the festal lace tablecloth a staring rebuke considering the lack of festiveness in the diners, I attempted to enliven the decorous atmosphere. I asked her what she thought about the Mae West jokes then prevalent. "Like which ones?" she asked. "Like the one about Mae West going into a bank and depositing some twenty-dollar gold pieces [they were outlawed during the war]. The bank teller said, 'Hoarding, eh?' to which Mae West replied, 'Never mind how I got 'em, just gimme the receipt.' "

She laughed, said, "No, I never heard that one," and then countered with, "Did you hear about Mae West and the . . ." and she launched into another Mae West joke, talking of Mae West in the third person, as if she were a fictional character. The remainder of the meal was rather jolly. I had hit upon a popular topic.

She liked the songs Jack played and we made an appointment for her to come to the apartment a week later — after dinner this time — so that we could rehearse her. In the meantime Jack would have a professional arranger make some orchestrations. When she appeared again on the appointed evening, the escorting chauffeur-companion remained in the apartment. Although he was properly deferential, they seemed to be on closer than employer-employee terms, unless I was reading into it more than was there. At the piano, when Jack asked me to get the lead sheet for one of our songs — "It's on my dresser in the bedroom" — she interposed jauntily, "My favorite room." It was the only time I heard her indulge in less than seemly badinage, but it was her public personality speaking, as if she were repeating a line from one of her plays.

The Columbia recording never came through. Al told us that they wouldn't agree to Miss West's terms. She had been offered the standard top percentage but had grasped for more. Some months later, the record shops around town began selling a Mae West album containing eight numbers, two of which were "My Man Friday" and "Pardon Me for Loving and Running." We were credited with the authorship but no contracts had been signed and we had never heard of the recording company. I obtained the distributor's address from a buyer at Doubleday's, but the company was not listed in the telephone book and a posted inquiry from Jack's lawyer elicited no response. The address was probably merely a letter drop. The lawyer said that in any event it would be difficult to win a suit because the material was "semi-salacious" and the action would most likely be tossed out of court. I was indignant. Doesn't semi-salacity have any legal rights? Since Miss West had made it pay during much of her theatrical career, and since she was noted for her business acumen, we wondered if in this instance she was an equally injured party.

She revived *Diamond Lil* for England, which had never seen her on a stage. We heard that she had interpolated "My Man Friday" as one of the songs in the show. She brought the revival to the United States, opening with it out of town. We had Jack's lawyer write the management requesting a $25 weekly royalty for the song. We then heard no more about it. When the revival reached New York, I went backstage to see her. I complimented her on the performance and on how well the show had retained its vitality. By the way, I added as an afterthought, we had never received a penny in royalties for her recording, and hadn't been able to trace the distributors. She said without interest, "That's funny. I don't know who they are. . . ." Her voice trailed off, as if to say, why pursue the unpursuable?

A New Year's Card from Polly Adler

AT ONE PERIOD in my life — I was chronologically adult but adolescent in spirit — I thought it amusing to play the imposter when answering my telephone. In response to a ring I would lift the receiver and give an outlandish identification, "Pasorelli's Shoe Shine" for instance, or "Club Hot-Cha." Once, when I was playing a recording of Mickey Rooney and Judy Garland singing "Treat 'em Rough" from the musical *Girl Crazy*, I answered the telephone's summons with "Can I help you? Mr. Drutman's onstage." The voice at the other end was Lee Gershwin's, wife of the show's lyricist, Ira, and she said, "Aren't you ashamed of yourself?" Indeed I was.

To my mind the most entertaining of these arch impersonations was "Polly Adler's, good evening," which I delivered in the monotonous singsong of a business switchboard operator. Miss Adler had not as yet published her autobiography with its provocative title, *A House Is Not A Home,* but she was even then — in 1940 — the most celebrated of the madams, "her name synonymous with

sin," according to the *Daily News,* her notoriety stemming from the
eminence of her clientele and dating from nine years earlier when
she had been a highly colorful (if unwilling) witness in the New
York State investigation conducted by Judge Samuel Seabury into
judicial bribe-taking and the extortion practices of the New York
City police vice squad. There was no doubt that Polly's customers
had status, including as they did many of the most influential
politicians, gangsters, writers, film stars and millionaires. "From the
parlor of my house," she later wrote, "I had a backstage, three-way
view. I could look into the underworld, the half-world and the
high."

At the start of the Seabury investigation, Polly had hidden out so
that she wouldn't have to testify, which gave the newspaper headline writers a field day. She had her choice of sobriquets: Red
Light Czarina, Notorious Vice Entrepreneuse, or just simply Vice
Queen. MIDTOWN MADAM OF MANY MAGDALENES MISSING ran one
of the heads, followed by POLLY ADLER SURRENDERS, and GIVE LA
ADLER LEADING ROLE IN QUIZ SHOW. She was apparently a frustrating
witness; she could remember no names of customers, no dates, no
police personnel she had paid off, and she was eventually dismissed.

One day when Spivy, the burly nightclub entertainer who was an
acquaintance of mine, telephoned, she laughed at my greeting and
said, "Would you like to meet Polly?" I certainly would. "I'll
arrange it," she said.

Spivy (it was her lone professional name, her supposed patro-
nymic LeVoe being for private consumption only) was coarse-fea-
tured and squat, and she was burdened with a lot of weight, no
inconsiderable portion being consigned to her imposing bosom. She
had made a midnight reputation singing for the social, theatrical
and literary demimonde who patronized the back room of Tony's
Restaurant on West Fifty-second Street; moving among the crowd
in that good-natured, raffish atmosphere, she was not unlike some
eccentric figure out of Lautrec's Montmartre. After a disagreement
with Tony, she left and opened her own nightclub at the northeast
corner of Lexington Avenue and Fifty-seventh Street in the building's penthouse (there were some unkind suggestions that she call it

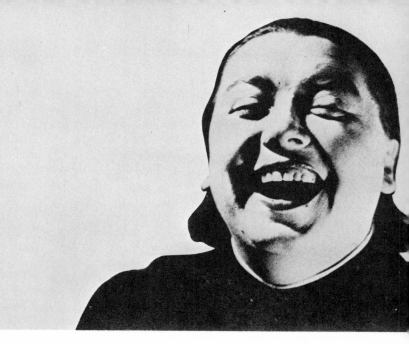

Spivy — "This is a very sad song and you must be very quiet."

Polly Adler — Midtown Madam of Many Magdalenes

ARTHUR L. MITCHELL

La Vache sur le toit.) Although still informal, the ambience here was slicked-up East Side, and Spivy had been slicked up too by her retinue of girl friends (she was, incidentally, considered a great catch by some of her set). She now sported a well-coiffed pompadour with a fashionable streak of gray running through it and the imposing bosom looked even more imposing under the alternating black or white gown sparked with glitter that she wore for her performance.

She would sit down at the piano and solemnly inform the audience that "this is a very sad song and you must be very quiet." She would then race her fingers over the keys fortissimo and launch into the lyrics of her special material in a contralto growl, a phrase at a time, punctuating each division of words with her virile arpeggios. She was a slow study and her entire repertory consisted of not more than eight or ten songs, among her staples being Noel Coward's "I'm the Wife of an Acrobat," Everett Marcy's impish twitting of the celebrity-hunting Mabel Dodge, "I Brought Culture to Buffalo in the '90s" (When Wilde was there, he visited my home) — a historical inaccuracy but no one minded — and Charlotte Kent's "The Madam's Lament" (They all go upstairs but me). In time the habitués got to know the words as well as she did and occasionally there would be an outburst of temperament when their conversational buzz would serve as an unwelcome counterpoint to her performance. In the middle of a number she would then split the air with an ominous crash on the piano keys and stalk out through the terrace door.

Not that such behavior was the rule at Spivy's; there were moments of ladylike gentility, too. One night Belle Baker, the vaudeville singer who was identified in particular with Irving Berlin's "Blue Skies," was introduced and there were calls for her to sing that song, an invitation which she graciously declined. I was seated near her and I added my appeal to the others'. Miss Baker smiled at me hazily and pointing to her half-filled glass of whiskey and soda, said, "I can't, dear. I've had one sherry too many."

In a relaxed mood Spivy could be good company and she wasn't shy of wit. When I was in the hospital recuperating from a tonsillectomy she sent me a telegram, "Next time you want to be clipped come to Spivy's." And I still recall with amusement a late hour excursion after closing her club at 4 A.M., when she suggested to a group of us that we have a little breakfast way up on 117th Street at Patsy's Italian Restaurant, the little breakfast consisting of clams possilipo, spaghetti and meatballs, salad and coffee but — she had to be prudent because of her weight — no dessert. Coming back, with no taxi in sight, we settled for a bus. Somehow Spivy got into a conversation with a sotted derelict seated near her, who told her he had just been released from prison. "What were you in for?" she asked. "Forgery." Spivy was sympathetic. "I didn't know you could write," she said.

Polly Adler had suggested that we come to dinner at her home — not her house, it was emphasized — where Polly would cook for us one of her specialties, pot roast. I called for Spivy at her apartment and she and a young man with her and I set out for Polly's address, which was a conventional red-brick apartment house on East Forty-seventh Street. Polly opened the door herself and she was blazing mad. She told us that upon returning home the night before, she had discovered that she had been robbed. She was not overly concerned about the value of the articles taken — a silver fox scarf, a case of liquor, a semi-precious jeweled pin — but she was still indignant at finding her scrapbooks of clippings spread out open on her bed. "Imagine, the nerve," she exclaimed. "All that stuff from the Sea-bury Investigation!" The very notion that the burglars had paused in their flight to read, no doubt with awe, of the lurid career of their unwitting benefactress, the tabloid heroine of her day, seemed to me ineffably romantic, but of course I didn't dare to express any such sentiment.

Polly's apartment was not at all in keeping with her exotic vocation; it was that of a moderately prosperous middle-class couple (although, so far as I could tell, she was unmarried and lived alone) whose taste had not been contaminated by the decorator magazines. An entrance foyer led into a "dinette" furnished with a Grand Rapids table, four straight-backed chairs and a stool, with an enclosed kitchen off that. A few steps down from the dinette was a dropped living room, an iron balustrade serving to separate the two areas. The living room contained an upholstered suite of the kind featured in installment-plan shops, some imitation-Meissen figurines serving as bases for fringed silk lampshades and, as wall decorations, silhouettes of eighteen-century ladies and gentlemen with mirrored mats and frames. The rest of the apartment consisted of two bedrooms leading off a long corridor.

Polly was a tough little woman, slightly under five feet tall, with a work-worn face, plain of feature, and a look of candor that made her immediately likable and must have been an inestimable business asset. She was homey; one would have placed her, and how mistakenly, as the ubiquitous mama in a family-run delicatessen, and indeed Spivy later told me that often some of the clients came just to have a couple of drinks and a chat with Polly rather than to make use of the establishment's girls.

She spoke pure New Yorkese — "Now, I've got a perfectly fine Delancey Street accent," she declared shortly after our arrival, in telling us about some fancy someone who had tried to hoity-toity her. She was good with an anecdote, even when it was slightly denigrating to herself. She mentioned a well-known millionaire sportsman whom she had recently encountered at the racetrack. He was strolling with "a society girl" and he didn't acknowledge Polly as she passed. "The son-of-a-bitch," she said, without rancor. "All the times he's been to my house; the least he could of done was to wink."

She and Spivy were obviously old friends who were completely at ease with each other. In the general euphoria, I blossomed and told funny stories and said funny things, to which they responded most appreciatively. By the time the Negro maid who had been working in the kitchen announced dinner, I felt pleasantly that I was a prince of wits.

Earlier in the evening, a delicate blonde girl had been admitted. Polly, barely glancing at her, had gestured her to one of the bedrooms, excused herself to follow her in, and had remained about ten minutes or so before returning alone to us. Now, when the four of us were seated at the dinette table, Polly shouted to her down the hall, "Come in and have your dinner," and the girl reappeared. Polly introduced her offhandedly as "This is Dottie" (I don't actually remember the name) and the young man who had come with Spivy and who had been content to remain in the background rose and so did I to acknowledge the introduction. Since the stool was the only piece of furniture on which she could sit, I offered her my chair but Polly said, "The stool's good enough for her," and Dottie sat down submissively on the stool. Polly's disdainful manner to what we could assume was one of her girls, in such contrast to her genial deportment with us, possibly was due to a priggish social distinction she made between guest and employee. It was the only disconcerting element of the evening.

The pot roast cooked by Polly was good enough, although not as good as my mother's — nobody's pot roast is as good as a Jewish boy's mother's. During the meal, Polly, Spivy and I continued in high form, the other two being mainly silent, apparently content to serve as passive listeners.

Polly and Spivy reminisced about their childhood and their strict orthodox Jewish upbringing. Both told me that they had had rabbinical tutoring. I was skeptical. It's too perfect, I thought, the drop from piety too classically steep. They were having fun at my expense. "I'll show you," said Polly. "Next week is Rosh Hashonah. We'll write you a greeting." She opened a desk drawer and brought out a specially printed New Year's card, bare of any identification except for a parrot, Polly's trademark, which, since she was so famous in her profession, she held to be identification enough. On it she wrote in Hebrew script her good wishes for the New Year. She then handed it to Spivy, sister hedonist, who inscribed a similar Hebrew greeting for the high Holy Day. I have kept the card as evidence. A child's early training is of importance in later life.

8

Bread and Butter Letter

MY FRIEND COLIN MCPHEE, when informed that a fellow guest at the Yaddo artists' colony had written a blistering novel about the place after having partaken of its free hospitality, remarked, "Of course. The bread-and-butter letter." This is *my* thank-you note to the movie business in which I served for more than twenty years as a publicity man; which provided me with a comfortable livelihood, with a goodly portion of laughs as well as no small amount of irritation and upset, and upon which I look back without regret but also without the least degree of affection.

In the usual order, I had been a journalist before I became a press agent; therefore I arrived at the latter occupation somewhat ashamed of my new profession as a step downward. I was in an anomalous position, for I continued to write pieces for the *Herald-Tribune* and for magazines all the time I was publicizing films, but there was seldom a conflict of interest. For my journalism, I wrote mostly about the theater, touching only occasionally upon movie personalities when they had a stage background. Nor was there any subterfuge. My editors were aware of the situation and to my film employers it was a distinct advantage for me to be a free-lance contributor to various publications that might at some point be of use in promoting their pictures.

The reason I was propelled into a film publicity job in the first place was an article I wrote for the *Saturday Evening Post* on Paul Draper, called "18-Karat Hoofer," which was published in mid-December, 1942. The Post advertised it in a quarter-page advertisement in *Variety:* "The only tap dancer ever to be billed at Carnegie Hall. . . . $50,000 a year for cabrioles, arabesques, tours jetés and entrechats. . . . He threw away the gold spoon he was born with and climbed the ladder of success the hard way. . . . A dozen stories of his spectacular off-stage pranks. . . . How he works and plays. Color photos. The Life Story of PAUL DRAPER by Irving Drutman. Out Today. 10¢." I was thrilled. I had never been advertised before.

Mort Nathanson, a theatrical publicity man, had just been hired by Samuel Goldwyn to be his New York press representative. Mort needed an assistant. Al Tamarin, another theatrical publicity man with whom I was acquainted, saw the *Variety* advertisement and suggested me. I was agreeable to taking the job because, although I felt it would be demeaning to become a supplicant for journalistic favors, I would have a subsidiary vocation to fall back on and also the salary, $75 a week, would keep me from scrambling around for my living expenses. My *Tribune* articles paid very little and while I had received $500 each for my recent magazine pieces, it had taken several months for me to gather the material for them and to write them, after which a couple of months might elapse before I could get another assignment from a magazine editor. Free-lance writing was a financially hazardous occupation.

Goldwyn had a busy schedule planned for the following year. To start with, *They Got Me Covered,* a comedy-melodrama in which Bob Hope played a war correspondent, was about to be released, and *The North Star,* with the first original screenplay by Lillian Hellman, was ready to go into production. I liked Hope's films — he had not yet become a tiresome rubber stamp — and Hellman was of course one of the most considerable American dramatists. I felt that I should enjoy my new job.

Goldwyn remained on the Coast during my first two months and I had no opportunity to make his acquaintance and gather my own little bouquet of malapropisms. In fact, I never did get to meet him because when he was in town my boss Nathanson didn't introduce us; while we were having private screenings of *The North Star,* Oscar Levant told him I had asked him to a showing and Goldwyn querulously wanted to know from Nathanson about this strange man who was going around inviting people to see his picture. I had then been in his New York office for almost a year.

I more than earned my small salary the first few months by devising a cute scheme for *They Got Me Covered.* Hope's role was that of a maladroit foreign correspondent whose career is pock-marked by the big stories he's missed. I thought a by-line piece by him, in which he asked some actual foreign correspondents to tell of *their* grand boners, could be placed in *This Week* magazine, the Sunday supplement which was subscribed to by papers all over the country and which had the largest circulation of any periodical in the United States. I telephoned some correspondents I had become acquainted with in preparing a *Town and Country* article on lecture agents and got four of them to consent to contribute about one hundred and fifty words each. *This Week* was to pay $750, which sum Goldwyn would match, the proceeds to go to the Overseas Press Club's Emergency Fund. I wrote the by-line piece and it appeared as a double-page spread with a two-column photograph of Hope and full credits to the film.

It was an auspicious start for me and for Mort Nathanson, who wrote Goldwyn emphasizing that the two-page layout was the equivalent of $15,000 in paid advertising, with a cost to him of only $750. Goldwyn had to be reminded constantly of any bargains he was getting, since he was a past master at denigrating his employees. Another press agent of his had once come to him with an advance copy of *Coronet,* a *Reader's Digest*-size periodical, to point out exultantly a sixteen-page spread on a Goldwyn picture. Goldwyn thumbed through the magazine, counting with his lips, then said, "You call this sixteen pages? Such a *little* magazine!"

The North Star was to be his prestige release for 1943. Its genesis had been a conference in Washington, to which all the big studios had been bidden. As war propaganda, they were asked to make a film that would help the allied cause. Each production chief was assigned a different country. Goldwyn drew the Soviet Union. He went around anxiously asking friends and acquaintances whether people would think he was a Communist if he did the film. The idea of Goldwyn the Communist was a concept beyond the imagining of the most inventive fabulist.

On the theory that very famous names were a guarantee of excellence, Lillian Hellman, whom Goldwyn esteemed possibly above all other writers, was signed to prepare an original screenplay, Lewis Milestone, noted for his *All Quiet On The Western Front,* was chosen to direct — he was an expert with battle scenes — and Aaron Copland was to write the musical score, with song lyrics by Ira Gershwin.

The participants were all high-grade but the project was fated from the start. It was impossible for Goldwyn to leave a film unembellished; his trademark was opulence. Lillian Hellman's script detailed the effect of the Nazis' invasion on a group of children in a Soviet village called the North Star. Simplicity was the keynote.

I immediately fell under her spell when I went to see her to get background on the film. There is an attractive humorous quality to her face, an intelligent I-don't-fool-myself-and-don't-you-try-to-fool-me challenge that has lured a long line of distinguished beaus. On that initial visit she told me wryly that Goldwyn used to stop in the midst of story conferences to point a finger at her and say with astonishment, "Men *like* her!"

She was in good spirits then. She had just come back from the Coast where she had been shown the early rushes of the battle sequences. "Milly," which was Milestone's nickname, was doing a good job. We had received wires from Goldwyn instructing us to stress Lillian in the publicity. She was by far the most impressive name we had to work with. The cast that had been selected for the film contained not one potent draw: Dana Andrews, not yet a big star, Anne Baxter, Ann Harding, Walter Huston, Dean Jagger,

Walter Brennan and a teenage Farley Granger, making his first film appearance. There wasn't a box-office ticket among them.

Some weeks later we had another wire from the Coast. Lillian's name was not to be mentioned in any further *North Star* publicity. We of course ignored it; we had no other selling point. What had happened was that Goldwyn had sent for her to look at some more rushes. She came out of the screening room appalled; as she later related to us, he and Milestone (now no longer referred to as "Milly") had bent over backward, so that every Russian had *three* eggs for breakfast. The houses in the little Russian village looked all new and shiny, the peasants scrubbed clean. Dick Maney, when he later saw the finished picture, suggested that it must have been made by the fashionable dressmaker Hattie Carnegie. Lillian had had a big blowup at Goldwyn's house that evening, with Goldwyn ordering her out.

In line with his Big Name policy, Goldwyn had hired one of the *Life* magazine stars, Margaret Bourke-White, as "photographer extraordinary," to shoot publicity stills on the set. She had three published books on the Soviet Union to her credit and was regarded as the most authoritative American photographer of Russia. When she returned from the Coast, I did a *Tribune* interview with her and also sat in on an interview Mort had arranged with Eileen Creelman, motion picture critic of the *Sun*. Creelman was ultra-conservative and a relentless Red-baiter. She began by saying maliciously, "I liked *Ninotchka* [in which the dour Communists are converted to capitalism in gay Paree], didn't you?" Bourke-White, who had been out of this country in various war zones for the past few years, didn't understand her reference. She just said, "Mmmm," and continued with what she had been saying. Creelman persisted, "The Russians are just like the Nazis anyway, I don't see the difference." I was very uncomfortable; Bourke-White just stared at her in astonishment and said, "Well, that's a matter of opinion, we won't discuss it." But Creelman pounded away, asking in what way they weren't similar, and Bourke-White, with perfect aplomb, tried to explain patiently, as if to a stubborn child. I said with forced gaiety, "Hey, let's get back to Mr. Goldwyn," but my antic didn't

THE NORTH STAR
Goldwyn's Soviet village, at peace

The village at war

work. Creelman replied, "That won't be necessary, I'm finished," then got up, said cuttingly to me, "I'll conduct the interview," and left. Bourke-White and I had a stiff drink and she said, "That's one big favor Goldwyn owes me."

She worked with a multitude of cameras and lenses, and used hundreds of rolls of film. The most spectacular scene in the picture was the burning of the extensive village which had been built on the Goldwyn lot, and which naturally was left for the end, when all other village sequences had been shot. Bourke-White wanted to keep trying for perfection. Accustomed to Luce plenitude, she asked if the holocaust could be repeated, so she might get shots at different angles.

Goldwyn brought the finished picture to New York and began a series of conferences with RKO, his releasing company. He was interviewed by Mary Braggiotti of the New York *Post:*

> M.B.: I've been looking through clippings and I read that in 1928 you proclaimed that sex was finished in the movies.
>
> S.G.: My dear young lady, I could never have said such a thing. Sex is too important. It will outlive us all.

At last, a genuine Goldwynism. We began screening the picture for the magazine press. Jim Agee was then reviewing films for *Time.* I had a drink with him. How did he like the film? Not much. I told Mort that we wouldn't be getting a good review from him. Mort told Goldwyn. I was horrified. I had assumed ingenuously that it was a matter of confidence. About a week later, Jim phoned me at the office, stuttering a little from embarrassment, and asked if I could arrange another screening for *Time.* Henry Luce had noted that because Russia was our ally in the war against the Nazis, he would like to have another opinion about the film. Jim said that generally Luce didn't interfere, that it only happened two or three times a year and he didn't mind. He was quite cynical about his work on *Time,* anyway, saving his proper criticism for his spot on *The Nation.* I apologized to Jim for my innocent part in the affair.

Goldwyn was a smooth operator. He hadn't gone directly to Luce with a complaint. He had asked Elsa Maxwell, who arranged parties for café society, to give a dinner for him and to invite the Luces. They had talked of *The North Star* at the dinner. Miss Maxwell was later presented with a nice gift of jewelry in appreciation. Jim's review was scrapped. Another staff member obliged with a favorable report.

Goldwyn arranged for a double opening, at the Palace Theater and at the Victoria, diagonally across on Broadway. We were all busy trying to get celebrities to come to the two gala events. The more prestigious, which would be attended by Goldwyn and his friends, was to be at the Victoria. I telephoned Fanny Holtzmann, Gertrude Lawrence's manager and lawyer. Miss Holtzmann had attained notoriety by winning a large settlement from British M.G.M. for Princess Irina Youssoupoff, who claimed to have been libeled in *Rasputin and the Empress*. She was very good at getting and saving money for her clients. She knew many famous people. Alfred Katz, a friend of mine, had told me that one night at her house, when he was looking through the books on her shelves, she had cautioned "Alfred, if you're gonna browse, browse where they're autographed." I asked Miss Holtzmann if she would like to attend the opening with Gertrude Lawrence. Gertrude Lawrence then had a regular radio program, presenting a different drama for each broadcast. She used up lots of material. Miss Holtzmann called back the next day. Yes, Gertie would come to the opening. And there was a tiny favor that she would ask of Mr. Goldwyn. He owned a property (I've now forgotten which) that Gertie would like to have adapted for her series. It was an old film and shouldn't mean very much to him. It did mean much to him. There was a fee of some thousands of dollars that he wasn't ready to give up in exchange for her presence. I don't remember seeing Gertie at the opening.

It was a disaster. Two days earlier, we had learned — through what Goldwyn called "the grapevine," a term he had picked up somewhere — that Hearst had given orders for all his papers to slam the film as being the worst sort of Soviet propaganda. One million, five hundred thousand copies of the *Sunday Mirror*'s magazine section, with a picture layout and an enthusiastic notice by Frank Quinn, the staff reviewer — "by far the outstanding cinema effort dealing with any one phase of the global conflict" — had already been run off and couldn't be recalled. When Hearst's orders came through, another review was hastily substituted, on the "insidious propaganda" line, which appeared in the remaining three hundred thousand copies. Goldwyn was extremely upset, since the Hearst chain still had tremendous influence throughout the country. However, he had only himself to blame, for he had sent a special advance print to San Simeon asking for the publisher's approval.

A little comedy was enacted at the Palace Theater opening, when a starlet arrived in a limousine, was photographed, and made her way into the auditorium. She had been slated to bring the illustrator James Montgomery Flagg, but he hadn't wanted to come. One of the RKO press men dashed in after her, got her out of the theater and into a cab, with instructions to persuade Flagg — the means were obvious — to return with her. She was back twenty minutes later, with a reluctant, inebriated Flagg in tow. The pair were photographed and went into the theater. But in the meantime two other people had preempted their seats and couldn't be got out of them. That left an outraged Flagg with his Circe in back of the theater, having to stand to look at a picture he hadn't wanted to see in the first place.

The showing at the Victoria was calamitous. The house was filled with Goldwyn's fanciest friends, with Lillian Hellman (definitely *not* in the Goldwyn party), with the pick of the available celebrities. At the end of the first reel, the film began to splutter and crackle and suddenly, poof, the screen went dark. I was standing in the lobby when an agonized Goldwyn rushed by crying for the theater manager. Lillian came out for a cigarette, holding her sides to try to suppress her laughter. Ordinarily, she said, the accident would have made her stomach turn. I had to show her the way to the ladies' room when she could no longer contain herself. The lobby was filling up with people who had left their seats thinking there was an unexpected intermission, and Goldwyn was shooing them back into the theater. After some minutes the projection machine was put to rights again — it hadn't been properly over-hauled — and the film continued, only to break down twice more during the evening. Goldwyn was in tears, mumbling "the goddam bastards," unusual language for him, since he was not a casual user of profanity.

The reviews the next day were not good. The general verdict was that the picture was overdressed, overscored, overproduced. In *The Nation,* Jim Agee called it "a film drowned in ornament." Lillian had been vindicated and she was delighted. When I suggested that she had stuck pins in her producer's effigy the night before, she grinned and said, "Are you accusing me of being a witch?" And the thing Goldwyn had been dreading all along, happened. The *Mirror* came out in heated print implying that he was a Red.

We were not yet finished with *The North Star*. Two weeks later Lillian was booked to appear on a popular radio program called *Author Meets the Critics.* We had wired Goldwyn, now back in California, to listen in to this publicity coup. The critics — Aaron Copland, Lewis Gannett and Burnett Hershey — spoke favorably of the film. Then it was the author's turn. The author didn't accept the praise. On the contrary, she said, "I think it's a bad film." Mort and I, sitting in the studio, looked at each other and wished the wire to Goldwyn had never been sent. Lillian especially disliked the first third, which Goldwyn had changed from her original script. She rightly thought that writers should be more respected in Holly-wood. Gannett made some reference to "mere writers, if I may use that phrase," and Lillian quickly denied him the privilege, saying "You may not!" Then Aaron chimed in to say Hollywood was the place where writers should cooperate with directors and producers because the medium imposed collaboration, and writers might learn from the latter's experience. This did not fit in with Lillian's sentiments at all and there ensued a rather acrimonious dialogue between them. When the program had ended, she said to him with mock-bitterness, "And to think how I fought to have you do the music, instead of Stravinsky [who had been Goldwyn's first choice]."

We weren't surprised when we learned from fellow press agents that Goldwyn was looking for a replacement for Mort. *They Got Me Covered* had hardly been a blockbuster and *The North Star* was doing bad business all over the country. In such cases, the publicity department is usually blamed, never the pictures. We had already started advance work on the next film, which was to be Danny Kaye's first, *Up In Arms*. I suggested to Mort how to head off being fired. We prepared a two-page telegram reading: UNDERSTAND YOU WANT TO REPLACE ME STOP CANNOT UNDERSTAND WHY STOP HAVE ALREADY LINED UP FEATURE STORIES AND PICTURE LAYOUTS ON DANNY KAYE IN LIFE LOOK COLLIERS SATURDAY EVENING POST THIS WEEK PARADE WOMANS HOME COMPANION MCCALLS REDBOOK, etc. etc., mentioning almost every popular magazine then in existence.

Very little of this was true. Mort was apprehensive lest his perfidy be discovered; I justified it by saying that Goldwyn had been planning to fire him with very little notice and the least that could happen would be to stave off the sack for a few months. Besides, we *were* getting a good response to Danny. The day after Goldwyn received Mort's wire, he phoned James Mulvey, his New York representative, and asked him to tell Mort not to send such long, expensive telegrams; a letter would do just as well. The replacement rumors stopped. If only temporarily, the ploy had worked.

We managed a very good publicity campaign for *Up In Arms,* and the picture was a critical and commercial success. I wrote articles on Danny under my by-line, under his by-line, under Sylvia Fine's (she fashioned intricate song lyrics for him under her maiden name and he was accustomed to introduce her with her full credits as "my wife, Sylvia Fine"). I knew his chronology and the incidents of his professional life backward; sometimes, sitting in on an interview we had arranged, I would doze off and wake up suddenly to find Danny still droning on.

Goldwyn was taking his time preparing a second Kaye picture; meanwhile, there was nothing much for Mort and me to do. We would spend the late morning playing gin rummy in Mort's office, with the door shut, while our secretary read a book at her desk; in the afternoons, we would go across the street to Mike Beck's office and play there with a couple of other inactive publicity men. Mike was an excellent press agent and an excellent gin rummy player. He would conduct business with the phone in one hand while he played his cards with the other, and he usually was successful at both occupations. The movie people met for lunch at the downtown Lindy's, near Forty-ninth Street, on the second floor. We would sit at a long table with some of the other publicists we knew from Columbia and United Artists. Occasionally outsiders would find their way into the area. I remember the unbelievable moment when above the din we heard the genteel Gentile voice of a large lady saying, "Waiter! May we have some more of those little round Jew-rolls, please." You could have heard a bagel drop before the conversational hum started up again.

This dilatory state of affairs couldn't last long. One day late in the fall, Mort was called in to Mulvey's office and told we were through. I had learned a new trade in the two years I had worked for Goldwyn but I still hadn't met Goldwyn and never did.

With the termination of my job at Goldwyn Pictures, where I handled all the elements in a publicity campaign, I became a circumscribed writer for United Artists. The principal function of a writer in the departmentalized New York publicity offices of the large companies was to prepare press releases and to rewrite the squibs that came from the Coast on each picture. These were euphemistically known as "stories" and the forwarded copies of the originals, on thin second-sheets (before Xerox), were called "flimsies." The manner of composition was small-town journalese; from two paragraphs to two pages in length, they were frequently barely literate. As a writer, my job was to wade through this mass of trivia and try to rework some of it into acceptable feature items for the metropolitan press.

I remained at United Artists for only a short time, the one bright spot being when I was sent to pick up Fred Allen at Pennsylvania Station, arriving from the Coast, where he had recently released his tart opinion of California: that it was all right if you were an orange. After six boring weeks, I asked the theatrical producer

Herman Shumlin if I might use his name to apply for work at Warner Brothers. Herman was under contract to Warner's and was then in excellent standing with the studio, having to his credit *The Watch on the Rhine,* which had been a success, and the recently completed *The Corn Is Green,* which, with Bette Davis in the leading role, was bound to be profitable. Herman very kindly telephoned Mort Blumenstock, the executive head of New York publicity and advertising, who made an appointment for me to see his lieutenant, Larry Golub. Larry had been deeply impressed by Warner's leading male contract player, Humphrey Bogart, whom he slightly resembled and whose patterns of speech he unconsciously imitated. There was a job open for a writer and I was hired at $110 a week, an increase in my former salary, plus an expense account of about — Larry wrote the figure down conspiratorially — $25. The expense account as additional income was standard practice in the movie business.

I was one of two writers who reworked the flimsies from the Coast. I was also assigned to deal with three "class" papers, the *Times,* the *Herald-Tribune* and the *Christian Science Monitor.* My immediate supervisor was a former Hearst journalist; in that ethnically overbalanced organization, he was known as "Warner's goy," and he was generally disliked.

In looking over the folder for *The Corn Is Green,* I encountered a gem. A choir had been employed in the film, conducted, so the flimsy informed me, by A. Capella. I used to trade these with my peers from other companies. At M.G.M., Mike de Lisio savored two of his favorites: one began "Greer Garson is a phenomena," and another was ready to tell the world that "there is not two ways about it. Van Johnson must grow a mustache."

Warner's publicity department was run along fraternal lines. The weekly staff meetings in Mort Blumenstock's office often generated more laughs than the picture under discussion, especially if it was one of the studio's dismal comedies of that period. We were supposed to arrive for work at 9:30 in the morning, but only the timid were in that early. I usually made it by 10:20. The elite squad — Sid Garfield, Jack Tierman and Milton Berger — were seldom in before 11:00 ("Ah," Blumenstock would say, encountering one of the incoming trio in the corridor, "here's Jack Tierman, bright and shining at the crack of," checking with his watch, "11:22").

These three, who handled the Broadway columns and the off-the-entertainment-page sections of the evening papers, were the protégés of Irving Hoffman. How to explain Irving, the publicity eminence behind many a Broadway and Hollywood magnate? Show business executives hired him for the prestige of being known as one of his clients. His charm for many of them lay in the fact that he treated them like trash. His accolade, "You're an ignorant sonofabitch," to Jack Warner would be treasured far beyond any yes-man's obsequious praise. Irving was a genial, easygoing individual, with the look of a bright college student. He wore spectacles with thick lenses, since his vision was deplorable. The secret, an open secret, of his power was his close friendship with Walter Winchell, to whom he regularly supplied material; he also wrote his own column of chit-chat in the trade paper, the *Hollywood Reporter*. He was a devoted son. Movie press agents sent him invitations to screenings, which he passed on to his parents. If they liked the film, it was sure to appear in Winchell under *Recommended to Diversion Seekers*.

Irving's office staff attended to the mundane details of his business. His apartment above Billy LaHiff's Tavern on West Forty-eighth Street was a hangout for assorted Broadway characters and their ladies of occasion. Here Irving spent much of his time lying in bed, working under a magnifying glass on his detailed, outsize drawings of female pudenda.

About every two months, we would receive a memorandum from Mort informing us that Charlie Einfeld, vice-president in charge of publicity and advertising on the West Coast, was due in New York and for us to cut down on our expense accounts for the period. We readily acquiesced, knowing that when he returned to Hollywood we could make up the difference in subsequent weeks. Einfeld was purely a Hollywood product; he spoke in go-getter gibberish and it was a fascinating game to try to translate what he was saying into comprehensible English. Copies of his wires from the studio would be sent to us: "Just saw the new Ida Lupino the funniest picture ever." The print would arrive, the New York staff would be herded up to the screening room to sit glumly through something like *Pillow to Post* or *A Salesgirl and a Soldier,* each a sterling candidate for *un*funniest picture ever.

That was when the teamwork of the department came into play. We would be called in by Mort or Larry and told that since the film was such a stinker, we would have to do our utmost to get out a good advance campaign. I couldn't do much — my three proper papers would have been irritated by pleas for favors. But the boys who handled the syndicates and the less discriminating magazines and dailies pulled out all the stops. Garfield, Tierman and Berger piled into one cab and made the rounds downtown armed with girlie stills for the obliging picture and feature editors of the afternoon journals. Their connections were good, and the department could be generous with gifts of bottles of liquor.

The years 1944–45, which covered my Warner's employment, were not prestige years for the company. There were good writers on the Hollywood payroll, including William Faulkner, known to Jack Warner simply as "that drunk." Star players, headed by such shining lights as Bogart, Bette Davis, James Cagney, Errol Flynn (none of whom ever came near the New York publicity department when they were in town), also included Ida Lupino, Eleanor Parker, Alexis Smith, Helmut Dantine, Zachary Scott, Dane Clark, Dennis Morgan, Joan Leslie, Faye Emerson — an uninspiring lot. The subsidiary actors, canny veterans like Peter Lorre, Sydney Greenstreet, Charles Coburn, easily outshone these luminaries-by-contract.

Rhapsody In Blue, based (blandly) on the life of George Gershwin, was to be Warner's big summer picture for 1945. The advance credits made it sound more promising than most film biographies of composers. George's brother-collaborator Ira was around to advise on details (Ira is a great detail man; even after fifty years he can remember the menu and price of meals he had in Atlantic City during the tryout of a Gershwin show); Oscar Levant, who had been a disciple from the mid-Twenties until George's death and had played the piano with him at concerts, was cast in what we called

his real-life role, and also recorded the title piece and *Concerto in F*
for the sound track; for further authenticity the producer had
rounded up such of George's music executants and associates as
Paul Whiteman, Al Jolson, George White, Rouben Mamoulian,
Anne Brown, Tom Patricola and Hazel Scott.

I was to write a piece for the *Times* on my friend Levant and his
connection with Gershwin and the film. Oscar invited me to spend
Saturday at his house in Westport, Connecticut, which he had
recently moved into. A letter I wrote to Mike de Lisio describes the
occasion:

"Oscar was both his old and new self, behaving as though he had
a priority on neuroses. First he wouldn't give me a drink because
he's very prim about people getting drunk; then he gave me a drink
and was somewhat comforted when he saw I didn't gulp it down.
Then we had the interview, in the middle of which he suddenly got
an acute stomach pain. 'It's that interview,' he said, but his wife
said, 'Oh Oscar, now don't make something neurotic out of this too.'
Then he was genial again for a while, then I said something
innocuous which irritated him and he walked out of the room, then
I called him on it and asked him to tell me explicitly what I had
said that had disturbed him and he had to end in blustering, since
there was nothing he could really pin down. Then June said something innocuous that disturbed him, then we had dinner, very good
and very pleasant, then I played gin rummy with June so Oscar
could practice but he couldn't practice and lay down on the couch
brooding — 'the lion is as quiet as a mouse' I said but June [who
was pregnant] was too nervous to laugh at that — then finally they
both drove me to the train, after Oscar had asked me to stay
overnight, but I wasn't going to get into that because I knew he'd
hate himself for having given the invitation — 'I can be cordial for
just a minute,' he says — and while we were waiting for the train he
bludgeoned me into promising to show him the article before I
turned it in to the *Times*."

The biggest difficulty in devising a Gershwin screenplay had been
to find some conflict in George's life — "He was the most extroverted
person I've ever known," said Oscar. Clifford Odets was the first

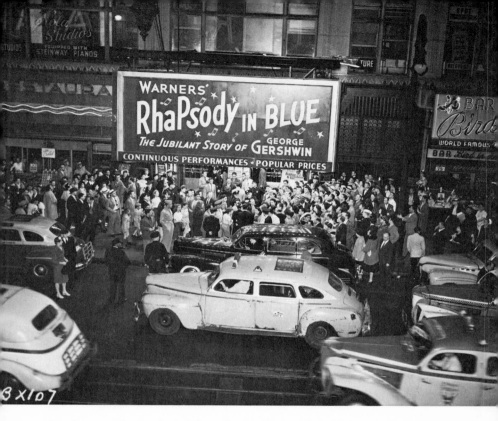

Broadway movie opening — Rhapsody in Blue. I am standing to left of box office, under the "o" in Rhapsody

writer assigned to the script. Clifford so identified himself with his subject that he turned out a plot, against all the known facts, in which George was constantly being torn between popular music and serious composition. When Oscar read it, he said, "You know what Cliff's done? He's written his own life — but with song hits."

Our publicity staff was given a briefing the afternoon before the big klieg-light premiere. With great solemnity, we were all assigned stations in the theater lobby. Although Blumenstock and Larry Golub were very serious — this was to be an important occasion — the rest of us at the briefing behaved in our usual schoolboy manner. Someone referred to the lobby as "the terrain," someone else pretended to be confused about whether he was the Reds or the Blues. I suggested that we hold a dress rehearsal, using second-rate celebrities as stand-ins. Top Brass was not amused. Because I had met George and Ira's mother at Ira's, I was to be stationed at the street door so that I could have her picture taken and escort her inside. I was also to be there to identify other notables. I have been nearsighted since childhood although I only wear spectacles for reading and for close work. I also have no talent at all for remembering faces. How could I tell them that I would be useless as a celebrity-indicator?

I arrived to take up my post only half an hour before the movie was scheduled to start and was told that Mrs. Gershwin had preceded me and was already seated. In fact, my only contributions were Edna Ferber, whom I had interviewed a few years earlier and whose face was unmistakable, and Thyra Samter Winslow and Muriel Draper, who were friends of mine. Oscar had come in for a few hectic minutes after the picture had started, asked Mort Blumenstock where I was, and when told I had already left — we were only on duty until the film began — declared it was a betrayal and he too departed. He called me the next day and I read him the first review, which said he was very funny. His comment was, "Don't they say anything about my warmth?"

My carefree association with Warner's ended when I was offered an autonomous job at more money to handle publicity for Loew's International Company, M.G.M.'s foreign distributing organization. Howard Dietz, head of Eastern publicity for Metro from its formation, had recommended me to Arthur Loew, president of the division, as someone who "knows everybody." If not an accurate assessment, it was certainly a flattering one.

With the end of World War II, Metro was about to launch an ambitious program which [I wrote for the *Times* in announcing the venture] "for the first time will enable the general American public to see outstanding foreign films with synchronized English dialogue. Although sound business reasoning rather than altruism is behind the move, the company's program, if successful, should prove to be of great cultural advantage to all concerned." The sentiments were noble, but what had really induced M.G.M. to engage in the film-import business was that earnings in postwar European countries were blocked and had therefore to be spent in the land of origin. In an attempt to deplete this surplus, executives were given a black market rate of exchange when on vacations abroad; marble was imported from Italy to refurbish the Loew's State Building lobby; scenes with foreign locales were written into films, with second units being sent to shoot on location; and the hitherto-ignored alien films were bought for United States distribution. This last was also a diplomatic move to salve the pocketbooks of the European picture industry and thus prevent further quota laws against the extremely popular American movies. The original announcement by Loew's called for about fifteen to twenty releases a year, "the number to be limited only by the amount of good product that can be secured."

Ilya Lopert, Lithuanian by birth, polylingual, with a European background in dubbing American films into foreign languages, was put in charge of the operation. Lazar Wechsler's *The Last Chance,* from Switzerland, about the underground shuttling of war refugees to neutral safety, was the first to be released. A Mexican film about peasants, *Portrait of Maria,* with Dolores del Rio and Pedro Armendariz, followed, then a lusty French peasant comedy, *Goupi Mains Rouge,* retitled *It Happened At The Inn,* and *Remorques,* about a tugboat captain simultaneously in love with two women, in which Jean Gabin and Michele Morgan played the leads. Dialogue of *The Last Chance* was mostly in English and an effort was made by Loew's to give it some kind of distribution; the others, in the original language with subtitles, were presented in small art theaters, were well reviewed and well patronized by New York's staunch foreign film public and were then put away in storage. Some attempt was made at dubbing into English, but M.G.M. was not really interested in the project, since the potential profits would be minimal by its standards, and the entire program languished.

I went to Hollywood for several weeks of vacation where by inadvertence I was domiciled at company expense in a luxurious mansion kept by Metro for its chief executives (Dave Blum, a Loew's International factotum, had written the Coast office asking that accommodations be found for me, without explaining that I was not on a business trip). My song collaborator, Jack Lawrence, and I, having sold two songs to films, toured the music departments of several of the studios to try to get additional assignments. At M.G.M. a music arranger was working on a movie with a Mexican background. He told us righteously that he had dissuaded the producer from using Aaron Copland's *El Salón México* by saying, "What did Copland do? He just took some old folk themes and made a concert piece. We can take the same themes and score them right here." The Copland original turned up later, anyway, as background for an Esther Williams picture.

When I returned to my job in New York, Lopert screened for me an exceptional Italian film he was trying to get Arthur Loew to buy. *Shoeshine* had been made in Rome right after the Occupation by a prewar matinee idol, Vittorio de Sica. Loew hadn't seemed much interested in it. I sent him a memorandum, with a copy to Howard Dietz, excitedly urging its acquisition. It was, and remains, the most heart-catching film I have ever seen. Dietz wasn't even curious enough to have it shown to him. Since we had no program of releases, I fretted away my time for several months until Dietz asked me to stop by to see him. My office was in the Capitol Theater Building; M.G.M.'s publicity offices were in the building over Loew's State Theater. The reason for the summons was that Dave Blum, in charge of the Capitol Theater enclave (Dietz referred to him as "a humorless Mark Twain," whom he resembled), had inquired if I could be moved to the Loew's State building, since he was cramped for space for his own department.

When I appeared in Dietz's office he asked what I had been doing. I told him I was waiting for the next picture to be released. He telephoned Arthur Loew and was informed that at the moment there were no such plans. I said irritably that I had come back from Hollywood thinking I could start work; otherwise, I would have stayed to write some more songs for films. What do you want to write songs for? asked songwriter Dietz, which I thought was humorless of *him*. It was an uncomfortable meeting. He said that unfortunately there was no position open for me there (thank Heaven, since he ran an authoritarian department, where the raffish camaraderie of Warner's would not have been tolerated; I had heard a staff member's comment once when Dietz's secretary was to pick him up at the airport, "Of course it takes two to lift that ego off a plane"). How much notice did I want, asked Dietz. I said two weeks, although I could have asked for at least twice that, but I had been so bored being paid for doing nothing that I was glad to be free. I could see that stories I had heard about Hollywood's forgotten employees were not exaggerated. If Blum had not required my office space, I, along with my assistant and my secretary, could have remained on salary for many more months, undetected, unremarked. The ambitious import program of course expired of inanition. Forgotten was "the great cultural advantage to all concerned."

Ilya Lopert decided to go into the foreign film distribution business for himself and hired me on an individual fee basis to publicize the pictures he had wanted M.G.M. to purchase. Free-lancing suited my temperament much better than being a salaried worker, and the volatile Lopert, too, was happier operating as an independent. Thereafter, for the eighteen succeeding years before I retired from the field, I was my own agent, contracting to handle one film at a time on special assignment for the limited period of its promotion campaign.

When I began, there were but two or three press agents working on foreign pictures. Distribution of the films was also in the hands of only a few promoters, since there was a limited market concentrated in the biggest cities and some college towns throughout the country. In New York the pictures, with English subtitles, could be booked into a handful of what were then known as "art" theaters, with a small seating capacity.

Lopert's first release was the work of André Malraux called, after his novel, *Man's Hope*. This consisted of seventy minutes of ragged, intense footage that had been shot by Malraux during the last days of the Spanish Civil War. An unadorned documentary of a tragic, lost cause, it had only recently been exhumed. The exceptional final sequence, lasting about half an hour, consisted of a torturous procession of stoic peasants escorting their dead and wounded down a mountainside into a valley still held by the Loyalists. Jim Agee's

response in *The Nation* to this "collossal dirge for heroes" was that
"it towered above most successes, and most attempts, that I have
ever seen in films."

The picture had a musical score by Darius Milhaud. I discovered
that he was then visiting in New York, staying down the street from
Lopert's Fifty-seventh Street offices, at the Great Northern Hotel. I
went to see him to ask if he would consent to a series of interviews as
publicity for the picture. He and his wife and son were having their
midday meal in their small suite: a picnic lunch consisting of
cheese, bread and fruit out of a brown grocer's bag. Milhaud had
recently finished the background score for *The Private Affairs of
Bel-Ami,* to which Jack Lawrence and I had contributed the interpolated theme song. I said, "We're sort of collaborators," identifying myself as one of the song's authors. This information was met
with a blank stare. I asked how he had liked the song. Silence. Then
he suddenly burst out, "They gave me the picture with the song
already in it. It was a *fait accompli.* What could I do about it?"

De Sica's *Shoeshine* put Lopert in business. Along with Rossellini's *Open City,* it was in the vanguard of the Italian neo-realist
movement. The story of two Roman street urchins, close companions, caught in a petty black market transaction, it moves inex-
orably to their imprisonment, the poisoning of their friendship
while in jail, the death of one of the boys and the psychological
destruction of the other in a most poignant climax.

The movie had been shot with leftover prewar film stock and the
photographic stills I received for publicity were clouded and dark.
Some months earlier, *The New Yorker*'s Janet Flanner had sent in a
glowing report in her "Letter from Paris," where she had seen
Shoeshine. She had written of it as "one more of those remarkable
European films that have been made with a poverty of equipment
and with rich emotion [that] are putting the slicker, emptier
Hollywood productions to shame. . . . The two boys undergo the
complete human disaster that is usually harvested only by the adult
man. This bootblack film provides the most informative, alarming,
and concise picture of poverty-ridden, demoralized postwar European childhood that has yet been seen here."

I included a reprint of this vivid report with my advance screening notices. In view of the murky stills I had to work with, I knew I had no chance with *Life,* the goal of all cinema press agents. Like every other popular magazine, *Life* then paid little attention to foreign films. But I also knew that the publisher Henry Luce had a keen interest in the plight of Italian war orphans. I sent Luce an invitation, along with my Flanner reprint; the result was that *Life*'s movie department telephoned to ask me to set up a special showing for the boss, his wife Clare, and the top editors. No one seeing the film could help but be emotionally drained by it. Luce requested his staff to give it a picture spread as the Movie of the Week which, with *Life*'s enormous circulation, almost guaranteed a financial bonanza.

For Cocteau's *Beauty and the Beast,* which followed, I wrote the English subtitles, in addition to my work on the publicity campaign. My knowledge of French is minimal; I used a literal translation along with a bilingual dictionary as aides. Title-writing has advanced since those early days. At that time distributors assumed that a majority of their audiences understood not one word of a foreign language. When an actor said "Non," it was not unusual for an explicative "No" to appear at the bottom of the screen. One comedy dealing with a mythological country opened with a close-up of a plaque on a building: *Consul de Patagonia.* An explanatory title had been considered necessary to keep the audience from being befuddled: *Consul of Patagonia.*

The flatness of some titles as adjuncts to a pungent bit of dialogue is sometimes caused by technical considerations. The length of reading time possible for the duration of an accompanying speech is marked out by a restricted number of letters and spaces for each frame. If the original line is spoken very quickly, as in many French films, the frame would change before a precise translation could be absorbed. The audience will laugh when a verbose speech is approximated with "She says 'all right,'" but twenty-one letters and spaces may be all that the reading time prescribed.

Cocteau's elegant version of Perrault's old Beauty and the Beast fairy tale was a poetic recreation, with stunning visual effects by

Christian Bérard, most memorable being the Beast's castle, with its wall candelabra supported by disembodied hands and the stone statues with human moving faces. Such a *rara avis* required a suitable launching. The membership of Lincoln Kirstein's Ballet Society, forerunner of the New York City Ballet, was composed of a cultural elite with a bias toward Paris. I offered Lincoln the film as a special event for his class A subscribers, to be held in the auditorium of the Museum of Modern Art. The invitations featured Bérard's portrait of Cocteau from the Museum's collection. Even the reclusive Garbo came to this private showing; when the Beast's animal countenance dissolves to reveal the classic features of Jean Marais, she was heard to moan, "Oh, I liked him better before!"

Advance word anticipated the laudatory notices; I was especially pleased that my titles were singled out by many of the reviewers as being notably literate. My success in publicizing Lopert's good films created a demand for my services by other distributors. I publicized a second Cocteau film, *The Eternal Return,* an up-to-date, tenuous version of the Tristan and Isolde legend; a Swedish film, *Torment,* whose screenplay was the work of Ingmar Bergman, as yet unknown as a director; *The Raven (Le Corbeau)* , a nihilistic effort by Henri Clouzot, which had created a scandal in France when it was filmed under German auspices during the Occupation, but which only puzzled New York audiences, who couldn't see what all the fuss had been about.

This last was presented by a new distribution firm, Westport Films, whose principals comprised as polytypic a group as I had yet encountered in the movie business. They consisted of Emil Lustig, a Czechoslovakian aristocrat who had been a producer at UFA until Hitler came to power and who had a wide experience in all phases of the film industry; Leonid Kipnis, a Russian art merchant of pervasive charm, who had almost no experience in any phase of the film industry; his close relative Alexander Kipnis, a retired Russian basso celebrated for his *Boris,* who knew absolutely nothing of the film industry. Aligned with this trio was a silent backer, originally from the Ukraine, who had a profitable concession for Mickey Mouse watches.

Westport Films' offices were down the street from Carnegie Hall, in a building consisting of huge duplex apartments, most of whose tenants were connected with the world of music. Heavy brown velvet draperies obscured the windows of the two-story drawing room, its gloomy atmosphere further weighted down by massive Jacobean tables and chests and bulky upholstered armchairs. When I first went to work there, a sizable painting by Titian of a bearded Venetian patriarch was prominently displayed on an easel. This would disappear to be replaced from time to time by a Degas oil or a suspicious-looking Renoir. Only the downstairs portion of the duplex was devoted to the moving- and art picture businesses; part of the upstairs was rented to the *New Yorker* cartoonist Alajalov.

Working through the Alien Property Custodian, Emil Lustig purchased the rights to Leni Riefenstahl's staggering *Olympiad*, Part One; renamed *King of the Olympics*, it was given for distribution to United Artists, who siphoned off a lot of expenses, booked a costly and ill-advised Broadway theater opening, then let the picture fizzle and expire. Unfortunately, fired by Leonid Kipnis's rosy predictions of the film's financial future, I had invested $1,500 in the project and had gotten Mike de Lisio to put up an equal amount. I was determined somehow to recoup this loss. Kipnis had acquired, through his connections with the art world, the American rights to an ingenious short film biography of Van Gogh, in which the high points of the artist's history were narrated while the camera roamed over those intimate details in his paintings which seemed to forecast the melodramatic events of his life. I agreed to publicize the film for a 30 percent share in its ownership.

The Metropolitan Museum of Art was planning a big Van Gogh loan show. I went to see the Museum's director, Francis Henry Taylor, and laid out a plan whereby for $2,500 he could have the short for continuous daily showings during the entire run of the exhibition. The museum would make back its advance by charging the public ten cents admission. Taylor thought the film would enhance the educational aspect of the exhibit and agreed to the experiment.

The paintings that had been used in the film were of the most rigid authenticity. Prior to its announced release, a Hollywood producer who prided himself on his art collection offered to give us $1,500 if we would include one shot of the oil he owned, which had been refused the imprimatur of the Van Gogh foundation. Happily, Kipnis turned it down. At the same time as the museum showing, the short was booked commercially and was in demand as a special attraction to bolster regular theater programming.

I also publicized an hour-long film on the art and the experimental inventions of Leonardo da Vinci. As an advertising logo, we used the well-known Proportions of the Human Figure drawing from the Accademia di Belle Arti in Venice, in which a male nude's movements are indicated by a double set of extended arms and legs. I was successful in having a blowup of this drawing placed in the window of Scribner's Fifth Avenue bookstore, to promote the film. Both Scribner's and the *Times,* in which advertisements were placed, mortised out the genitals of this most famous of Leonardo's sketches.

When a distributor sought to round out an art-film series and wanted to purchase the Van Gogh, I held out until I got $3,500 for my 30 percent share, which I split with Mike de Lisio. I had retrieved our *King of the Olympics* losses and made a $500 profit. I had also learned a lesson, and never again invested in any movie enterprise, which for all but hardened professionals is like buying into the Brooklyn Bridge.

As an independent publicity agent rather than a regular employee of any producing studio, I was called in by the big companies to work only on what were thought to be "difficult" pictures. Those from the assembly line could be managed by the staff at hand in its usual routine manner. For Stanley Kramer's *Home of the Brave,* one of the earliest Negro-problem films, United Artists hired me to supplement the departmental campaign. Shortly thereafter when Louis de Rochemont's *Lost Boundaries,* which dealt with another Negro-white theme — that of the light-skinned black who has "passed" — was about to be released, Emil Lustig recommended me as an expert on that type of film. Then, again on Lustig's recommendation, I was asked by Italian Films Export to publicize *The Little World of Don Camillo,* based on the stories by Giovanni Guareschi. This led to my first contact with an international star. I.F.E. was composed of a group of independent Italian film producers who had formed a communal distribution organization to release their pictures in this country. As promotion for the industry, some of the most succulent native stars were sent to the United States on publicity junkets. Perhaps as contrast, Anna Magnani, whose main asset was her emotional acting ability, had been induced to make the trip. Magnani was Italy's distaff film eminence, a position earned by her wracking performance in Roberto Rossellini's *Open City.* She had become a worldwide household name when Rossellini, her domestic partner of some years' duration, left her for Ingrid Bergman. During this affair her truculent, public refusal to accept the situation enriched and prolonged the scandal.

I had first been a witness to Magnani's impetuous behavior in Rome in 1948 when the screenwriter Piero Tellini brought me to a restaurant called Nino's, off the Bocca di Leone, where the local film people were likely to congregate. We were invited to sit down at a table whose setup included Rossellini, among others. He was reading a newspaper, looking up occasionally to contribute casually to the animated general talk. Magnani burst suddenly into the long, narrow room, came up to the table and by way of greeting smashed the newspaper into his face. Having established her vigorous presence, she proclaimed loudly that she was going to supervise the cooking of the pasta and strode into the kitchen. She was in a good humor when she returned to sit with us, her dark-ringed brooding eyes impersonally taking in the other diners, who perforce had now turned into spectators. She was apparently being provocative with Rossellini, making fun of him (I don't understand Italian but I could tell from her tone and the amused reaction of our companions that he was being made the butt of her uninhibited wit). In an aside, I asked Piero if she spoke English. Piero, a Florentine, answered, "English? She doesn't even speak Italian. She speaks Roman."

Now, five years later, her celebrity having increased immeasur-

ably, she was to be introduced to the American public. Jonas
Rosenfield, head of publicity at I.F.E., hired me to take charge of
the campaign. Since her English was still rudimentary, an interpreter would have to be found to assist at interviews and to be with her
on social occasions. Natalia Danesi Murray, a friend of mine, a
native Roman, who at that time was the American representative
for the Italian publishing house Mondadori, consented to serve as
duenna. Natalia was acquainted with Magnani, having toured in a
musical revue with her in Italy in the Thirties.

Magnani's ship arrived early on a cool April morning. She was
met on board by a gratifying number of reporters and photographers, fended off questions about Rossellini and Ingrid Bergman,
and posed for pictures. She had left her dark hair unkempt, retain-
ing the image she projected in many of her bellicose film roles.
Unlike other visiting Italian movie stars, who exploited a plunging
bosom line, she cannily wore a simple skirt and turtleneck sweater.
The most typical, and engaging, newspaper shot showed her waving
in salute to New York, thereby exposing a hole in the black sweater's armpit. As we guessed, that unassuming introductory costume
was premeditated, for she had brought with her a sizable wardrobe
designed by the leading Roman couturiers.

At the St. Regis Hotel, where a large suite had been engaged for
her, some of the I.F.E. executives met for a welcoming glass of
champagne. Accompanying her on the transatlantic voyage had
been two Italian film men sent along to keep her fraternal company
in a strange land. Both were dandies, both were familiar with New
York, both couldn't wait to get to the girls at the El Morocco nightclub. To her increasing bitterness, she was to see very little of them
during her stay.

We gave a welcoming party for her at which an impressive
number of acting notables were on hand but it was a self-conscious
affair, with Magnani ill at ease because of her limited knowledge of
English. She knew almost none of the guests, even by reputation.
Dorothy Gish she mistook for her sister Lillian. Nor had she ever
heard of Judith Anderson or Shirley Booth. She did flare with
excitement at meeting Danny Kaye, whose films she had admired.

She remained for a little more than an hour, then told Jonas Rosenfield that she would like to continue the party in her St. Regis suite, if she could be the hostess for just a few of the guests. We whispered invitations to those we thought would interest her. That gathering was much livelier. She was more relaxed in her own quarters, with not so many people around. I was berating Danny Kaye's manager, in language he would understand, for having been remiss about a message I had left for him, saying, "You fuck, why didn't you call me?" when Magnani passed and spoke to me for the first time in English. *"That* word I know!" she said mischeviously.

She could not or would not understand about interviews; she thought the mass shipboard encounter should have been sufficient press coverage. Jonas and I explained about the importance of individual meetings and she finally consented to allow two a day, starting not earlier than noon. She was irked by the full schedule I and some of the I.F.E. staff had arranged for her but was somewhat mollified once she saw the printed results. Nor was she innocent about what made good copy. I had told her that Hal Boyle of the Associated Press was important, since he was published in approximately five hundred papers and was probably the most widely read columnist in the country. When he appeared for his five o'clock appointment, she asked me to bring him into the bedroom. She was sitting up in bed, puffing away on a cigar. Natalia and I looked at each other in astonishment; we had seldom seen her even light a cigarette. She told Hal, who later headed his piece CIGAR-SMOKING ITALIAN ACTRESS, that she habitually smoked several a day.

Danny Kaye was performing in a one-man show at the Palace Theater, which she was anxious to see. One of the two Italian playboys was to be her companion for the evening, but reneged almost at the last minute. She had to go alone with Natalia, which upset her sense of propriety. "Imagine," she said, "two women going by themselves to a theater!" The playboy telephoned her room the next evening. He had a young actress in the hotel lobby with him, who was desirous of meeting Magnani. "If you want to lay her, do it on your own," she said. "Don't try to use me as a decoy," and banged down the receiver.

She was exhilarating to be with, but exhausting. She wore us out. She would rest all morning long while Natalia worked at her Mondadori office and I was busy arranging details of her publicity campaign. We would meet about noon; Natalia would remain with her for most of the afternoon, while I returned to my office after sitting in on one of her interviews, to compose releases, column items and newspaper features. At four or five, I would be back at the hotel for another interview. Anna was just springing to life. She had her bath; we had our aperitifs; if Natalia hadn't arranged an evening for her with the local Italian colony, I would try to think of an amusing place for us to dine. After dinner, at about 10:30, when Natalia and I were ready to collapse, she would say, "Where do we go now?" Once it would be to El Morocco, once to Sammy's on the Bowery, with Anna preferring the knockabout atmosphere of the latter.

She wanted to see *Porgy and Bess,* and she wanted to go to Harlem. The Gershwin opera was then having a successful revival at the Ziegfeld Theater. I arranged with the show's press agent to have a photographer backstage after the performance. I telephoned John McCarten at *The New Yorker* and suggested that the evening might make a good Talk of the Town piece for him. Harlem was still hospitable to white sightseers but there wasn't much in the way of entertainment going on. Anna wanted the prewar Harlem she had heard about and had seen in American films. I inquired around and was advised to take her to the bar and restaurant that prizefighter Sugar Ray Robinson had recently opened, and to the legendary Savoy Ballroom, which was still going strong.

Sugar Ray's place was decorated with huge photographic murals of the owner. He was as handsome as Muhammad Ali and as vain. He sat down beside Anna and said, "I go for you" and gave her the flashing smile. She just looked at him, uncomprehending. He said, "I guess she don't understand English." He was chewing gum and Anna said, in parody of the noise he made, "Boom, boom." While we were eating the chicken-in-a-basket supper, he brought out some autographed pictures of himself to present to Anna, saying, "Pass them around to your friends."

At the Savoy Ballroom, she was fascinated by the dancers jitter-bugging. Then she wanted to see a Harlem nightclub show. There were none uptown: I was told the closest was Jimmy Daniels's in the Village. Mae Barnes, in the eupeptic Harlem tradition, was on the platform when we arrived. Then Jimmy sat down to do his turn at the piano. I had known him casually for many years. His performing repertory consisted entirely of Broadway show tunes. Anna said, "Ask him to sing some spirituals." I thought it would be entertaining to get his reaction and approached the piano with her request. Jimmy looked at me as if I had just called him Nigger, then he swung into his specialty, Cole Porter's "Just One of Those Things."

We had a premiere of Anna's picture, *Bellisima* (directed by Luchino Visconti), for an invited celebrity audience at the Museum of Modern Art. She received a vociferous welcome and was very pleased with her reception. Jonas presented her with a bulging scrapbook of clippings the next day. When she sailed for home, we kissed and parted fondly. From the S.S. *America* she cabled me: IRVING DEAR I MADE YOU CRAZY MANY TIMES AM SORRY BUT NOW I KNOW HOW UNEASY YOUR WORK WAS NEAR ME STOP FOR THIS I AM TUA GRANDE AMICA UN GROSSO ABBRACCIO ANNA.

Upon her return to Italy, she was interviewed by the press. She gave a glowing account of her New York visit. Of course, she told the reporters, she hadn't seen much of the two men, well known in Rome, who had accompanied her, since they were always busy chasing girls. Both were married men with families. Anna had been biding her time for her revenge.

When I remarked to Federico Fellini a few years later (I was working on *Il Bidone*), "Isn't Magnani wonderful?" he raised his eyes heavenward (a more religious man might have crossed himself). "*Too* wonderful," he said.

On the Waterfront, one of the most acclaimed pictures of the Fifties, was in preparation for four years before its producer, Sam Spiegel, finally got the backing for the project. Budd Schulberg's

Anna Magnani and I.D. at Sugar Ray Robinson's in Harlem

screenplay about corruption on the Hoboken waterfront had been judged a questionable financial gamble, especially since Frank Sinatra had been chosen to play the leading role of a hoodlum who develops a conscience. (Sinatra was then at a low point in his career.) Prospects grew brighter when the director, Elia Kazan, succeeded in procuring Marlon Brando to replace Sinatra. With an assured box-office favorite, Columbia Pictures was ready to guarantee the $1,000,000 estimated budget.

There were stipulations, among which were that Columbia would install their own business agent to check on expenditures, and that they would have final approval on who was to handle the publicity during the making of the film. I had worked with them on two Louis de Rochemont pictures they had released. They recommended me for the job, their recommendation being tantamount to my being hired.

For his previous pictures, Spiegel had made an ingenious word play of his name, the billing reading *S. P. Eagle presents.* The comic pseudonym had exposed him to a certain amount of ridicule and he

On The Waterfront. *Sam Spiegel, extreme left next to Marlon Brando. I.D. extreme right*

was sensitive about it. Before preparing my initial release, I asked him, "Are you going to be Sam Spiegel or S. P. Eagle for this?" He was embarrassed by the question. Sam Spiegel, he said, after a bit of hesitation. He was displeased, some weeks later, when I brought John McCarten of *The New Yorker* out to Hoboken, where most of the shooting took place. "A man who makes puns on my name!" he said. Under cover of his pseudonym, Spiegel had produced *The African Queen*, which was very well received, following it with a ponderous film biography of the Victorian singer Nellie Melba. McCarten's summation was: "This time the eagle failed to soar."

When film production started in Hoboken, Kazan and Spiegel were still casting. They had not yet settled on a girl for the lead. I drove out to the location with Sam (the use of first names on short acquaintance is a show-business convention, not necessarily implying intimacy or even familiarity) and asked that he introduce me to Brando. Like a trainer with difficult animals, I usually kept clear of the stars of a film for the first few days, until they got used to seeing me around. I already knew "Gadg" Kazan as a theater director, having interviewed him several times for the *Tribune,* and also had encountered him in Hollywood and at Tennessee Williams's house. I also knew the prize cameraman Boris Kaufman, who had worked with de Rochemont. But I was unacquainted with Brando, except for a casual backstage introduction, which he would have no reason to remember, just before a performance in *A Streetcar Named Desire.*

From professional associates of his and from a domestic service we both patronized, I had heard of patterns of eccentric behavior. Before he finally moved to Hollywood and gave up the stage entirely, he lived on West Fifty-second Street in a top-floor flat of a brownstone house. We shared the same laundryman, shared him also with Katharine Hepburn in Turtle Bay. The laundryman knew that I was connected in some way with the theater. He would puff up the stairs to *my* top-floor brownstone flat on Lexington near Fifty-sixth; to deliver and pick up the weekly wash. Every once in a while he would say, *"He's* in town." "Who's in town?" "Spencer Tracy. I got some of his shirts in Hepburn's laundry." I didn't need a gossip columnist, I had a personal informant. "You know this Marlon Brando? He's crazy. He tells me if he don't answer the bell, to come on up, the door's open and the laundry's in the closet. I go up, I open the closet door and Brando pops out, all naked, and says, 'Boo!' "

The impulse to be seen with his clothes off was apparently a continuing diversion. When he left *Streetcar,* he went to Hollywood for his first film, *The Men.* He went, as many actors do, intending to return to the stage. He kept his apartment and when the picture was finished, came back to New York. Mike Beck, my gin rummy friend of the Goldwyn days, was handling the publicity for the film and arranged some interviews for him. He didn't keep the first appointment, his excuse being that he had been delayed by having to stand in line for his unemployment check. Getting the unemployment check was apparently a matter of principle to the most sought-after male actor of the decade. Mike Beck is wily. He invented a game with Brando, saying he would give him five dollars for every interview. The game appealed to Marlon, who insisted on payment in advance. Mike rescheduled the appointment. Eleven o'clock the next morning. The interviewer, in accordance with Brando's instructions, was to ring the bell and proceed upstairs without waiting for the answering buzzer. When he did so, he beheld a tableau that had been arranged for him: a young female was in the bed and Marlon was in the act of putting on his shorts.

I was provided with no such opportunity to admire his physique. Perhaps, by the time of *On the Waterfront,* he had tired of that prank. He still indulged in practical jokes when in high spirits, such as giving the hotfoot to dozing longshoremen who had been hired as extras. But in general, his behavior those first few weeks was exemplary. He had apparently decided to resist any action that would maintain the reputation for eccentricity he had gained in Hollywood. He was being a gentle, brooding, well-spoken young man; off camera, his thin reedy voice emitted none of the truculent Kowalski undertones that were his acting trademark.

The only flare-up I was to witness occurred one afternoon during exterior shooting in the scraggly waterfront park. Spiegel was saving money by not providing the customary publicity car for my transportation to Hoboken; since I wouldn't leave at seven in the morning when the rest of the company was picked up, I would wait until Sam was ready to make the trip and ride with him in his chauffeur-driven limousine. On this day we arrived close to four in the afternoon to find that all production had stopped. The entire crew — Kazan, the day's extras, Eva Marie Saint, who had finally been chosen to play the part of the girl — were standing around idly. Marlon was sitting off by himself on a rock, stubbornness emphasizing the weak structure of the lower half of his face. The cause of the trouble was easy to discover. Marlon followed each day's shooting with a visit to his New York psychiatrist. Since he couldn't arrive before six, the psychiatrist was charging double his $50 rate. To circumvent the after-hours fee, Marlon wanted to stop work at four, so he could get to the psychiatrist by five. Impasse. The extra hour's shooting was necessary if the picture was to meet its nine-week schedule. It seemed to me that the sensible solution would have been to pay the additional clinical fee ($250 a week) as an added production charge, since a crew unable to function without its star was costing ten times more. No one of course asked me. It must have been settled, I don't know by what means (appealing to reason?), for the shooting continued according to plan.

I was amused to see that, although the few minor roles for tarts needed for the saloon sequences had already been filled, girls kept appearing at Spiegel's office at the end of the day. One such sat down close to the desk of his secretary, who was busily typing away. "Gee, that looks like hard work," she said companionably. "Not as hard as the work you do," answered the secretary, her fingers continuing to fly over the keys.

The outstanding ego on the film was Kazan's. He surrounded himself with his own court, a pair of crew members who had worked with him for years; who would, without question, do whatever he asked of them. Hoboken was picturesque but grubby. There was an odor of neglect in the row of late nineteenth- and early twentieth-century houses. The town seemed to have been breathing dust for years. This setting was of course ideal for a film on waterfront corruption, but the grime seemed to invade nervous systems. Everyone was on edge, Kazan, because he would have to bear responsibility for the picture, more so than others.

When he directed intimate scenes, he would ask that the set be cleared of all but members of the crew, of which I considered myself one. An important part of my function was to observe what was going on, for items to send to columnists, for possible vignettes, or for facts tucked away to be used in production stories when the movie was finished. I would stand behind the cameraman, behind the lights, keeping myself as much as possible out of view. We were in a bar that had been rented as a location for the day. Gadg was instructing Marlon, boy to boy. "Now," he said, "you pick up the fuckin' bottle and you walk down the fuckin' bar, and you lift the fuckin' bottle and throw it at the fuckin' wall" and so on. In the midst of this demonstration, his eye lighted on me. "Irving, get out," he said. I left, thinking, "Is this the way for two grown men to communicate with each other?" When I later reported on my ejection to Spiegel, wanting to know why I couldn't have stayed, Sam shrewdly said, "Because he's probably embarrassed with you listening."

Outwardly, my relations with Kazan were very genial, but then I would discover that he complained to Sam about my bringing journalists to the location without informing him and asking his permission. I operated in my own way, which was to take advantage of the impromptu occasion; if I could get a newspaperman or magazine editor out to Hoboken on short notice, I would do so. During the shooting, I tried to get general-atmosphere coverage. The concentration on our star personalities would come later. I always prudently asked Marlon, as a possibly explosive element, if he would talk to a reporter informally, but didn't think it was necessary with Gadg, whose consuming project this had been for four years and who, I thought, should be pleased with any publicity that could come its way.

Tensions built as work on the production accelerated. There was a flare-up with Gadg; there was a flare-up with Eva Marie Saint, whose husband pretentiously said he didn't want her publicized on her looks but on her acting ability (this was her first picture). After six weeks, I told Columbia I wanted to quit as soon as a replacement could be found. I was fed up with the lot of them, the silly girl, the duplicitous Gadg, and Sam, who kept changing his mind and found it difficult to keep to any decision.

Sam asked me to stay. Gadg said he hoped he wasn't the cause of my leaving. I replied that there were too many stars on the project — "you, me, Sam. . . ." I didn't mention the actual star, Marlon, who, contrary to expectations, had comported himself with unaccustomed restraint.

Anna Magnani was intrigued with the image of Brando. She had promised Tennessee Williams that she would make her American stage debut in *The Rose Tattoo*, which he had written with her in mind, if she could play opposite Marlon. (She finally appeared in the film version but had to do it without him.) He was one of two actors she was intent on meeting during her first visit here, the other being Bette Davis. She had spent a mutual-admiration afternoon with Davis, and she and Brando, with Natalia Murray as interpreter, shared an evening that included a ride on the Staten Island ferry. No sparks were ignited since, to her regret, he was interested in her only as an actress.

Two years after that meeting, when she had made several Hollywood films and each had been blessed with an Academy Award, Magnani for *The Rose Tattoo* to match his for *On the Waterfront,* Anna achieved her desire to perform with him. I had no connection with *The Fugitive Kind,* but from reports, the shooting period was a nightmare. Marlon was at his worst, playing a cat-and-mouse game with Anna, who finally exploded and gave a counter exhibition, proving that her Roman reputation as a virago was justified. When the production came to a merciful end, one of the staff complimented the film's third star, Joanne Woodward, saying, "At least, *you* behaved well during all this." "I don't want to behave well," she replied. "That's why I'm going to an analyst. I want to be *interesting,* too!"

As a respite from interesting stars (*too* interesting, as Fellini might have said) my next few years of publicizing films were devoted to luminaries of a different order — such figures as Martin Luther, Helen Keller and Albert Schweitzer. *Martin Luther,* with the Scotch actor Niall McGinnis giving a rousing performance as the willful Reformation leader, was commissioned by the Lutheran Church of America. Borden Mace, president of the de Rochemont organization, which had produced the film, opened it first in Minneapolis, a Lutheran stronghold. Its success was instantaneous, not only with churchgoers who had a stake in its fate, but also with unaffiliated movie patrons. Borden, who was most responsible for its success, booked it in other large midwestern cities, its prosperity accelerating as news of its excellence spread. By the time we opened in New York, it was a proven box-office commodity.

Jerome Hill, a grandson of the late nineteenth century railroad magnate James J. Hill, had produced a documentary film on Albert Schweitzer, which he asked Borden to help him distribute. Borden recommended me to do the publicity. I had as little knowledge of the sanctified cult figure of Schweitzer as I had had of

Luther, but at this stage was adept at promoting problem pictures. I started by screening the film for the National Council of Churches, which had been of great help with Luther. The Council would only give its support if there were a scene showing Schweitzer conducting a religious service in his African hospital-compound at Lambaréné. Such a touchingly simple scene had already been shot, but Schweitzer had requested that it be taken out of the film; he didn't wish to exploit his piety. I told Jerome Hill that he must convince the good doctor/theologian that its inclusion was necessary if the documentary were to be a success in the United States. Jerome had allocated all profits to the Schweitzer Foundation. Schweitzer overcame his scruples in the interests of his hospital's need.

Albert Schweitzer, a reverent portrayal of a dedicated man, was exhibited successfully in this country. He was shown in his African outpost in Lambaréné, treating the sick natives by primitive methods; he wouldn't allow modern equipment in his jungle hospital. I traveled with Jerome and some of his staff for its showing at the Edinburgh Festival. From there we went to Günsbach in Alsace, Schweitzer's European home, where he spent his summers. Jerome had given the money for a new church organ, on which we were to hear Schweitzer play Bach. We were also to have dinner with Schweitzer at his house. The dinner materialized, the concert did not (I think the workmen hadn't finished installing the organ). Like most messianic figures, Schweitzer seemed to be completely surrounded by women — his secretary, his housekeeper, the violinist Erica Morini, and Erica Anderson, who had photographed the Lambaréné sections of the film. They tiptoed around him as if he were made of glass.

The dinner was a torture to me. I was then a heavy cigarette smoker and smoking was forbidden. Schweitzer did not believe in killing any creature, so of course there was no meat or fish. We were served frugal portions of vegetables, although his plate was kept amply supplied by his henchwomen with a succulent-looking dish that wasn't on our menu. A small glass of wine was set before each place and there was no encouragement for the guests to help themselves to a refill. Conversation was strangled because of The Presence. Any attempt at frivolity, I felt, would have meant instant banishment. I was sitting close to a myth, a deity, but if I were a praying person, I would have prayed for instant deliverance, which came none too soon.

The next morning we drove across France to Jerome's house in Cassis, where a non-believing Belgian countess was one of the guests. "Can you tell me," she asked wickedly, "why a cure has been found for leprosy everywhere but in Lambaréné?"

Columbia Pictures was filming *The Eddie Duchin Story*. The popular society band leader of the Twenties and Thirties had died of leukemia five years earlier. The producers were afraid that he had been forgotten. I was hired to revivify his name. I was not to mention that it had any connection with a movie. Where to begin?

I decided that the best strategy would be to promote a benefit and chose the American Theater Wing as the lucky recipient. With the hired help of a press agent I knew who worked for musical organizations, I arranged for a vaudeville concert to be given at Town Hall. The proceeds would go toward the establishment of the Eddie Duchin Fund for piano students. For our letterhead we recruited a board of impressive names which included Marie Harriman, wife of the New York State governor, and Mrs. Donald Stralem, both of whose husbands were guardians of Duchin's son Peter, who had not yet started in his father's profession. I thought it would be amusing to inveigle Howard Dietz, of the rival M.G.M. company, onto the list, and had my associate make the request. Dietz, who should have smelled a publicity tie-up, asked a Columbia executive if it had anything to do with the projected film and agreed to participate when he was solemnly assured that it had not. My friend Hiram Sherman, celebrated as a master of ceremonies, agreed to perform for the occasion. Other recruits included Hermione Gingold, Leonard Bernstein, Eugene List, Pierre Fournier, the Dave Brubeck Quartet, and Benny Goodman, the only one who didn't show up and didn't even bother to send his regrets.

Nate Spingold, Columbia's vice-president in charge of publicity, suggested that we end the program with a spotlighted piano on an otherwise empty stage, while an old Duchin record was piped in over the sound system. I thought it a gruesome plan but was not about to commit lese majesty by saying so. The concert went off splendidly, except that all the big executives were out of town and were not present to see what had been accomplished. When we reached the finale, the vintage Duchin solo was run off on a phonograph under the stage and its ghostly sound tinkled through the house. The record came to an end and started all over again. I was in the rear of the auditorium; by the time I got backstage and was able to find the technician to get him to turn it off, it had played three times. With the spotlight firmly on the piano, as a surrogate for Duchin, the audience was immobilized. We certainly gave them more than they had paid for.

The American Theater Wing received the proceeds from the concert. I don't know if the Eddie Duchin Fund was ever implemented. The movie, with Tyrone Power and Kim Novak, was terrible.

Warner's — an entirely new setup after all those years — asked me if I would serve as unit publicity man for *Act One,* based on Moss Hart's autobiographical memoir, which was to be shot in New York. Dore Schary was to direct and produce and while his simplistic pious films (*The Next Voice You Hear,* the voice of course being God's) had struck no sympathetic chord, the ambience of this new venture was one I was familiar with from my youth. I had been acquainted with Moss, I had been to the tryout and to the triumphant first night of *Once In A Lifetime,* which was the climax of the story.

The picture was to be made on the cheap, mostly in a studio in the West Twenties usually given over to television productions. Schary, who had known Moss when both were young, had gotten his start in Hollywood B pictures and had risen to be head of M.G.M. during that giant's declining years. He still operated on the B-picture principle. The shooting quarters were cramped. There was only one dressing room, no larger than a walk-in closet, for the cast. The two leading roles were to be filled by Jason Robards as George S. Kaufman and George Hamilton as Moss. Jason had acquired his information about the part he was to play from Kaufman's friends and acquaintances and had settled on the playwright's habit of peering quizzically over his spectacles as the main point in his characterization.

I don't think George Hamilton intellectualized his conception of Moss even to that extent. At our first meeting, he told me he wanted his image as a playboy changed. Changed to what? I asked. He was anxious to get ahead in a high social sphere and a few years later managed some sort of image-transformation when he became the publicly acknowledged escort of President Johnson's daughter Lynda.

Schary (I called him "Mr." instead of the customary "Dore" not out of respect but because I didn't like the Uriah-Heepishness I sensed in him) went to some lengths to shoot in the original locales of Moss's early life . . . the exterior of a Brooklyn tenement in which the family had lived, the Newark Y.M.H.A. where the fledgling playwright had directed an amateur group. One day I came to the studio and saw a sign that had been prepared to go outside the Music Box Theater for Moss's first produced comedy, *Once In A Lifetime.* The sign began, "Sam Harris presents." I reminded Schary that it was inaccurate, that Harris's billing had always been Sam H. Harris. Almost no one would know what Moss's tenement had looked like, but theatergoers of a certain age would remember how a prominent producer advertised himself. The sign was not changed; it probably would have added ten dollars more to the budget.

I had screaming bouts with Schary's nephew, who was the production functionary and expense-cutting hatchetman. I worked very hard and got as much publicity as if it had been an A picture, instead of a quickie. I had been hired with the understanding that I would be employed for six weeks. At the end of five, when the picture finished shooting, I was thanked by Schary for what I had accomplished and told by his nephew that I would no longer be needed. They were saving a week's salary. The picture was not even terrible. It was just flat and dull, proving that whatever one's gift, it will usually come through.

9

Eminent Friends

W. H. Auden
Janet Flanner
Ira Gershwin
Virgil Thomson

JOHN D. SCHIFF

*W. H. Auden, sculpture by
Michael de Lisio*

BOB SERATING PHOTO

Janet Flanner

COLUMBIA PICTURES CORP.

Ira Gershwin

MAURICE GROSSER

Virgil Thomson and I.D.

W. H. Auden

"MY, YOU HAVE EMINENT FRIENDS," said my London landlady as I
waved good-bye to two of them who were getting into a cab from
which she had just emerged. Miss Tibbs's recognition of Wystan
Auden was no exceptional feat: by July, 1973, his craggy face was
almost as well known as that of any ranking movie star or head of
foreign state.

I had just come from lunch with Wystan and Chester Kallman,
who were in London to participate in the annual Poetry International Week. It was the last time I would see either of them. Two
months later, Chester discovered Wystan dead of a heart attack in
his Vienna hotel room, as he was himself to be found in his Athens
apartment a year after that. Neither of them seemed to be in ill
health at the time of our final meeting. The meal was gobble and
gossip, interspersed with the usual bickering between Wystan and
Chester that had been going on ever since I'd first met them twenty-
six years earlier.

That was at Fire Island, where Wystan spent the hot weather

months in a squalid cottage he had bought with the English writer James Stern and his wife, Tania. The plan was that he and the Sterns were to spend alternate summers there. Wystan was a man of unbreakable routine. He worked all morning and interruptions were not allowed during those hours. After lunch he would join a few of us on the beach for a period of relaxation, then back to work. Four o'clock was coffee time, six o'clock martini time. He was gregarious. Once his labors were finished he enjoyed being in company and was perplexed that season because so few of the regulars invited him for social occasions. He later discovered that Tania had spread the word that he was not to be bothered. An intimidated hostess sent a note by way of a feeler: *if* she were to ask him to dinner, *would* he accept? The natives from the mainland were in awe of him and even the more forward summer renters kept their distance.

One celebratory weekend two intimates of his youth, Christopher Isherwood and Stephen Spender, came to visit. He had had a falling-out with Spender and this was to be a rapprochement. Twelve of us, including companions they had brought and neighbors like Lincoln Kirstein, Mike de Lisio and myself, crowded into that small cottage. Chester was too flustered to make coffee for such a mob. I boiled some in a large soup pot and ladled it out, institution-style, into cups, mugs and glass tumblers. Lots of photographs were taken; there was a consciousness of its being a momentous literary occasion.

Wystan was a domestic person. Possibly his greatest pleasure was dining at the homes of friends or having them dine with him. The apartment in 77 St. Marks Place, where he lived for nineteen years, was usually messy, for both he and Chester were slovenly housekeepers, but the bonhomie made the place inviting. At dinner's end, having, on top of three or four martinis, drunk at least two bottles of wine (a vintage premier cru to be gulped down as indiscriminately as California-by-the-jug), he would mumble, "Time for bed," and shuffle off to his room, leaving us to finish the evening with Chester. We would catch two more glimpses of him as he crossed the sitting room on his way to his bath — a lightning-quick submersion — then back again dripping soapsuds. After he had been elected Professor of Poetry at Oxford, he would use his ceremonial gown as a robe to and from these ablutions.

He liked to invent games, one of his favorites being to pair two people of one's acquaintance who would be most distressed at being in purgatory together. For instance, the youthful prodigies Truman Capote and Gore Vidal, or Edith Sitwell and Diana Trilling, strong-minded women with diametrically opposed minds. He liked schoolboy jokes, saying, "Chester, tell about the two old maids who . . ." and then he would naively give the point away before Chester could even start at the beginning. People were compartmentalized, kept in their proper pigeonholes. Chester would be chided if he related a theatrical anecdote — "You shouldn't tell that, it's not your place"; because I wrote about the theater, it was in my jurisdiction. Chester could tell stories about opera singers, which was in his. Chester's obsession with opera had kindled a spark in Wystan, and Chester contributed a good deal to their libretto collaborations, beginning with *The Rake's Progress.*

Wystan's strict moral sense would manifest itself in judgments like "That's just not done" or "He ain't a gent." I told him I had been to a party at Dwight Macdonald's where Mary McCarthy, who has savaged many a writer, was in tears, crying, "What are my friends doing to me?" because of two unfavorable criticisms of *The Group* in the *New York Review of Books.* He was unsympathetic, saying, "Why is she complaining? She's written a bad book, out of which she's making pots of money." He himself refused to review books he didn't like if they were by a living writer. When Robert Lowell, in a literary *cause célèbre,* interpolated in a published verse sequence emotional letters written to him by his wife, from whom he had separated, Wystan declared, "I shall never speak to him again." During Poetry International Week in London, he wouldn't appear on the same platform with him and the schedule had to be rearranged.

When Enid Bagnold came from London to oversee the New York opening of her high comedy *The Chinese Prime Minister,* I interviewed her for the *Herald-Tribune* (I wanted to transcribe what she said accurately and asked her to speak more slowly; she did, but as if she were dictating into a machine, including marks of punctuation — "You don't choose a way of writing comma it chooses you period therefore comma I write as I talk no comma and as lots of people talk comma . . ."). I knew that my friends Lillian and Dorothy Gish, who had taken her play *The Chalk Garden* on a summer tour, would like to meet her and that she would be interested in meeting them. I arranged for them to have tea at my apartment. Wystan hadn't met her and as I knew he liked her writing, I invited him too.

They all arrived promptly — like Wystan, Dorothy usually had to be restrained from being too early for an engagement. I introduced Wystan to Enid not by his public initials of course but by his given name (he had already met the Gishes many times before at parties of mine). Enid acknowledged the introduction but there seemed to be no recognition on her part that he was anyone special. She spent all her time looking at and talking to the Gishes. Several times I tried to bring him into the conversation but couldn't manage to get past Enid's theatrical chatter. Wystan sat politely through it all and finally left, wondering, I could see, why he had been invited.

A week or so later, Enid suddenly asked, "The Auden that I met at your house — was he any relation to the poet?" I assured her that he *was* the poet. She was quite upset. "To think," she said, "that I had gold in my hands and let it slip through my fingers!" When I told that to Wystan, as expiation, he was not appeased. He said it made no difference whether or not she knew who he was; she shouldn't have behaved like that toward anyone. And so she shouldn't have.

He was frequently dogmatic and would not budge from a stated opinion. He disapproved of the labeling of eras — the Naughty Nineties, the Age of Innocence, the Jazz Age — and would not retreat from his position even after I pointed out that he himself had contributed, with his Age of Anxiety. Yet he could also be indulgent. When Susan Sontag published her lengthy, humorless explication of "camp," the master of that effervescent (and evanescent) form said commiseratingly, "Poor dear, she got it all wrong."

In the foreword to his collection of essays, *The Dyer's Hand,* he wrote, and it was a schoolmaster's instruction, "The order of the chapters . . . is deliberate, and I would like them to be read in sequence." I told him that he had inhibited me, that I enjoyed reading essays at random, and he relented, inscribing in my copy, "Irving Drutman may skip as he likes."

Wystan was pro-kraut and anti-frog, which is how he obdurately referred to the Germans and the French. His generation in England had sought the intellectual and erotic stimulation in Berlin which their American counterparts looked for in Paris. When I edited Janet Flanner's *Paris Was Yesterday* and asked the publishers to send him a copy, his idea of a usable advertising quote was "I found it fascinating and, since I am a Francophobe, I know it must be."

He had no interest in and little feeling for the visual arts. He would come to my apartment to dine at least once a month when he was in New York and so far as I know he never more than glanced at the modest but noteworthy accumulation of pictures on the walls. He had a Blake colored etching hanging in St. Marks Place above a bookcase, but it was usually covered over by books piled high in front of it. I am certain he had bought it because of its connection with poetry rather than graphic art. Other pictures in his flat were there because they were the work of friends. He was very complimentary about the bust of him sculptured by Mike de Lisio and was tempted to buy it, but thought it would not be proper to own a three-dimensional reflection of himself. Bronze casts of the sculpture are now in the collections of Christ Church at Oxford, where he went to school and spent his last two winters, and the Smith College Museum of Art.

He made quite a point of asking his friends to destroy his letters when he was gone and was not pleased when I said (accurately, I believe), "Of course they won't." "[A writer's] private life should be of no concern to anybody except himself, his family and his friends," he wrote in the foreword to his Commonplace Book, *A Certain World,* and it was a sentiment he repeated frequently in conversation. His friends took a skeptical view of this attitude since he himself delighted in reading about other writers. He was particularly laudatory in a review he wrote of Leslie Marchand's three-volume *Life of Byron,* but when faced with this and similar commendations, would dismiss the subject with "Nevertheless, I think it wrong." In *The New Yorker* he wrote a combined review of the memoirs of Evelyn Waugh and of Leonard Woolf, comparing their early lives with his own English upbringing, and was very pleased when the editors sent him a check at the Profile rate rather than the lower book review rate. I asked him if the article was part of a projected memoir of his own, but he said firmly, "That's all the autobiography you're going to get."

Yet he was an indiscreet gossip about himself not only to intimates but to journalists as well. When articles about him appeared with detailed and candid quotes based on interviews he had given, he was perturbed and would say ingenuously, "They said they would show it to me first." Roy Perrott of the London *Observer,* whose article did not displease him, told me that he had admired Wystan's poetry since he was a schoolboy and had especially asked for the assignment to write about him. He arrived at the house in Kirchstetten, outside Vienna, where Wystan spent the year's middle six months, on a wet morning. The muddy road caused his car to skid and land in a flower border. Wystan came tearing out of the house and the first words Roy heard from the Master he had waited so long to meet were, "I shall be very cross if you do that again on the way out." Wystan himself was an incautious driver, feeling that it was up to others to be on the lookout. "Riding with him," said the witty artist Dan Maloney, "you feel you're there not so much as a passenger but as a witness."

He was sentimental about occasions. Once, when I was staying with him in Kirchstetten, he even put on the heavy black shoes he detested but wouldn't throw away, to go into Vienna for a dinner celebrating my birthday. In New York, his annual birthday party on February 21st was an evening to look forward to. The card announcing the event (engraved, in the early years, his only bit of ostentation) would carry the legend: Carriages at 1 A.M. He meant it, too. As the stated hour approached, Wystan — quite "tiddly," in his word, from champagne — would announce to everyone who was left, "Time to go, time to go." The guests were a motley group, consisting of many writers, composers, musicians, singers, an artist or two, a priest or two, some college professors, some business people. One year Edith Sitwell was there, her presence deposited in a solid upholstered chair which had been moved to the center of the front room, where she could hold court. As I arrived, Hermione Gingold was leaving (theatrical performers were a novelty at Wystan's; she had been invited because he had been discussing with Lincoln Kirstein an English Christmas pantomime he wanted to write for the New York City Center, in which she would play the fairy godmother). Hermione was in a rage. "I always avoided those Bloomsbury people in London, and there's no reason I should put up with them here," she said as she hastened down the stairs. I gathered that Dame Edith had been capturing all the attention.

The annual party given for Chester's birthday was a smaller affair, confined to intimate friends. The date was the same as Vera Stravinsky's and she and the composer would be there whenever they were in New York. I never got to talk to him; I was intimidated by my lack of musical knowledge. Similarly, I was too shy to approach Edmund Wilson at the bigger parties and there was never an opportunity, alas, to meet him in a more intimate circumstance.

The parties ceased when Chester left New York to live in Athens during the winter months, joining Wystan in Kirchstetten for the spring and summer. Wystan was lonely in New York without him. He didn't like living alone and grew increasingly morose. Since Chester wasn't there to check him, he would repeat favorite anecdotes, frequently retelling incidents like his experiment with LSD, which he undertook with medical supervision. It had no effect on him and he thought he must be immune to its hallucinatory properties. Returning from lunch early in the afternoon, he imagined he saw his postman greeting him across the street. The postman made his rounds in the morning. This must be an illusion and meant the LSD was working. The next day the postman said to him, "Mr. Auden, I guess you didn't see me when I waved to you yesterday."

To entertain him, one abided strictly by his rules. He would be invited for seven in the evening, with the understanding that dinner would be at quarter to eight, since his habit was to eat early. But he would almost always arrive, wearing his carpet slippers, ten to twenty minutes before the scheduled time, that precious period when the untidyness of the day must be hastily thrown into closets, when ice cubes are to be taken out of the refrigerator, when parsley is to be chopped. . . . I would set a martini before him — the other guests certainly had not yet arrived — and tell him he was on his own, that I couldn't pay any attention to him for a while. He would agree that that was just, but then after five minutes he would grow restive. He had finished his day's work and now he was ready for sociability. He would talk and I would have to come in from the kitchen to listen. I would give him another martini. "Now, Wystan, dinner isn't until an hour from now, because you came early." "Very well," he would answer, "then I shall get tiddly." By the time we got to table, he would be well on the road.

His talk was a pleasure to listen to, bright and expansive even at its most pontifical. Food — preferably meat and potatoes, no green vegetable, no salad, no dessert — would be served quickly, so he could get that out of the way, and continue with the wine. By the time he was ready to go, shortly after nine, he would be quite drunk, but he could leave easily under his own steam.

It was at such a dinner party that he made one of those pronouncements that none of us would think of questioning. "I shall live to be eighty-four," he said. We all implicitly believed that he would. When I heard the radio announcement that he had died in his sixty-seventh year, my first thought, before the tears came, was "He never made it to eighty-four." It didn't seem fitting that his forecast should have been disregarded.

Janet Flanner

AS A PRECOCIOUS reader at the age of fifteen, I first saw the signature *Genêt* attached to a Letter from Paris in an October 1925 issue of

The New Yorker. The *nom de journalisme* belonged to Janet Flanner. I have been enamored of her elegant, trenchant style, replete with comic ironies, ever since.

When she was a fellow guest at a party given in New York by Larry Adler in the early 1940s, I couldn't wait to talk to her. *The New Yorker* had just published her two-part profile of Thomas Mann, called "Goethe In Hollywood," an impressive exploration of a complex, canonical figure, the writing of which must have given her a great deal of trouble. I was so envious, I told her fatuously, that I had cried when I read it. "I cried when I wrote it," she replied as someone mercifully distracted her attention.

A dozen years later we were to meet again through Natalia Murray and soon grew to be close friends. She is exceptional in that her spoken words come out with the precision and wit of her sentences on paper, with no pause for editorial restructuring between thought and utterance. She lived in Paris for half a century, except for the war years, which she spent in New York. American tourists who were literate and could manage an introduction considered her a necessary Paris landmark; travelers less fortunately situated would have to make do with the Eiffel Tower and the Louvre. She kept a room overlooking the Tuilleries at the Hotel Continental, and from the mid-Fifties on, when I was frequently abroad, drinks with her in the commodious Continental bar (or at the Ritz when she moved there) and dinner later in some favorite bistro like the Louis XIV was an anticipated pleasure.

Although a local resident of long standing, she was not immune to the incivilities of the crusty natives. We were in a taxi once on our way to a Left Bank restaurant which the driver was having difficulty in locating. She tried to attract his attention so she could help with directions, saying, "Monsieur, monsieur," but he ignored her. In exasperation she called "Chauffeur!," at which he turned around angrily, saying "Monsieur!" She said she had tried to call him that but he had paid no attention. The encounter made her cross, and I could see that she was still fuming about it when after dinner we got into another cab for the return trip. This driver was a young man with hair modishly down to his shoulders. We settled into the rear seat and started off. Malevolently, Janet leaned forward and said, "Mademoiselle." He whipped around in a rage and corrected her with "Monsieur!" Janet was content. She had gotten a bit of her own back.

Another taxi ride: The summer of 1973, in London, where we had gone for the English publication of her book *Paris Was Yesterday*. Of one laudatory review, she remarked, "I am not a vanitous woman, but I was real thrilled." She was then eighty-one. I helped her out of the cab with a cautionary "Watch your head." "It's the only good thing I have left," she answered, banging it anyway.

Ira Gershwin

AS A MODEST MEMBER of an egocentric profession, Ira Gershwin is an anomaly. When some youngsters crowded around him to ask for autographs after a matinee of *Park Avenue*, his last new Broadway venture, he was puzzled, but then calculated that it was a result of his being a character in *Rhapsody In Blue*, the film biography of his brother George. His wife Leonore persuaded him to hire me, as an old friend, to publicize his book, *Lyrics on Several Occasions*, when it was about to be published. He consented only to please her. For the occasion, they came to New York from Beverly Hills, where they have resided since the mid-Thirties. I arranged several newspaper interviews. I also arranged for Ira's participation on a radio show. Lee called me the next morning. Would I mind canceling? Ira had been up most of the night worrying about such a public invasion.

Of the three prodigious show-lyric writers of the Twenties and Thirties, he had long been my favorite, with a glancing touch lighter than that of his estimable peers Porter and Hart. In his foreword, Ira explained why *Lyrics on Several Occasions* is *sui generis:* "This book is unique in that its author isn't looking forward to doing another." It is a witty compendium, not only of Ira's irreplaceable lyrics, but of his wry, irreplaceable comments as well on the craft of songwriting and the idiosyncrasies of theatrical producers and stars. But it is typical of its self-effacing author to downgrade it as being rare only by arithmetical definition.

Ira wrote the lyrics for his first Broadway success, *Two Little Girls in Blue,* with Vincent Youmans. Because he didn't want to trade on the reputation of his brother George, who was already established as a composer, Ira hid under the pseudonym Arthur Francis, which combined the given names of his youngest brother and his sister. He subsequently collaborated with George on seventeen shows in one of the most felicitous partnerships in our musical stage history. Before and after George's untimely death in 1937, he also worked with every leading theater composer except Cole Porter, who wrote his own lyrics, and Richard Rodgers (who asked him to follow the late Larry Hart, but geographical preferences — Ira wouldn't live in New York and Rodgers wouldn't live in California — deprived us of that combination).

When he was collaborating with the whimful Jerome Kern on the movie *Cover Girl,* Kern asked if he had read his biography by David Ewen, recently published. "Did you read about your brother George standing outside my window when he was a kid, listening to me composing?" Ira tried to douse this reminiscence with fact, saying that at the time, Kern was living in a large apartment house, on a high floor; George couldn't possibly have heard him even if he *had* stood outside the building. Kern would not be deterred. "It says so in the book," he insisted.

I first met Ira when he was working with Kurt Weill on the score for *Lady In The Dark.* I wanted some material for an article on Oscar Levant. It didn't confound Ira that, with an enterprise of his own in progress, I should be interviewing him about someone else. When he came to New York again for his next musical with Kurt, *The Firebrand of Florence,* I had my job with Warner Brothers. *Rhapsody In Blue* was about to open. I got an assignment from the *Herald-Tribune.* At the hour of my appointment, I rang the bell of his hotel suite. Lee Gershwin opened the door. I gave her my name and rushed past her down the hall, so anxious was I to renew my brief acquaintance with the Master. She said, "Young man, you go right out and ring the bell again and come in properly." Abashed, I did as I was told.

Ira wove his cocoon of meticulous reminiscence. When the Gershwin brothers were writing half the score for Ziegfeld's *Rosalie* (with the schmalzy operetta composer Sigmund Romberg writing the music for the other half), they were working without a contract. The opening was imminent, but Ziegfeld kept putting off signing the papers. One day Ira brought Lee to the theater to watch a rehearsal. Ziegfeld thought Ira's wife was there to press his claim. Intimidated by a pretty woman, he tore a piece of brown wrapping paper from a recently opened case containing props and scribbled an informal agreement.

Of Thee I Sing was the first musical to win a Pulitzer Prize. The two authors of the libretto, George S. Kaufman and Morrie Ryskind, and Ira, author of the lyrics, each received $333.33 of the one thousand dollar award, George Gershwin being deemed ineligible since he was a composer. In recounting this event, Ira disappointed me, the only time in our continuing relationship. He couldn't remember which of the three collaborators got the extra penny.

After George's death, Rudolph Friml visited Ira's house in Beverly Hills. "Is that George's piano?" he asked. It was. "Then why does it have a vase of flowers on it? Does Heifetz put a rose on his violin?"

Ira is a skeptic. When his sister-in-law Emily Paley wanted to know, "Why is it, on some days you feel better than on other days?" he shook his head. "That's not the way it is. On some days I feel worse than on other days."

I once asked him, in one of those idle suppositional games, what he would like to have been if he hadn't become a lyric writer. "A lyric writer," he said. He couldn't conceive of wanting to be anything else. During the McCarthy Red-baiting era, he was one of the many requested to come into a California court to testify if he had observed any Communist infiltration into Hollywood films. In the midst of the heated proceedings, the judge suddenly asked, "Are you the brother of George Gershwin, who wrote all those wonderful tunes?" "Scared as I was," Ira said later, "I couldn't help thinking, 'You son-of-a-bitch, what about me? I wrote the words.' "

Virgil Thomson

"HE REMINDS ME OF one of those intimidating English butlers," Wystan Auden once said of Virgil Thomson. They weren't particularly cozy in each other's company; indeed, I escaped giving a disastrous dinner party to which I was about to invite Virgil, when I happened to mention that Wystan would be another of the guests. Virgil told me it wouldn't be a good idea, since he had just published his opinion, which I had not yet read, that the libretto for *The Rake's Progress* was one of the silliest of any opera in his memory (no mean accomplishment).

Virgil can be formidably explicative on most given subjects, no matter how remote from his experience. He will supply as facts what may be merely conjectures or misconceptions and he dislikes being challenged. Many years ago, when I contradicted him on some point about which he was being adamant, he laced into me with "You're stupid . . . you're ignorant . . ." then, since he is by profession a critic as well as a composer, he balanced the judgment, adding, "but you're loyal . . . and you've kept your figure." I assumed he was ticking off these qualities in an ascending order of importance.

I was writing for the *Herald-Tribune* when Virgil was its stimulating music reviewer, a gadfly making life uncomfortable for the stolid, entrenched directors of the New York Philharmonic and the Metropolitan Opera. In a conversational style no less perspicacious for sounding matter-of-fact, he would pinpoint what was lacking in the body of a composition, the tempi of a conductor, or the expressiveness of a soloist. This was especially notable considering that he almost invariably snoozed through portions of the performance. When I told him I had seen him napping while on duty, he dismissed the implied censure as an irrelevancy, saying "I know the music."

Since I *don't* know the music, I have never had a hassle with him about his best subject and could therefore sit back and be the delighted auditor of some witty cantankerousness. Once he had given up daily reviewing, he could devote a greater portion of his time to composing and was no longer under the necessity of attending performances. He spent part of a summer near Tanglewood and I asked him if he had been present at any of the Festival evenings. "What would I go as," he said, "a spy? I only go to concerts when they're playing my music. I'm not a voyeur."

He was invited by the mayor of Jerusalem to be an honored guest of the city. He didn't know anyone there and I suggested that he get some names from Leonard Bernstein, who had frequently performed in Israel. "He's the king of the Jewish Musical Mafia," he said. "He won't do anything for a goy." I thought the king was Aaron Copland, I continued, to egg him on. "Emeritus," he said.

One evening he was being especially sententious, ranking anyone he could think of in the musical orbit. "There's that phony Bartók," he would begin, going on to deliver a homily on the subject which, when exhausted, he would switch to a celebrated pianist, the efficacy of whose keyboard renderings depended on the shifting barometer of his love life, then on to the venality of an equally celebrated conductor who could only be aroused by a woman who was rich. It was all uproariously funny and devastating. Finally he got down to a fellow composer whose output was at a standstill "because he spends all his time chasing after sex." For the first time that evening, I chimed in, commenting, "Well, at least it keeps him from writing operas," a form in which the composer had been least successful. Virgil gave me a baleful look. "You're awfully hard on people," he said.